T0270919

MONETARY WAR AND PEACE

The international monetary system imploded during the Great Depression. As the conventional narrative goes, the collapse of the gold standard and the rise of competitive devaluation sparked a monetary war that sundered the system, darkened the decade, and still serves as a warning to policymakers today. But this familiar tale is only half the story. With the Tripartite Agreement of 1936, Britain, America, and France united to end their monetary war and make peace. This agreement articulated a new vision, one in which the democracies promised to consult on exchange rate policy and uphold a liberal international system – at the very time fascist forces sought to destroy it. Max Harris explores this little-known but pathbreaking and successful effort to revolutionize monetary relations, tracing the evolution of the monetary system in the twilight years before the Second World War and demonstrating that this history is not one solely of despair.

Max Harris received his doctorate in economics from Harvard University.

STUDIES IN MACROECONOMIC HISTORY

Series Editor: Michael D. Bordo, *Rutgers University*

Editors:
Owen F. Humpage, *Federal Reserve Bank of Cleveland*
Christopher M. Meissner, *University of California, Davis*
Kris James Mitchener, *Santa Clara University*
David C. Wheelock, *Federal Reserve Bank of St. Louis*

The titles in this series investigate themes of interest to economists and economic historians in the rapidly developing field of macroeconomic history. The four areas covered include the application of monetary and finance theory, international economics, and quantitative methods to historical problems; the historical application of growth and development theory and theories of business fluctuations; the history of domestic and international monetary, financial, and other macroeconomic institutions; and the history of international monetary and financial systems. The series amalgamates the former Cambridge University Press series Studies in Monetary and Financial History and Studies in Quantitative Economic History.

Monetary War and Peace

London, Washington, Paris, and the Tripartite Agreement of 1936

MAX HARRIS

CAMBRIDGE
UNIVERSITY PRESS

CAMBRIDGE
UNIVERSITY PRESS

University Printing House, Cambridge CB2 8BS, United Kingdom

One Liberty Plaza, 20th Floor, New York, NY 10006, USA

477 Williamstown Road, Port Melbourne, VIC 3207, Australia

314–321, 3rd Floor, Plot 3, Splendor Forum, Jasola District Centre, New Delhi – 110025, India

79 Anson Road, #06–04/06, Singapore 079906

Cambridge University Press is part of the University of Cambridge.

It furthers the University's mission by disseminating knowledge in the pursuit of education, learning, and research at the highest international levels of excellence.

www.cambridge.org
Information on this title: www.cambridge.org/9781108484954
DOI: 10.1017/9781108754187

© Max Harris 2021

First published 2021

A catalogue record for this publication is available from the British Library.

ISBN 978-1-108-48495-4 Hardback

Contents

Figures

Tables

Acknowledgments

This book began as a dissertation, and I thank my advisors – Ken Rogoff, Ben Friedman, and Jeff Frieden – for all of their guidance and encouragement during and after graduate school. This book simply would not have been possible without them.

For helpful comments and discussions, I thank Lisa Abraham, Olivier Accominotti, Yazan Al-Karablieh, Olivier Blanchard, Tom Ferguson, Joe Gagnon, Claudia Goldin, Doug Irwin, Emmanuel Mourlon-Druol, Jeremy Patashnik, Brad Setser, Nathan Sheets, Mark Sobel, Paul Tucker, and Mike Wong. I received valuable feedback from seminar participants at Harvard, the Peterson Institute, and Rutgers, as well as attendees at Cambridge-INET's Centenary Conference on Keynes's *Economic Consequences of the Peace*. Kendrick Foster provided excellent research assistance, and I thank Guilhem Flouzat for translation assistance.

Many people read parts of the manuscript, whether in dissertation or book form, and I thank them all for their suggestions: William Allen, Forrest Capie, Sebastian Edwards, Susan Howson, Amaan Mitha, Eric Monnet, Kenneth Mouré, Alain Naef, Ishan Nath, George Peden, Eric Rauchway, Greg Rosston, Kurt Schuler, Scott Sumner, Stan Veuger, Chenzi Xu, and two anonymous referees. Nathan Means provided expert editorial advice. All remaining errors of fact, interpretation, and style are mine.

I am indebted to countless archivists who assisted me at the following institutions: the Bank of England, the National Archives of the United Kingdom, the Banque de France, Service des archives économiques et financières, the Bank for International Settlements, the Swiss National Bank, the National Bank of Belgium, De Nederlandsche Bank, the Nationaal Archief at The Hague, the Baker Library at Harvard, the

Federal Reserve Bank of New York, the Morgan Library & Museum, and the Mudd Manuscript Library at Princeton.

One of the highlights of this project was spending the afternoon with Cameron Lochhead, learning about his grandfather, Archie, and exploring his collection of clippings from Archie's extraordinary career. I thank him for sharing these files.

I am grateful for the financial support provided by the Smith Richardson Foundation and I am particularly thankful for Mark Steinmeyer's continuous encouragement. I am deeply appreciative of Adam Posen for facilitating the grant and generously opening up Peterson's doors.

While working on this project – indeed, throughout graduate school – Gene Sperling made sure I always kept an eye on current policy issues. I thank him for his many years of mentorship.

The late Marty Feldstein offered advice and guidance throughout my years at Harvard. His support for this project – as with so many others – was invaluable.

It has been a pleasure to get to know Mike Bordo while writing this book. Few combine Mike's breadth of knowledge with his kindness. I first became interested in monetary history after reading some of his work. I am delighted to now publish this book as part of his series.

At Cambridge, I thank Karen Maloney and Rachel Blaifeder for getting this project started and Robert Dreesen, Erika Walsh, and Laura Simmons for guiding it to completion.

Finally, any merit in this book is a product of my family's support. To Mom, Dad, and Sam, thank you for everything. And to my fiancée, Karen, thank you and I can't wait to see what life brings us.

Abbreviations

BdF	Banque de France
BIS	Bank for International Settlements
BoE	Bank of England
ECB	European Central Bank
EEA	Exchange Equalisation Account
ESF	Exchange Stabilization Fund
FRBNY	Federal Reserve Bank of New York
IMF	International Monetary Fund

Introduction

The two men did not much like each other, not that they had ever met. Personalities and politics ruled out a warm relationship. Neville Chamberlain, entering his fifth year as Britain's chancellor of the exchequer in 1936, was reserved by nature. He was more at ease watching birds or catching trout than shaking hands and slapping backs. But such was his skill that he ascended the political ladder all the same, from local council to Parliament, junior ministerial posts, and now to one of the great offices of state. Through hard work, mastery of detail, and preternatural self-confidence, he had become the dominant minister in Cabinet, a prime minister-in-waiting who often acted as if he already had the job. Chamberlain was sure his talents amply justified his influence and, as a result, did not handle dissent well. He treated those who saw the world differently than he with condescension, from members of Parliament at home to whole peoples abroad. The upstart Americans, seemingly too powerful for their own good, were a favorite target – "a nation of cads," he complained.[1]

Across the Atlantic, Chamberlain's counterpart, Secretary of the Treasury Henry Morgenthau, Jr., reached the halls of power in a less orthodox way. The son of a prosperous Jewish real estate mogul and ambassador, Morgenthau decided to strike his own path, buying a farm in the Hudson Valley in 1913. He soon became friends with his neighbor Franklin Roosevelt, and when the latter won election to the presidency two decades later, he brought Morgenthau to Washington, eventually installing him as the nation's top economic official. Given that Morgenthau's rise from farmer to chief financier depended entirely on a personal

---

[1] Neville to Hilda Chamberlain, February 4, 1933, in Chamberlain (2002, 374). This description builds on Parker (2002, chapter 1) and Self (2006, chapter 1).

relationship, he was sensitive to slights and instinctively suspicious, always on guard lest someone outmaneuver him. The financiers of London, with their reputation for cunning, were among those he most distrusted. He thus felt it best to keep Chamberlain, and the British generally, at a distance.[2]

This mutual distaste was at its strongest on matters of international monetary policy. As the Great Depression unfolded, both powers had shocked the world by leaving the gold standard. Yet they had done so at different times and in different ways. By 1936, neither trusted the other's currency policy, interpreting every move as an attempt to rig the international monetary system. Though the disputes could be arcane, emotions ran high. London viewed Washington's management of the dollar as ignorant and dangerous; Washington considered London's management of the pound selfish and destabilizing. The countries were locked in a monetary battle, one front of a larger monetary war convulsing the world in the 1930s. And the generals, Chamberlain and Morgenthau – finance ministers of the two most important economies – had no line of communication, so wary was each of the other.

But in the spring of 1936, with France headed toward a currency crisis, Morgenthau tried to put the past behind him and reach an understanding with London. He feared that French devaluation would unleash a new round of competitive depreciation and drag the world further down the abyss. It could worsen France's already fraught political situation and sow further discord between the democracies, all to the benefit of an increasingly aggressive Germany. To forestall these dangers, Morgenthau asked for permission from Roosevelt to open a dialogue with the British. Convincing the president took some persuading – Roosevelt exceeded Morgenthau in distrusting Chamberlain, sure that the latter "thoroughly dislikes Americans" – but Morgenthau eventually got the green light and sent out a feeler.[3] Though Chamberlain was initially reluctant, he soon came around. A stream of cables commenced, first between the two capitals, then including Paris, working out the terms of a monetary truce. Over several months and in fits and starts, the finance ministers devised a plan whereby London and Washington would accept the franc's devaluation and not retaliate, preventing a renewed race to the bottom. In addition, all three countries would contribute to the "restoration of order in international

---

[2] Blum (1959) is the standard reference on Morgenthau.
[3] Morgenthau conversation with Roosevelt, April 29, 1936, MD 22/155.

economic relations" by renouncing competitive depreciation generally and consulting on international monetary policy moving forward.[4]

Announced on September 26, 1936, the Tripartite Agreement, as it became known, offered the hope of a better future, one of cooperation rather than confrontation.[5] "[T]he three great democracies," *The New York Times* enthused, "have given evidence of their ability to work together in behalf of economic peace, recovery and order." With the Agreement, "the world breathed a new hope. A streak of sunlight had broken through the dark clouds of nationalism."[6]

Morgenthau was so pleased with the public's reception that he informed a British representative of wanting one day to shake Chamberlain's hand.[7] The two had accomplished much, he thought, and could still do more. After hearing of Morgenthau's gesture, Chamberlain, unable to take the compliment without a sneer, wrote to his sister, "I trust Providence will not put me to any such ordeal." As it turned out, distance saved him from ever having to suffer Morgenthau's handshake. But even Chamberlain was "glad to have produced such a change of heart" in Morgenthau and the Americans, claiming to have nudged them into a "more sympathetic mood" (Chamberlain's pride would not let him admit that it was really Washington that had prodded London.)[8]

Friends, no, but the two men and their governments, as well as the French, could perhaps now be partners working toward a more stable monetary system. What was needed was trust. Slowly, the countries started to build confidence in one another. They began communicating as a matter of routine, discussing monetary developments and policies. While the Agreement, informal by design, did not bind countries to fixed exchange rates, the parties promised to intervene in markets to limit fluctuations and established new technical arrangements between central banks to facilitate these operations. Rather quickly, a monetary alliance took root.

---

[4] See Appendix C for the text of the British statement and Bank for International Settlements (1937) for all of the statements.

[5] The announcement occurred around 1 a.m. Paris time on September 26, which was still early evening on September 25 in Washington. This book dates the Agreement as having occurred on September 26 since Paris was the first to announce, but other sources date it as September 25.

[6] "Toward Stabilization," *The New York Times*, September 26, 1936; "Restoring Monetary Order," *The New York Times*, October 4, 1936.

[7] Mallet to Waley, September 29, 1936, T 160/840/7. The British representative reported that "Morgenthau was so delighted with the way things had gone that he became quite genial and human!"

[8] Neville to Ida Chamberlain, October 10, 1936, in Chamberlain (2005, 210–11).

To a public yearning for good news, the Tripartite Agreement was a bright light, promising and captivating. For ministers and officials, it provided the backdrop to just about every issue of exchange rate policy, becoming the fundamental organizing principle of the international monetary system until the outbreak of the Second World War. At a time when little was going right, when relentless economic conflict seemed to be the natural order, the liberal powers – "rulers of the three master-currencies of the world" in the words of one City columnist – managed to defy the trend and find peace in their monetary relations.[9]

Yet, squeezed between the demise of the gold standard and the creation of the postwar monetary system, the Agreement is largely forgotten today. Few know of this pact that in many ways serves as the foundation of modern monetary cooperation; fewer still know how it worked. Research into the accord has been sparse. Save for a couple of works several decades ago, it usually receives a sentence at most, a paragraph on occasion, a page almost never.

Indeed, despite the centrality of the 1930s to monetary history, much of the decade's story – not just that of the Tripartite Agreement – remains little known. Too often, the narrative peaks at the collapse of the gold standard and the fury over competitive depreciations and then ignores all that came after. But what came after was no less important. In fact, for most countries, the bulk of the decade was not pre- but post-collapse. Britain left the confines of the gold standard in 1931, the United States in 1933, France in 1936 (past the midpoint but still far from the end). Figuring out what to do in this chaotic situation was no easy task and went well beyond pushing exchange rates down. It was a time of trial and error, with the future of the global economy at stake. By not giving full weight to what happened after the breakdown of the gold standard, the conventional history oversimplifies the monetary war – portraying it as just a battle over exchange rates rather than a fight over the very design of the international monetary system – and disregards the peace. There is thus the need to reexamine the period to better understand how the former unfolded and how the latter emerged and operated. This book aims to do just that.

***

The 1930s was a time of immense deprivation. The statistics continue to astound. Production plummeted, trade evaporated, prices cratered,

---

[9] "World's Hopes from New Currency Compact," *The Daily Telegraph*, October 7, 1936.

unemployment soared. The volume of global trade dropped nearly 30 percent from 1929 to 1932. The United States, which experienced one of the most devastating downturns, saw industrial production fall by almost 50 percent. Unemployment reached one in four. Britain's economy had not climbed as high as others in the 1920s so its crash in the 1930s was less precipitous. But its slump was nevertheless severe. Industrial production fell 17 percent, and unemployment hit one in six. Behind these raw numbers, people starved and anger mounted. While Britain, France, and America made it through without the collapse of society, elsewhere fascism took hold, further compounding the misery.

The Depression was not only grim: It was also incredibly disorienting for everyone living through it, monetary policymakers included. Events moved and ideas changed so rapidly that it was difficult to see straight. As a top official in the British Treasury lamented, "everything in the currency sphere has been kaleidoscopic," making what was clear one moment doubtful the next.[10] To fight the Depression, countries threw off the chains of the gold standard, but then they wavered, unsure of the end goal and how best to get there. The old orthodoxy had lost its grip, but a new religion had yet to take hold. The result was a mishmash of monetary systems, no two precisely the same. Conflict filled the gaps as countries accused one another of distorting their currency policies. They fought not only over the movements of exchange rates – that is, the customary concern about competitive advantage – but also the flexibility of those rates, the connection between currencies and gold, the regulations surrounding gold, the freedom to deal in currencies, virtually every dimension of international monetary policy. Confusion was common, mercantilism ascendant, and confrontation frequent.

But there was also experimentation and innovation. However bewildering the moment, inaction was not a viable option – no politician could long survive in office doing nothing as people went without work and food. Governments had to design and execute policy, often with limited precedent to turn to. Britain, in particular, had little historical guidance with which to map its future after suspending gold convertibility – the promise to exchange currency for gold at a fixed rate – in September 1931. For centuries, sterling's gold value had been constant, except for times of war and its aftermath; suddenly that constraint vanished. The pound dropped 20 percent on impact against the dollar, franc, and other gold currencies, and was down 30 percent by the end of the year.

---

[10] Hopkins, Untitled memo, May 25, 1937, T 177/39.

To better control sterling's movements, Britain devised one of the decade's key monetary inventions in 1932: the Exchange Equalisation Account (EEA). Endowed with assets of £171 million (4.1 percent of GDP) and ultimately growing to over £571 million (10.7 percent of GDP), the fund inaugurated a new era of exchange intervention, with governments actively managing their currencies in the market through the purchase and sale of foreign exchange and gold. At the same time, the EEA inflamed tensions around the world. Its statutory mandate of "checking undue fluctuations of the exchange value of sterling" left wide latitude, and many abroad viewed the secretive hoard as a weapon to depreciate the pound and gain a competitive advantage. America responded by establishing the Exchange Stabilization Fund (ESF) in 1934. The two funds blanketed both sides of the Atlantic in a haze of suspicion. All the while, France, seeking salvation in purity, clung to gold, blaming Anglo-American heretics for its economic plight.

Bitterness and rivalry seemed to be the order of the day until the most important innovation of all: the Tripartite Agreement. Through it, France, conceding to the inevitable, left the gold standard but did so in a way that, far from poisoning relations, drastically improved them. Under the Agreement, rather than protest or retaliate, London and Washington "welcomed" France's decision. Though the arrangement was not a treaty or even a single text – each nation issued its own virtually identical five-paragraph statement – the parties indicated their commitment moving forward to avoid competitive depreciation and exchange control, as well as to work toward easing restrictions on trade. The aim was to achieve "the greatest possible equilibrium in the system of international exchanges," while reserving the right always to "take into full account the requirements of internal prosperity." That is, the countries would no longer act without regard to the impact on others, but neither would they return to a system, such as the gold standard, that required sacrificing the domestic economy at the altar of fixed exchange rates.

Among the many consequences of this entente was a revamping of technical arrangements between the members. Now working in concert, exchange managers were to use their funds to dampen currency fluctuations. But doing so was more complicated than simply buying and selling foreign exchange. Precisely because currencies were no longer fastened to gold, managers did not want foreign exchange on their balance sheets. If a currency depreciated, the fund could take a hit: better to hold gold, which seemed unlikely ever to lose value. To reconcile the need to intervene with the insistence on holding reserves in gold, the Tripartite countries developed a new structure of reciprocal gold facilities, whereby they exchanged their currencies for gold with one another on a daily basis. Britain, for example, would now give gold to France in return for any pounds the latter purchased even though Britain no longer had any legal obligation to convert sterling into gold. This "24-hour gold standard" was a hallmark of the Tripartite years. Besides stitching together the members' disparate monetary systems, this "new type of gold standard," as Morgenthau called it, demonstrated the continued pull of the past: The old gold standard was dead, but the metal remained indispensable.[11]

In November 1936, Belgium, the Netherlands, and Switzerland joined the "currency club." Though "junior members" in the eyes of the founders, smaller influence befitting smaller economies, the club's expansion provided further proof that a corner had been turned.[12] This new cordiality, however, was not universal. Not every country belonged to the club, most notably, Germany, Italy, Japan, and Russia.[13] Their exclusion was on purpose. Part of the motivation behind the Tripartite Agreement was to strengthen the liberal order of free exchange against the proliferation of exchange controls – regulations that governments imposed to restrict transactions in foreign currencies – which the democracies deemed totalitarian. Since Berlin, Rome, Tokyo, and Moscow relied on these methods, their membership would have been incongruous at best. In addition, the Agreement was a tool to unify the democratic powers and demonstrate their resolve to friend and foe alike. A primary motivation for the pact was, its preamble declared, to "safeguard peace." Though London, always trying to keep open the possibility of appeasement, was more hesitant than Paris and Washington in ascribing overtly political intentions to the Agreement, it grew to view the club as an instrument to bring the democracies closer together. The Tripartite Agreement thus became, to its members, the public, and the world, a measure of and force for democratic cooperation.

All of this is to say that the collapse of the gold standard was more than the end of an era: It was just as much the beginning of another. This book picks up the baton, considering what happened after the fall. Three themes ground the narrative. First, understanding why the democratic powers locked horns during the early years of the decade requires looking beyond charts of the pound, dollar, and franc. The monetary war encompassed far

---

[11] Press conference, October 12, 1936, MD 39/34.
[12] See, for instance, Simon to Morgenthau, July 19, 1937, BoE C43/327.
[13] See Chapter 8, however, for the various attempts to bring some of these countries into the fold.

more than a disagreement over the level of exchange rates: It involved all aspects of currency management. For instance, Paris and Washington were to some extent less concerned with the pound's initial depreciation in 1931 than with London's refusal to return to the gold standard and reestablish a fixed rate quickly thereafter. When the Americans left the gold standard in 1933, they did so over a chaotic, drawn-out period, throwing Europe off-balance to a far greater degree than had a clean, one-time devaluation occurred. The way in which Roosevelt devalued, not just the fact that he did, helps explain why relations soured. London and Washington also refused to share information on exchange intervention, leading each to assume that the other was up to no good with their funds. None of these points negate the predominant role of exchange rates, but grasping the full extent of the conflict requires examining each dimension on which it played out. It then becomes clear why tensions remained so high for so long, even during times when countries were generally satisfied with the level of exchange rates.

Second, the Tripartite Agreement was a watershed, fundamentally altering monetary relations. The members pivoted from fighting over their fiercest disagreements to finding areas of consensus on which they could build. Though they differed as to whether exchange rates should be fixed, they all believed that less volatility was better than more, so they set up a system to enable stabilizing intervention through reciprocal gold facilities. Exchange funds, previously suspect, now embodied the new collaborative spirit. Members talked constantly, detailing their actions, getting advice, and coordinating efforts – gone were the days when London and Washington guarded information on intervention from each other as a state secret. The Agreement provided the framework through which all issues of international monetary policy were considered, by both policymakers and the public. As Sir Frederick Leith-Ross, one of Britain's top financial diplomats, recalled, it was "the basis of our currency policy."[14]

To be sure, the Tripartite Agreement was not perfect. It was limited by design, leaving many problems unsolved. None of the members were willing to lend to one another, meaning that there was no long-term support for balance of payments problems. Officials, ministers, and observers wondered at times exactly what the Agreement required given its purposeful ambiguity, and more than a few crises tested its viability, particularly repeated problems with the franc. But there is no question

---

[14] Leith-Ross (1968, 170).

that it marked a momentous shift. Countries no longer viewed the international monetary system as an arena in which to fight for maximum advantage but as a structure that needed to be upheld for the benefit of all.

Finally, giving the Tripartite system its due sheds light on the evolution of the international monetary system, particularly the role of gold. Monetary systems are not binary: They exist on a continuum. The breakdown of the gold standard did not mean the end of gold's influence; in fact, it solidified the metal's preeminence as a reserve asset among the democratic powers. Many central banks had held foreign exchange on their balance sheets in the 1920s and the beginning of the 1930s when the gold standard was in operation. They then suffered enormous losses on these assets as the system disintegrated and currencies depreciated during the first half of the 1930s. As a result, monetary authorities rebalanced their portfolios away from foreign exchange and toward gold. The irony, then, was that when the gold standard was credible, foreign exchange was an acceptable reserve asset; once the gold standard fell apart, only gold seemed safe.[15] Studying the evolving principles of foreign exchange management, including the first in-depth analysis of the reciprocal gold facilities, brings these considerations into relief and helps bridge the gap in the literature between the end of the gold standard and the birth of the postwar system at Bretton Woods.

What follows then is a story about international monetary policy and relations in the wake of the gold standard's collapse. It examines the triangle joining London, Paris, and Washington (with some branching out to Amsterdam, Berne, and Brussels), looking at why the connections frayed and how, with the Tripartite Agreement, they became stronger than ever. Though all three sides are integral to this history, the emphasis is on the London–Washington link. It suffered the greatest strain at the decade's beginning, nearly snapping in half from the pressure, but went on to mend and rejuvenate during the Tripartite years. Indeed, the Anglo-American relationship formed the backbone of the currency club.

And while this book is international in scope, it focuses on Britain's management of the pound to structure the narrative. There are many reasons for doing so. As the first major country to depreciate and suspend

---

[15] This dynamic applied to countries with key currencies, the focus of this book. There was an opposite tendency to move away from gold and toward foreign exchange for smaller countries whose economies were closely connected to larger trading partners. For instance, much of the British Empire, as well as Scandinavia and some other countries, pegged to sterling and turned most of their reserves into sterling. See Chapter 3 for more on what became known as the Sterling Area.

gold convertibility, Britain launched the era that this book seeks to explain. The Bank of England (BoE), exhorted on by the Treasury, lowered its policy rate to 2 percent in the summer of 1932 in pursuit of a "cheap money" program and kept it there for an unprecedented seven years until the outbreak of war. With this policy lever pushed to and held at an all-time low, exchange rate management became the dominant day-to-day and month-to-month concern. The EEA thus turned into Britain's main monetary policy instrument. Records of its operations – the longest available since it predated other funds by several years – provide a window into the changing strategies of exchange managers and the ups and downs of international monetary relations. Sterling was also a linchpin of the international monetary system, with roughly one-fifth of the world's population living in a country that either used sterling or pegged to it.[16] Finally, though there has been brilliant work on various aspects of Britain's story – Howson (1980) on the EEA, Sayers (1976) on the BoE, Drummond (1979, 1981) on the relationship with America, all of which provide the foundation for this book – it has yet to be told in full. London, then, is the ideal vantage point from which to explore the new monetary world of the 1930s.

***

The literature on the Great Depression is vast, and monetary policy plays an important role in any economic history of the period. Of course, it is a largely ignominious role. As Ahamed (2009, 7) writes, central bankers of the leading powers – the "lords of finance" – "broke the world" by forcing it into the "straitjacket" of the gold standard in the aftermath of the First World War. Under their stewardship, countries pegged their currencies to gold and thereby to one another, bringing about, by the end of the 1920s, a system of fixed rates. But as the downturn set in, the gold standard became a trap. The first rule of the gold standard was to maintain the peg, which meant keeping interest rates high enough to prevent gold from flowing out. The perverse result was that, even as economic prospects worsened, monetary authorities fought to attract gold, raising interest rates. Friedman and Schwartz (1963) show how in the United States the collapse in money supply brought about a grinding deflation that debilitated the economy, a story played out to varying degrees around the world.[17]

---

[16] Aldcroft (2004, 35).

[17] Eichengreen (1992) provides an invaluable panoramic view of the interwar monetary system. Country-specific studies include: for Britain, Drummond (1981), Howson (1975), and Sayers (1976); for the United States, Chandler (1971), Friedman and Schwartz

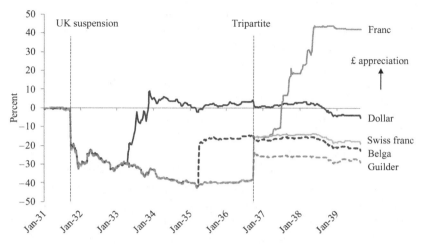

Figure I.1 Sterling exchange rate, 1931–1939 (percent deviation from pre-1931 parity).
Note: Upward movement indicates the pound appreciating relative to the listed currency.
Source: *Financial Times*

While the interwar gold standard's setup involved organized efforts to bring countries into the fold, its collapse was mayhem. Once deflation became too much to bear, countries freed themselves in a variety of ways: Some lessened the gold value of their currencies in a one-time devaluation, others depreciated their currencies by ending the gold link altogether, and the rest imposed exchange controls.[18] Finance ministries also assumed command over monetary policy, the central banks' lords of finance having lost much of their cachet. It took time for this process to play out. Britain acted in September 1931, the United States in 1933, Belgium in 1935, and France, the Netherlands, and Switzerland not until 1936. Figure I.1 depicts the pound's exchange rate against these currencies over the decade and the sharp changes associated with these depreciations.

With currencies no longer kept in tight confines by gold parities, countries managed their exchange rates by establishing exchange funds and intervening in markets. There is a long-running debate in the

(1963), and Meltzer (2003); for France, Mouré (1991, 2002); and for smaller European countries, Straumann (2010). For general histories of the interwar era, see Feinstein, Temin, and Toniolo (1997); Boyce (2009); and Tooze (2014).

[18] Devaluation in a strict sense refers to moving from one fixed rate to a lower fixed rate, whereas depreciation refers to a floating exchange rate losing value. This book does not stress the distinction and at times uses the terms interchangeably to refer generally to a reduction in the value of the currency.

economics literature about the efficacy of intervention, as summarized in Neely (2005). While the technical issues go well beyond the scope of this book, it bears mentioning that the frequency and scale of intervention in the 1930s likely made it more impactful than the more recent experience on which much of the literature is based – episodes in the 1980s and 1990s that tended to be one-off events.[19] More to the point, in the 1930s, policymakers took it as given that intervention was effective, indeed powerful. Monetary relations thus hinged on whether countries perceived exchange funds as acting competitively or cooperatively.

It was slowly realized at the time and later documented empirically – including by Choudhri and Kochin (1980) and Eichengreen and Sachs (1985) – that escape from the rigid gold standard was associated with faster recovery and could even be a boon to world growth.[20] In fact, some scholars, such as Eichengreen (2013), argue that the currency war was not all that bad. Countries needed to free themselves from the gold standard and launch an expansionary monetary policy to get their economies growing again. While a coordinated effort to lower interest rates would have been best, in its absence, the currency war did well enough, getting countries to where they needed to be. This book readily accepts the well-established fact that pursuing an expansionary monetary policy was imperative for recovery and that depreciation helped bring that about (though, it should be noted, countries often depreciated and then hesitated to lower interest rates, leading to competitive impacts first before boosting aggregate demand later).[21]

This book does, however, spotlight the giant chasm between the first and second best. The currency war did not happen instantaneously; it took place over years. Anger intensified. Retaliation kicked in. Countries responded on a variety of economic fronts. Many dimensions of international monetary policy became weaponized, which is why this book uses the term "monetary war" to stress the all-encompassing nature of the conflict, as opposed to "currency war," which usually connotes a confined battle over exchange rates. Trade policy entered the fray. Relations became so strained that, as in the case with London and Washington, authorities stopped talking, raising the risks for miscalculation. A monetary war may ultimately bring countries stuck in a deflationary spiral to the right place, but too much can go wrong en route for complacency. And even if the first

---

[19] Fratzscher et al. (2019) is a recent study that finds intervention to be effective.
[20] See also Bernanke and James (1991) and Mitchener and Wandschneider (2015).
[21] Eichengreen (1992, 288).

best was unattainable, the second best need not have been so bad. All the more important then to understand why the monetary war unfolded as it did, what was avoidable, and how the peace came to be.

That peace, reached in 1936 amid fears of a chaotic franc devaluation and smoothed by a new recognition that it was ludicrous for the countries to have their backs turned to one another at such a time, set forth a novel framework for cooperation that became the foundation of modern intergovernmental monetary collaboration. Some scholars have recognized this turn, Dam (1982, 49) arguing that the Tripartite Agreement "represented a move toward multilateralism and toward a recognition that exchange rates were matters for international and not merely domestic concern." Kindleberger (1986, 259) considers it a "milestone."[22] And Blum (1959, 181) concludes that, with much of the world sinking into totalitarianism, it was "an early reaction to fascism, the first evidence that the Western democracies could profit collectively from mutually acceptable concessions."

Yet, for the most part, researchers have downplayed the Agreement's significance, when they have acknowledged it at all. Toniolo (2005, 182), in his masterful history of central bank cooperation during the interwar and Bretton Woods periods, concludes that it "does not stand out in the eventful economic history of the late 1930s." Others contend that it was too informal to really mean anything. Drummond (1981, 223) has studied these years in the greatest detail and finds the Agreement lacking: The members made no promises about exchange rates, and "intergovernmental discussions" were "incomplete, spasmodic, and perfunctory." What resulted was "a shadow of international monetary cooperation but not its substance." Moreover, the franc continued to depreciate, from 105 francs to the pound right after the announcement of the pact to 179 to the pound by May 1938. The Agreement, in this telling, meant little and accomplished even less.[23]

---

[22] Kindleberger (1986, 259) qualifies his assessment, however, by characterizing the Tripartite Agreement as "half-hearted, or perhaps only an eighth-hearted." Additional works that view the Agreement as important and successful (to varying degrees) include Sayers (1976, 2:480–81) and Eichengreen (2015).

[23] Mouré (2002, 242–43) also sees little impact. Meltzer (2003, 544–45) considers the Agreement to have had "two basic flaws. The first was failure to distinguish between real and nominal exchange rates. . . . Second was the belief that international cooperation was a viable alternative to exchange rate adjustment." Meltzer is correct that the parties cared most about nominal stability – a preference that would continue into the Bretton Woods years. But policymakers understood that price changes impacted the viability of exchange rates. Moreover, they also recognized that exchange rate adjustment could become necessary at times and as such did not fix rates.

There is no question that, as Figure I.1 shows, exchange rates were not constant during the Tripartite years. But that was not the goal policy-makers set: They wanted stability, not rigidity. The question is not whether the Agreement achieved fixed rates – in fact, the parties never agreed to that, understanding that at times economic adjustment would need to go through exchange rates – but whether the signatories worked toward greater stability. The counterfactual, as ever, is unknowable. The method employed in this book is to dig underneath exchange rates to uncover policymakers' motives and actions. This book argues that the parties made good faith efforts to uphold the Tripartite Agreement, an understanding that, while informal, was nevertheless substantial, representing a new conception of an international monetary system predicated on cooperation. And sticking together was by no means easy during these years of intense strain, as war scares, politics, and recessions impacted exchange rates. Crises could have split the currency club asunder, but the bonds connecting members proved up to the task.

***

This book consists of ten chapters. Chapter 1 provides background on the classical gold standard. Chapter 2 looks at how that system fell apart during the First World War, how monetary authorities tried to reconstruct it in the 1920s, and how the new incarnation came crashing down in 1931 when Britain suspended convertibility. The next three chapters explore the monetary war. Chapter 3 recounts Britain's efforts to come to grips with a currency untethered to gold, focusing on the establishment of the EEA in 1932. Chapter 4 then describes Roosevelt's monetary experiments and the concomitant low point in relations. Chapter 5 details France's financial troubles and walks through the negotiations that led to the Tripartite Agreement.

Chapters 6 through 9 explore the Tripartite years. Chapter 6 discusses the creation of the reciprocal gold facilities and analyzes the operation of the Tripartite system. Chapter 7 investigates the Gold Scare and Dollar Scare, two crises centering on the price of gold that tested the new cooperative spirit and provide insight into gold's role during these years. Chapter 8 relates the chronic problems of the franc and the efforts by all three parties to keep the currency club together. Chapter 9 describes sterling's distress in the run-up to the Second World War and the Tripartite Agreement's lapse with the onset of fighting. Finally, Chapter 10 discusses the Agreement's legacy.

I began researching this project as a graduate student in 2015. It was a time when, despite innumerable political and economic problems, the demons of the 1930s seemed safely consigned to history. The world had largely recovered from the financial crisis, and the political order appeared stable. How much things have changed as I finish this book five years later. The connections to that awful decade seem to multiply by the day. Democracy is under attack. Economic nationalism is on the rise, with talk of currency wars rife. Though I do not examine current events, my hope is that shining a light on the Tripartite Agreement provides a jolt of optimism to those searching for a better way. Even in the darkest of times, progress can be made. To that end, Chapter 10 draws out some general lessons for monetary policymakers from these years – the importance of sharing information, the benefits of establishing routine forms of cooperation, and the power of informal arrangements.

Before proceeding, a few words about what this book is and is not. This book is not a history of the 1930s economy, nor of its politics, though both certainly enter the story. It is not about the trade war, war debts, or the many other disputes plaguing the world order. The monetary conflict was, of course, global, not only pitting democracy against democracy but democracies against dictatorships. However, this book does not delve into developments in Germany, Italy, Japan, Russia, or other countries – important though they were – except where they intersect directly with monetary relations between the democracies. The 1930s has given rise to an extensive literature for good reason, and this book relies on those works without attempting to pack so much of the decade's history into the narrative that it swerves off course.

This is a book, then, about a period in monetary history that has been neglected for far too long. It is about Britain's management of the pound during the 1930s and its monetary relations with the Tripartite countries. It is about a time of deep uncertainty, when the gold standard catechism was found wanting but a ready replacement did not yet exist. It is about innovations in exchange rate management. And it is about the move by the "great currency authorities" to band together, as one BoE official put it, in a "treaty of friendship" to restore some order to an international system decimated by unilateralism.[24]

This book is the product of archival research conducted in Britain, the United States, France, Belgium, the Netherlands, and Switzerland. It employs everything from transcripts of meetings in finance ministries to internal memoranda in central banks to exchange fund balance sheets.

---

[24] Clay, Untitled memo, January 10, 1939, BoE C43/100.

Throughout, we encounter a cast of characters, some well-known and others long forgotten. The Tripartite Agreement, though far from perfect, was their attempt to find solid ground after years in quicksand, to reach for something better when so much else was going wrong; their success in doing so redounds to their credit.

1

A Classical Prelude, 1880–1914

During the interwar era, there was no shortage of cranks, traditionalists, revolutionaries, reactionaries – indeed, thinkers and policymakers of all kinds – offering cures for society's ills. This was especially so in the monetary field, where proposals ranged from minor alterations to radical reconfigurations. Yet, to an astounding degree, this sweeping debate revolved around a shared reference point: the classical gold standard. A nebulous mixture of historical fact and economic abstraction, the classical gold standard represented an idea as much as it depicted the reality of the international monetary system in the decades before the First World War. As history, theory, and ideology, it permeated the discussions and influenced the decisions of the interwar period, from the near-universal desire to resurrect its tenets in the 1920s to the abandonment of many of those principles in the 1930s.[1] It was worshipped by some and reviled by others, but rarely a matter of indifference.

The classical gold standard is therefore the natural starting point for studying the monetary twists and turns of the Great Depression. What follows is a brief overview of the system's history and theory.[2] Along the way, this chapter introduces some institutional details of British monetary policymaking, such as the relationship between the Treasury and the Bank of England (BoE) as well as regulations surrounding the BoE's note issue, which play a crucial part in the interwar story. In addition, exploring the gold arbitrage mechanism in its classical form sets the stage for the 1930s,

---

[1] Eichengreen and Temin (2000) argue that the "mentality of the gold standard" conditioned policymakers' response to the Great Depression and delayed appropriate action to combat the downturn.

[2] For in-depth studies on the classical gold standard, see Bordo and Schwartz (1984), Eichengreen (1992, chapter 2), and Eichengreen and Flandreau (1997).

when gold and exchange markets were the focal points of monetary action, the arenas in which countries battled one another and eventually – after much damage had been done – worked to promote the common good.

Beyond providing context, surveying the classical era sheds light on a recurrent theme throughout this book: Gold is not monolithic. There is not one way to be "on" gold, and there are many ways to be "off" it. Even during the classical gold standard, when reality came as close as ever to approximating the textbook model, no two countries had precisely the same monetary setup. Decades later, once the Great Depression had demolished the world's monetary infrastructure, this multiplicity only intensified, and governments had to figure out how to operate in a fractious, balkanized system where every country treated gold differently.

✳✳✳

Today, the BoE is housed in a hulking structure that crams two massive stacks of columns, a narrow portico, a balcony, and a large pediment into its facade. While the building dates from the 1920s, the BoE's history and traditions stretch back much further into the past. Founded in 1694, the BoE has occupied the same area on Threadneedle Street in the City of London since 1734. Gatekeepers clad in a centuries-old uniform – black trousers, pink tailcoat over red waistcoat, black top hat with gold trimming – continue to greet visitors. For ceremonial occasions, they don red capes and carry bamboo staffs. Other connections to the past are less visible from the outside but no less significant. Several floors below ground level, nine vaults store 400,000 bars of gold on behalf of clients around the world. These vaults are not only important to owners of the gold, which is worth some £200 billion, but they also hearken back to a time when the metal was the foundation of the monetary system, when gold was money and money was gold.[3]

Exactly when the classical gold standard began is to some degree a matter of definitional preference. Britain went on gold in 1717, and save for a disruption of several decades during the Napoleonic Wars, continued at the same parity into the twentieth century. Most scholars date the international system as starting around 1880, by which point all the major Western powers were on gold.[4] It ended, far more abruptly, with the outbreak of war in 1914. During its heyday, the vast majority of countries – from the core of Britain, France, Germany, and the United States to much of the rest of Europe, Latin

---

[3] Bank of England (2020). For a general history of the BoE, see Kynaston (2017).
[4] Eichengreen and Flandreau (1997, 3).

America, and elsewhere – made gold the cornerstone of their monetary systems. Not that any treaty brought this about.[5] Rather, the international gold standard developed from the individual decisions of countries to connect their currencies to the metal, decisions that no doubt took into account the rising benefits of joining as globalization proceeded apace.

There were several steps to establishing a gold standard.[6] A country needed to (1) define its currency in terms of a specified weight of gold, (2) coin gold and designate the coins legal tender, (3) enforce the interchangeability between gold and paper currency, and (4) allow the export and import of gold without restriction. These measures did not imply that gold changed hands with every transaction. Monetary authorities issued paper currency and deposit banking became more advanced, and hence gold coin tended to play a decreasing role in everyday life. However, the legal obligation to convert paper currency into gold on demand constrained the amount issued by authorities – often but not exclusively central banks – as they had to hold a specified reserve of gold to back up the promise.[7] In addition, even though gold was at the center, not all gold was considered the same. Gold coin, minted by the government, was legal tender, whereas gold bullion (non-coined gold, such as gold in bar form) was not. For this reason, bars were worth less than coins, but as bars were easier to handle in large amounts, gold operators preferred this form of the metal.

Britain's monetary system followed these general tenets. First, the government defined sterling in terms of gold. The Coinage Act of 1816 set one standard ounce of gold (11/12 fine) at £3. 17s. 10½d.[8]

---

[5] There were some attempts at international cooperation on monetary matters, including a series of conferences during the second half of the nineteenth century, as discussed in Reti (1998). In addition, the Latin Monetary Union, formed by treaty in 1865, harmonized the then bimetallic monetary systems of Belgium, France, Italy, Switzerland, and, several years later, Greece, as recounted in Einaudi (2001).

[6] This section draws on Officer (1996, chapter 2).

[7] The United States notably had no central bank until the creation of the Federal Reserve in 1913.

[8] Governments measured gold content differently. Gold could be measured in fine ounces, which referred to the total amount of pure gold, or standard ounces, which referred to gold of a certain percentage of fineness. However, standard ounces were not standardized: Different countries used different ratios of fineness. The British measured gold in terms of standard ounces that were defined as gold that was 11/12 fine (11 parts gold to 1 part alloy). Some other countries, including the United States, defined a standard ounce as 9/10 fine. Since standard ounces are not always the same, fine gold measurements are best for comparing gold content. There are 480 grains of fine gold per troy ounce. With one standard ounce of gold 11/12 fine equal to £3.89, one pound sterling was equivalent to 113 grains of fine gold (Officer 1996, part I).

Prior to decimalization in the 1970s, there were 12 pence (d) to the shilling (s) and 20 shillings to the pound (£), hence the value of a standard ounce of gold in decimal form was roughly £3.89 (though the pre-decimal practice will be used in this book). Second, Britain allowed the coinage of bullion and the melting of coins; the former permitted gold to become money and the latter simplified the export of gold. Both gold coins and BoE notes were legal tender. Third, the BoE bought and sold gold at fixed prices against its notes. The prices were statutorily set at £3. 17s. 9d. per standard ounce for buying bullion and £3. 17s. 10½d. for selling coin, respectively.[9] This spread between buying and selling prices, in part a function of minting costs, was a key component in market operators' calculations as to when gold arbitrage was profitable, as discussed below. Finally, gold movements and exchange transactions were unrestricted so that holders of sterling could receive gold in exchange no matter where they resided.

Just how much gold the BoE had to hold in reserve was set out by the Bank Charter Act of 1844. This Act divided the BoE, which was privately owned at the time and would remain so until its nationalization in 1946, into two departments: the Issue Department and the Banking Department. The Issue Department had responsibility for supplying notes to the public as well as exchanging gold for notes. The Act allowed the BoE to create notes against a fixed Fiduciary Issue, composed of (mostly government) securities, and then required all notes beyond that to be backed one-for-one with gold. For instance, at the beginning of 1914, the Fiduciary Issue was £18 million and the Issue Department held £36 million in gold, and hence the total note issue was £54 million. If the BoE wanted to print an additional £1,000 of notes, it would have needed an additional £1,000 of gold. Clearly, the larger the Fiduciary Issue relative to the size of the note issue, the more fragile the commitment to convert notes on demand appeared.[10] The Banking Department, on the other hand, was that part of the BoE that, as its name suggests, acted as banker for the government and other banks.[11]

These policies, both those specific to Britain and the many variations adopted by other countries, created domestic and international gold

---

[9] Technically, the law required the BoE to pay at least £3. 17s. 9d. per standard ounce for bullion. It could pay more and did so at times when it employed gold devices as described below (Sayers 1953, 132–33).

[10] Some countries implemented this fiduciary system, while others enacted percentage-based gold covers, which mandated that there should be enough gold to back up a set percentage of liabilities (Eichengreen and Flandreau 1997, 5).

[11] Meltzer (2003, chapter 2).

standards. The domestic system resulted from the first three pillars: The currency was defined in terms of gold, bullion could become legal coin (and vice versa), and gold could be obtained in exchange for paper currency. A specie standard, whereby specie (coin) is in circulation, exists when all three of these conditions are in operation. Specie standards were common during the classical era, with coin and currency notes circulating freely and interchangeably. A gold bullion standard, on the other hand, occurs when coinage of bullion is not allowed, and the monetary authority converts currency into gold for large amounts only, requiring customers to purchase heavy bars instead of coin. The currency still revolves around gold, but coin does not circulate widely, allowing the monetary authority to centralize the nation's gold and exert greater influence over its movements. Britain, France, and many other countries would switch to the gold bullion standard in the 1920s.

The international aspect derived from the above in conjunction with the unrestricted movement of gold. Because countries defined their currencies in terms of gold, each pair of currencies had a mint parity that expressed their relative gold values. For example, the United States fixed the dollar at 23.22 grains of fine gold, meaning that one ounce of fine gold was worth $20.67. The mint parity between the dollar and the pound was then the ratio of the grains of gold in each currency. Since one pound sterling was worth 113 grains of fine gold, the mint parity was 113/23.22 = $4.8665 per pound, conventionally reported as $4.86. Equivalent calculations pinned down mint parities for all currencies tied to gold.

Importantly, exchange rates were not simply frozen at mint parities. Then as today, market trading – the balancing of supply and demand for each currency – determined exchange rates. But the mint parity acted as a fulcrum around which the exchange rate pivoted. The commitment to convert currency into gold and allow the import and export of gold kept the exchange rate close to parity because once the former drifted too far from the latter, market operators could capitalize on the gap and make a profit. For example, if sterling was trading significantly below parity, it was profitable to convert sterling into gold, sell the gold to the United States in exchange for dollars, and then use those dollars to purchase sterling: Arbitrageurs doing so would end up with more sterling than they began. As a result of these transactions, gold flowed from London to New York and the associated sale of dollars helped support the sterling exchange. Likewise, when sterling was well above parity, gold flowed from New York to London.

Arbitrageurs did not act the moment the exchange rate deviated from mint parity. After all, arbitrage was not riskless, nor was transporting a

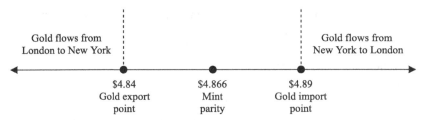

Figure 1.1 Sterling-dollar gold points.

heavy, valuable metal across vast distances free. There were many costs: insurance, brokerage, packing, freight, foregone interest, forward cover, just to name the most important. Monetary authorities also usually had a spread between buying and selling prices for gold. Because of these costs and spreads, arbitrage did not become profitable until there was a sufficient wedge between the exchange rate and mint parity.

The cutoffs for determining whether or not arbitrage transactions made sense were termed "gold points," the gold export point signaling that exporting gold was profitable and the gold import point that importing it was. Each pair of nations had its own such points with each other, so that, for example, the pound could be at gold import point relative to the franc (gold flowing from Paris to London) but at gold export point relative to the dollar (gold flowing from London to New York). Moreover, the gold points were not set in stone. They depended on the constellation of forces determining the costs of shipping as well as the statutory prices of gold. During the classical era, exchange rate movements tended to be confined to tight bounds, with the sterling-dollar gold points roughly one-half of a percent on either side of parity (around $4.84 and $4.89) in the decade before the war.[12] Figure 1.1 illustrates the sterling-dollar gold points.

The notion of ships crisscrossing the oceans to move tons of gold from one vault to another might seem odd today, but these transfers were foundational to the system as it then existed.[13] Gold flows settled balance of payments deficits and helped re-equilibrate the global economy. A nation running a persistent current account deficit, without offsetting capital inflows, would have its exchange rate fall below gold export point since demand for foreign currency exceeded demand for home currency. With the exchange rate below gold export point, the country would

---

[12] Officer (1996, 174).

[13] See Chapter 2 for a discussion of the rising preference for earmarking gold to reduce shipments.

transfer gold (by way of arbitrage shipments) to surplus countries. This transfer reduced the payments deficit and, under what would later be called the "rules of the game," signaled to policymakers the need to take steps that would work toward resolving the imbalance moving forward.[14] The country losing gold was to engage in monetary tightening, while the one gaining gold was to promote monetary expansion. Both of these actions helped to increase the price competitiveness of the deficit country and thus move the balance of payments back toward equilibrium.[15]

The policy interest rate was the usual lever for affecting credit conditions. For example, increasing the interest rate would help to attract short-term capital inflows or at least stanch outflows. A higher interest rate would also raise the cost of credit, acting as a force to reduce prices and thereby increase competitiveness. The BoE's policy rate, known as Bank Rate, was the minimum rate at which it would rediscount paper. It fell under the BoE's exclusive control, with the Treasury having no say in the decision process. "There has never been," wrote a former Treasury official in the 1920s, "either in my time or previously, any 'consultation' between the Bank of England and the Treasury in any shape or form with regard to changes in bank rate. In prewar days a change in bank rate was no more regarded as the business of the Treasury than the colour which the Bank painted its front door."[16] Responsibility for maintaining the gold standard rested squarely with the BoE, and its independence in carrying out this task went without question.

Gold flows in, lower the interest rate; gold flows out, raise the rate. The system seemed, to interwar observers at least, to have been automatic. So long as gold could move from country to country in response to market conditions and so long as central banks appropriately altered credit conditions, international balances would equilibrate and there would be little else to do. Monetary authorities simply had to maintain the gold parity. Achieving external equilibrium was thus the singular focus, even if the internal adjustments caused by a decrease or increase in credit might have been undesirable. In its fullest expression, then, the gold standard made domestic monetary conditions dependent on international ones.

---

[14] Keynes apparently coined the term in the 1920s (Bloomfield 1959, 47).

[15] In the mid-eighteenth century, David Hume described this process in his price-specie flow model (Eichengreen 1992, chapter 2).

[16] Quoted in Moggridge (1972, 160). Peden (2000, 12) writes that, in the prewar era, "the Governor of the Bank rarely had occasion to see the Chancellor—so much so that, when he did so during a financial crisis in 1914, his visit to the Treasury had to be concealed in case it caused further alarm."

There are qualifications to this account, however, that, while not negating its thrust, nevertheless reveal a more nuanced system. The unspoken rules implied that countries were expected to refrain from sterilizing gold flows – that is, neutralizing them – through offsetting open market operations. In other words, a country losing gold needed to contract the money supply and a country gaining gold needed to expand it. But officials might not have wanted to deflate or inflate as required. If a central bank losing gold went into the market and purchased government bonds in the same amount, the domestic monetary base would not change and the adjustment process would not occur; likewise, if a central bank gaining gold went into the market and sold government bonds. In these cases, countries gaining gold would continue to gain it, countries losing gold would continue to lose it, and there would be no tendency for international imbalances to decrease. Sterilization appears to have occurred somewhat regularly, making the classical gold standard less automatic and self-equilibrating than the idea it represented.[17]

Sometimes authorities merely wanted to ease, rather than completely avoid, the adjustment process. For instance, if a country was losing gold, officials could manipulate the gold points to hasten the import of gold – such as by offering interest-free advances to gold importers – or impose difficulties on its export without having to implement as drastic an increase in interest rates as would otherwise be necessary. Britain, and especially France and Germany, resorted to these "gold devices," which were an option because statutory regulations often left authorities wiggle room. The BoE, for example, could deal with foreign gold coins at whatever prices it desired; by altering these prices, it could impact the movement of gold between countries.[18] In addition, some central banks, notably those in France and Belgium, even had the option of converting their legal tender notes into silver coins instead of gold.[19]

The final qualification to the conventional story is the role of foreign exchange reserves. While Britain and the United States held the entirety of their reserves in gold, many other countries possessed considerable amounts of foreign exchange, whether as backing for their currencies or as supplemental resources. In 1913, foreign exchange accounted for almost 19 percent of reserves among thirty-five countries, including 21 percent for

---

[17] Bloomfield (1959, 47–51).
[18] Sayers (1953) details the BoE's use of gold devices. See also Eichengreen (1992, 37).
[19] These countries were on the so-called limping gold standard. Eichengreen and Flandreau (1997, 5).

Switzerland and over 60 percent for Belgium.[20] To the degree that foreign exchange reserves substituted for gold, they helped economize on the use of the metal. They could also provide central banks with interest income, a not insignificant factor given that central banks were private institutions still concerned with profitability and there were storage and handling costs associated with gold.

Most important, foreign exchange reserves provided yet another means to affect the flow of gold. As Bloomfield (1959, 55) writes, they "enabled the central banks in question to intervene directly in the exchange market when it was desired to smooth out excessive and erratic fluctuations in exchange rates within the gold points and, in particular, to prevent rates from moving to the gold export point at which private arbitrage outflows of gold would have become profitable." At the same time, foreign exchange reserves could increase the system's vulnerability: If official holders of sterling, say, began to distrust it, they could sell their sterling assets and purchase other currencies or gold. Given the size of central bank balances, such portfolio adjustments could put immense pressure on the target currency. This potential for trouble did not materialize during the classical era, but it would become a colossal problem in the interwar years.

Notwithstanding these important caveats, the classical gold standard largely operated in accordance with the stylizations that so entranced – or exasperated – interwar observers. And while it was not without problems, it functioned reasonably well. Gold flows kept exchange rates in tight bounds. After a prolonged period of deflation in the last quarter of the nineteenth century, discoveries of the metal in South Africa along with improvements in mining provided a large enough output to keep pace with the growing global economy as the twentieth century began.[21] Money traversed the world at record levels. Long-term capital flows were large, as Britain and other European nations invested in developing economies. And short-term capital flows tended to be stabilizing because faith in exchange rate pegs appeared justified. There was a tacit understanding that authorities would suspend convertibility only in the event of a national emergency, such as war, and that once the crisis had passed, they would work toward returning to convertibility at the old parity, just as Britain had done after the Napoleonic wars. Indeed, the credibility of the parity structure was an essential element of the system's success.[22]

---

[20] Lindert (1969, table 1).   [21] Friedman and Schwartz (1963, 90–91).
[22] Eichengreen (1992, chapter 2).

Sterling, and by implication the BoE, was at the center of this system, with the sterling bill serving as the predominant instrument for financing trade. As the economist John Maynard Keynes famously wrote, the BoE "could almost have claimed to be the conductor of the international orchestra," its moves to ease or tighten credit setting the tempo for the rest of the world.[23] The United States, on the other hand, did not even have a central bank, and its at times dysfunctional monetary system spread financial turmoil abroad. But the creation of the Federal Reserve in 1913 seemed to augur a more responsible future for the rising economic power. For the most part, the system operated through the independent actions of monetary authorities rather than collaboration between them. Despite a few episodes of cooperation between European central banks during crises, there was no sustained development of relations.[24] There did not seem to be much need: Each country just had to keep its own house in order and, the thinking went, all would be well.

At its height, the classical gold standard appeared, particularly to the elite, as self-evidently the optimal setup, a system that respected traditional verities and represented a triumph of civilization. The ministers and officials responsible for guiding policy in the 1930s began their professional lives in this milieu. Montagu Norman was already a director of the BoE in 1907, an institution he would later lead for nearly a quarter of a century. Neville Chamberlain, the future chancellor, won his first election for the Birmingham City Council in 1911. Harry Siepmann graduated from Oxford in 1912, earned the third-highest score on the civil service exam, and entered the Treasury, his first step in becoming an expert in international monetary affairs.[25] Frederick Phillips and Frederick Leith-Ross – both in time Sir Frederick – were getting their feet wet at the Treasury as well.[26]

Also in London, the Frenchman Charles Cariguel was learning the foreign exchange trade at Société Générale's office, a skill that would prove invaluable during his sixteen-year reign over the foreign department at the Banque de France.[27] In Paris, many of the politicians who would accept the seemingly cursed finance ministry portfolio were just starting their careers. Across the Atlantic, the future secretary of the

---

[23] Quoted in Eichengreen (1990, 289).

[24] Eichengreen (1992, chapter 2) argues that cooperation was essential to upholding the system; Flandreau (1997) considers it to have been far less important.

[25] "Mr. H. A. Siepmann," *The Times* (London), September 17, 1963.

[26] Peden (2008); Middleton (2008).

[27] "City Men and Matters," *Financial Times*, February 2, 1938.

Treasury, Henry Morgenthau, seemed destined for a more bucolic life in these last years of peace, buying an apple farm in upstate New York in 1913. There was little reason for any of these men or their colleagues to think twice about the gold standard. And then the world went to war.

2

Britain's Biggest Blunder, 1914–1931

Harry Siepmann was just one of the many millions of men and women whose lives were upended by the First World War. In his mid-20s when hostilities commenced, Siepmann was at the beginning of what seemed likely to be a brilliant career at the British Treasury. But war, in particular war against Germany, threw everything into confusion. During the tense summer months of 1914, his father, a German *émigré* with an "embarrassingly guttural accent," faced a torrent of insults. Siepmann himself was briefly arrested in the early days of August while walking near the Cornish shore with a lantern – the concern being that a man with a Germanic surname must be using the light to signal submarines, not, as he was, to avoid tripping in the fog. Siepmann had been born in Britain, attended top schools, played rugby, and served in government, but after his detainment in Cornwall, he feared those credentials might not be enough to demonstrate his family's loyalty. Hoping to dispel any question about his family's allegiance and compelled by a sense of duty to country, he soon volunteered for military service, the first Treasury official to do so.[1]

A captain in the Royal Field Artillery, Siepmann was deployed to Egypt, France, Italy, and Germany. After demobilization, the Treasury sent him to the peace conference in Paris to serve "under a man called Keynes, who complained of being shamefully overworked."[2] He then spent the first half of the postwar decade in the private sector and as a financial adviser to Hungary, before beginning his nearly thirty-year career at the Bank of England (BoE) in 1926, during which time he was instrumental in crafting

---

[1] Siepmann (1987, 13–16); "Mr. H. A. Siepmann," *The Times* (London), September 17, 1963. It took some time for the Treasury to allow him to join the army, however, as his superiors wanted all hands on deck in Whitehall.

[2] Siepmann (1987, 176).

Britain's international monetary policy. Colleagues universally recognized his intellect. But they also remembered him as a "loner," somewhat "bitter" at life's shortcomings and instinctively "pessimistic."[3] For, as with so many, the war never left him. Physically, his lungs were weakened from a poison gas attack during the last months of fighting. Mentally, he succumbed, in his son's words, to "moods of depression."[4]

Indeed, the world as a whole was traumatized from the war. Society was shaken to its core. The world had to be rebuilt and reorganized for it to be peaceful, and financial reconstruction was crucial to that end. Belligerents had abandoned the gold standard under the strain of financing the war. Resurrecting it seemed to many to be the natural goal for monetary policy – a return to normality after years of madness. Most policymakers assumed that reestablishing the interlocking system of fixed exchange rates, gold convertibility, and unhindered gold movements would foster the stability and discipline that economies needed to grow and democracies needed to survive.

Britain reestablished the gold standard to great fanfare in 1925. By the end of the decade, much of the world had as well. But no sooner had the system come into being than cracks started to appear. The pound, having returned to its prewar parity of $4.86, was overvalued: Britain's reserves dwindled, while French and American reserves kept growing. With the onset of the Great Depression, the cracks became craters. Sterling faced relentless pressure. Though the BoE attempted to hold the line – even using a secret reserve of dollars to intervene in exchange markets and prop up the pound – the efforts came to naught. Britain suspended gold convertibility in September 1931. Other countries followed suit, some immediately, some not until having endured much more hardship. The system, so laboriously built up, was now disintegrating.

This chapter explores these turbulent years, beginning with the breakdown of the international monetary system during the war and then discussing the reconstruction of the gold standard, its operation, and collapse. Throughout the 1920s, central bankers cooperated with one another to guide the world back to gold. To their dismay, however, fixed exchange rates and gold convertibility did not usher in nirvana. Britain, in particular, suffered from elevated unemployment and struggled to defend

---

[3] Interview with Cobbold, November 5, 1974, BoE ADM33/25; Interview with Ansiaux, January 29, 1970, BoE ADM33/25.

[4] Siepmann (1987, 9).

the sterling rate re-imposed in 1925. London's decision to give up and suspend convertibility in 1931 not only signaled the end of an era but was to many countries the first salvo in what would become the monetary war.

PANIC AND WAR

Before the First World War even began, financial crisis struck. As the international political situation grew evermore combustible in late July 1914, Europeans liquidated their investments in the United States to shore up their cash balances. The dollar depreciated and reached gold export point, leading to gold outflows. But shipping a lot of gold required sufficient tonnage and readily accessible insurance; with ocean transport suddenly more dangerous, both fell into short supply. Gold arbitrage ground to a halt. The dollar plummeted to unprecedented levels, with quotations reaching $7 to the pound, a depreciation of 30 percent from par.[5] Americans in Europe found themselves refugees, stranded in a continent at war, with their funds rapidly losing value. Such was their plight that Washington dispatched to Europe the armored cruiser *Tennessee*, carrying nearly $6 million in gold bars and coins, to bring aid.[6]

The exchange situation eventually calmed down. To ease the panic and in anticipation of the need to purchase materiel in North America, the BoE decided to accept gold in Canada – part of the British Empire and accessible from the United States by land – crediting the sellers with sterling funds at par in London. In this way, gold did not need to cross the Atlantic for arbitrage to function.[7] Moreover, as belligerents' demands for supplies kicked into gear, rising US exports of goods shifted the balance of payments in America's favor. By the end of November, the dollar was back near mint parity.

On a technical level, the panic made clear just how much the system revolved around the prosaic realities of shipping space, insurance facilities, and geography. Gold was a physical asset, and arbitrage worked by moving it from one central bank to another. The exceptional circumstances convinced the BoE to short-circuit the process by accepting gold deposits in Ottawa. Thereafter, monetary authorities would be more willing, though not without qualification, to hold gold abroad so as to reduce the need for physical transfers.

---

[5] Roberts (2013, 172–75).
[6] "Tennessee off with $5,867,000," *The New York Times*, August 7, 1914.
[7] Sayers (1976, 1:87).

More broadly, the crisis was the final spasm of the old economic order. The United States entered the summer of 1914 a net debtor, struggling to handle the mass withdrawal of foreign investments; it would emerge from the war a net creditor and the premiere economic power.[8] Britain began the war as lender to the world; it would win the war in part by disposing of much of this wealth. Coming to terms with these changes would not be easy, both for the United States – uncomfortable with the responsibilities of its newfound status – and Britain – struggling to align first power commitments with second power means.[9] But the balance of economic might had irrevocably shifted.

Another major transformation wrought by the war was the demise of the classical gold standard, which quickly crumbled with the onset of fighting. Since taxes and borrowing were insufficient to cover the costs associated with total war, governments spent gold reserves and resorted to inflationary finance, high doses of which were incompatible with the gold standard. Though belligerents maintained the official gold content of their currencies – prestige being of utmost importance during war – they dismantled, to varying degrees, the infrastructure that gave this value meaning. Many suspended convertibility, outlawed the export of gold, and requisitioned gold coin.[10] France launched a campaign to "harvest gold," eventually absorbing half the coin held by the public.[11] The United States retained domestic convertibility throughout these years but instituted regulations on the export of gold, thereby suspending the standard in practice if not in name.[12]

Britain kept up gold-standard appearances during the war as well, but regulations – and, just as often, moral suasion – meant that it too had left in all but name. Gold coin circulation effectively came to an end, with the government exhorting citizens and banks to hand over sovereigns to support the war effort. Convertibility and exportation remained permissible in theory, but, as Brown (1929, 6) explains, "pressure was brought to bear upon those who wished to redeem notes at the Bank of England or to secure gold for export to refrain from doing so by appeal to patriotism." As the fighting dragged on, the government resorted to more formal

---

[8] Silber (2007) argues that the US response to the crisis, in particular maintaining gold convertibility throughout, helped hasten America's displacement of Britain as the world's financial power.

[9] Indeed, as Kindleberger (1986) argues, much of the instability in the interwar era resulted from this gap in leadership.

[10] Eichengreen (1992, 70); Brown (1929, 6).   [11] Mouré (2002, 33).

[12] Crabbe (1989, 426).

restrictions, including export regulations.[13] On these matters and others, the Treasury and BoE worked closely together, if not always harmoniously, the latter's traditional independence pushed aside in the interest of a united war effort.[14]

Without the free flow of gold, there was no private arbitrage keeping exchange rates near their mint parities. As belligerents increased their imports, their exchange rates depreciated. Yet unstable, and especially depreciating, exchange rates were anathema during war, threatening the import of essential goods and the stability of the financial system. London therefore decided to peg sterling to the dollar at $4.76, somewhat below mint parity. It did so at first with the support of private dollar loans from the United States and then, when the United States entered the war as an Associated power, with the help of intergovernmental loans. Other Allies fixed their exchange rates near mint parity as well.[15]

Of course, this stability was manufactured and hid drastic differences in monetary developments. Britain and France, fighting a longer war, contracted much more debt than America, sold off more assets, and relied on monetary financing to a greater extent. Much of this debt was to the United States and would become a matter of heated contention in later years. But the immediate impact of these differences in financing showed up in inflation: While US wholesale prices rose by 92 percent from 1914 to 1918, British prices increased by 125 percent and French by 233 percent. The implication was that the pound and franc were not worth anywhere near their mint parities. Once wartime controls and intervention ended, there would be a reckoning in exchange rates. And given how far the world had swung from the gold standard, there would be much work to do for it to have any chance to return.

GETTING BACK TO GOLD

Allied exchange cooperation continued for some time after the Armistice in November 1918, but when it ceased in March 1919, the pound plunged.[16] Gold arbitrage was now highly profitable, and to prevent a massive depletion of the nation's reserves, London responded by officially prohibiting the export of gold, cementing its departure from the gold standard. Sterling reached a low of $3.18 in early 1920, just 65 percent of its prewar parity with the dollar. Other countries experienced even more

---

[13] Brown (1929, 6–7).   [14] Sayers (1976, 1:99–109).   [15] Moggridge (1972, 16–17).
[16] Eichengreen (1992, 100).

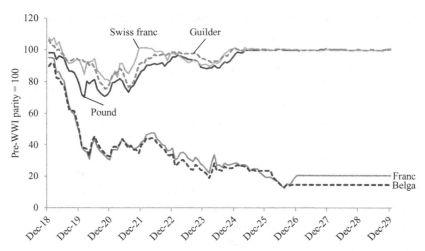

Figure 2.1 Exchange rates, 1918–1929 (pre-WWI parity = 100).
Note: Exchange rates are relative to the dollar.
Source: Accominotti (2020). I am grateful to Olivier Accominotti for sharing this data.

dramatic falls. The franc was worth roughly 30 percent of its prewar parity by the end of 1920 and had still not bottomed out. Only the United States was able to relax export regulations and quickly return to the gold standard. Figure 2.1 depicts exchange rates relative to the dollar and thus to prewar gold parities (since the dollar maintained its gold value) during the early postwar period.

The plan in Britain was to return to gold, in the sense that most ministers and officials assumed it would happen eventually and policy generally worked toward that end.[17] "The men of 1919," Sayers (1976, 1:111) writes, "believed that the best monetary system was that of 1913." The Cunliffe Committee – a group tasked with considering the postwar monetary transition – recommended a host of orthodox measures in 1918, including reinstalling the gold standard as quickly as possible and buttressing it with a minimum gold reserve of £150 million.[18] Conventional wisdom suggested that the nation should not only return to gold but should do so at the prewar parity rather than at a lower gold content; since America had not altered the gold content of the dollar, returning to the prewar parity in terms of gold meant returning to the $4.86 exchange

---

[17] Howson (1974) shows, however, that in the immediate postwar months, the government did not have a clear idea of its policy goals on gold.

[18] See Sayers (1976, 3:57–64) for a summary of the Cunliffe Committee's findings.

rate with the dollar. Such a move would reaffirm Britain's honor, the thinking went, as well as help the City maintain its status as the world's preeminent financial hub.

Perhaps the most fervent proponent for putting the pound back on gold was Montagu Norman.[19] Nearing fifty when he became governor of the BoE in 1920, Norman cut an odd figure. He was tall and had a white pointed beard, black slouch hat, occasional cape, and mischievous gaze. In looks and mannerisms, he was far from the typical City man. But his influence was prodigious, in the Square Mile and beyond. He held the governorship for twenty-four years, a reign of unprecedented length during a time of immense change. Part man, part myth, a magnet for intense loyalty and utter hatred, he had one overriding goal: to guide the international economy back to the glory of the gold standard with London at its center. He intended to use all of his might to achieve this dream. As *The Wall Street Journal* noted, some viewed him as a "Crusader," others as the "Currency Dictator of Europe," but none questioned his sway.[20]

Norman's design hinged on getting sterling back on gold at $4.86, which required realigning prices with those in the United States. But a postwar boom actually widened the price differential. To counter the boom, the BoE increased Bank Rate to 7 percent in the spring of 1920, among the highest levels in half a century. Norman obtained the chancellor's support for this move: In the early postwar period, monetary policy had not yet returned to the prewar practice of BoE independence. Norman believed strongly in the need for central banks to operate free from political interference, however, and soon succeeded in more or less reestablishing prewar custom.[21] With monetary policy on a restrictive footing, Britain experienced acute deflation, wholesale prices falling almost 50 percent from 1920 to 1923. Unemployment peaked at 12 percent in 1921 and did not fall below 7 percent for the remainder of the decade. Though the economy expanded after bottoming out in 1921, the distress of deflation – wage reductions, industrial disputes, comparatively sluggish growth – would make the populace and their representatives less willing to tolerate high interest rates in future years.

The silver lining was that the reduction in prices, while not closing the gap, helped sterling appreciate back toward $4.86. By the beginning of

---

[19] Ahamed (2009) provides a memorable portrait of Norman.
[20] "Montagu Norman has Big Influence," *The Wall Street Journal*, March 11, 1927.
[21] Sayers (1976, 1:119). See Howson (1974) for detail on the turn toward the "dear money" policy.

1925, return to the prewar parity seemed plausible and markets judged it increasingly likely. The prohibition on gold exports was set to expire at the end of the year, so the government needed either to renew the ban or let it lapse (and, by implication, return to gold). The chancellor of the exchequer in the new Conservative Government, Winston Churchill, was not yet set on what to do. In January, he articulated his concerns about the political and economic implications of returning to gold, including the prospect of higher interest rates and deflation, in a memorandum. The responses – from orthodox hands at the Treasury and BoE – seem to have allayed his fears. Norman's reply put the matter starkly. If Churchill chose gold, "he will be abused by the ignorant, the gamblers and the antiquated Industrialists;" if he chose not to go on gold, "he will be abused by the instructed and by posterity."[22] In this framing, there was little choice. And so, on March 20, 1925, a meeting of Prime Minister Stanley Baldwin, Churchill, Norman, and several others concluded with agreement to return and set Churchill's Budget Speech in April as the appropriate occasion for the announcement.[23] When Churchill informed the public, *The Times* of London lauded the move as a "historic feature of the first importance" and a "signal triumph."[24]

Even though the government chose what many believed to be the only honorable path, the action was not without dissent. Britain's economy had suffered from the war and was no longer in a dominant position. The loss in competitiveness suggested returning to gold at a lower parity. As one critic of establishment policy, economist G. D. H. Cole, fumed in 1924, "There is a Great God named Par who is worshipped daily at the Treasury.... Par likes unemployment, it is his form of human sacrifice. And on Par's altars the Treasury daily burns incense in the form of currency and credit."[25] Churchill had heard arguments for a lower rate first hand: In March 1925, he discussed the matter at a dinner that pitted John Maynard Keynes, who feared that $4.86 was too high, against Treasury stalwarts calling for a return to the old parity.[26] Keynes and his compatriots lost that battle, but within a few short years their view became accepted, as the public and government concluded that the return to $4.86 had overvalued the pound, perhaps by around 10 percent. Churchill came to this understanding as well, viewing his decision as the "biggest blunder of [my] life."[27]

---

[22] Moggridge (1972, 64–70).   [23] Ibid., 78.

[24] "City Notes," *The Times* (London), April 29, 1925.   [25] Quoted in Brown (1929, 253).

[26] Sayers (1960, 317); Skidelsky (1994, 197–200).   [27] Moran (1966, 326).

To make the return official, Parliament passed the Gold Standard Act of 1925.[28] The legislation required the BoE to sell gold for its notes at the previous rate of £3. 17s. 10½d. per standard ounce; the BoE continued to purchase gold bullion at the rate of £3. 17s. 9d. per standard ounce. The reinstated gold standard differed from its predecessor, however. So that the nation's gold holdings were centralized at the BoE, the Act implemented a bullion standard. The BoE would sell gold in the form of heavy bars – weighing roughly 400 fine ounces and worth over £1,700 each – rather than coin.[29] Convertibility was thus effectively restricted to gold arbitrageurs: Gone were the days of exchanging a couple notes for some sovereigns. As a result, the relationship between sterling and gold now mattered less in the day-to-day domestic environment and more in the international context of pegging exchange rates and effecting balance of payments transfers.

Britain was not the only country to return to gold. While London was considering the pound's relationship to gold, similar discussions took place in capitals around the world. By the end of the decade, most countries had returned to gold in one form or another. Unlike the classical gold standard, which, James (2001, 33) explains, "evolved by accident," the interwar version "corresponded to a plan." Conferences at Brussels in 1920 and Genoa in 1922 formulated principles for returning to gold and restructuring the international financial system. Norman was the foremost evangelist for these plans, preaching the benefits of gold convertibility, independent central banks, and monetary cooperation. These ideas were fairly uncontroversial when expressed in broad terms, but there was disagreement when it came to the details – disagreement that reflected fundamental ideological differences.

Gold convertibility was the goal, but what exactly did that entail? Some economists and policymakers worried that there might not be enough gold for every country to promise convertibility into the metal.[30] Not only had production of gold fallen during the war, but there was also concern that it would not keep pace with future needs. As Figure 2.2 shows, world gold output in 1923 was 21 percent below the record 1915 level, which would not be surpassed until 1932. Any competition to attract gold threatened

---

[28] See Sayers (1976, 3:85–86) for text of the Gold Standard Act.

[29] The Currency and Bank Notes Act of 1928 further centralized gold holdings by allowing the BoE to force any person with gold coin and bullion worth more than £10,000 to sell it to the BoE (Sayers 1976, 3:108–12).

[30] See Eichengreen (1992, chapter 6) for an overview of all of the issues discussed in this section.

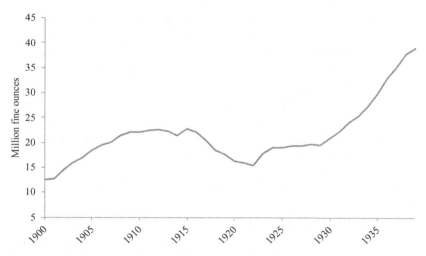

Figure 2.2 World gold production, 1900–1939 (million fine ounces).
Source: US Gold Commission (1982, table SC-2)

deflation, since central banks would attempt to outbid one another by raising interest rates.

In an effort to lessen the scramble for gold, Britain recommended that smaller countries increase the use of foreign exchange as central bank reserves. While never formally institutionalized in any binding international agreement, this "gold-exchange standard" sought to concentrate gold among certain key countries, such as Britain and the United States, which would continue to convert their currencies into gold.[31] Other countries would then hold these gold-backed currencies as part or all of their reserves, committing to convert their currency into sterling or dollars as the case might be. Central banks would not need to compete in a potentially ruinous battle to obtain gold. Many countries followed this advice, which, after all, was built on prewar practice, and by 1927, foreign exchange holdings constituted 42 percent of total international reserves among a sample of twenty-four European countries.[32]

---

[31] The Genoa resolutions supported the gold-exchange standard, but the declaration was nonbinding.

[32] Nurkse (1944, appendix II). Lindert (1969, 15) calculates an average of 25 percent in 1928 for a sample of sixty-eight countries as compared to 19 percent in 1913 for his sample of thirty-five countries. Whatever the chosen sample, it is clear that many prominent central banks were holding more foreign exchange after the war. The Netherlands was at 9 percent in 1913, 29 percent in 1927, and 37 percent in 1930; Switzerland was at 21 percent in 1913, 28 percent in 1927, and 38 percent in 1930; France

To be sure, not everyone supported lessening gold's role. US officials worried that doing so would lead to monetary extravagance; the further the world drifted from gold, the further it would from orthodox economic policies. The French likewise had conservative monetary tastes and were strident in their opposition, sharing American fears and also concerned lest the system strengthen London and New York at the expense of Paris. Others worried that greater reliance on foreign exchange could make the system less stable, as central banks might shift from one currency to another or from currencies to gold.[33]

Notwithstanding these disagreements, the process of stabilizing exchange rates and returning to gold proceeded. Cooperation on this front occurred through central banks, still seen as the guardians of monetary stability, rather than finance ministries. It reached its zenith in the friendship between Norman and Benjamin Strong, governor of the powerful Federal Reserve Bank of New York (FRBNY). Strong shared Norman's desire to resurrect a gold standard orchestrated by independent central banks. The United States had assisted Britain's return by maintaining low interest rates in 1924 and offering a gold credit line in 1925. America, Britain, and France also worked together to help smaller countries stabilize with guidance and credits.[34] In the end, some countries, notably Britain, the Netherlands, and Switzerland, made it back to the prewar parity; others devalued significantly, with Belgium choosing one-seventh of its prewar value; and still others, including Germany, had to start anew after hyperinflation rendered its currency worthless.

Following Britain's return to gold, Paris stabilized the franc de facto in 1926 and de jure in 1928.[35] The resultant franc Poincaré, named for Raymond Poincaré, the dual-hatted premier and finance minister, was one-fifth the prewar value of the franc, implying a mint parity of 124.21 francs to the pound and representing a considerable undervaluation.[36] In the period between de facto and de jure stabilization, the Banque de France (BdF) acquired massive amounts of sterling and dollars as it worked to

---

was at 1 percent in 1913, 47 percent in 1927, and 33 percent in 1930. Belgium, however, declined from 62 percent in 1913 to 42 percent in 1927.

[33] Eichengreen (1992, 161–62 and 202–03).

[34] See Clarke (1967) and Mouré (1992) for discussions of monetary cooperation during these years. Though working together to bring the world back to gold, Britain and France did strain each other's nerves as they competed with each other for monetary influence in Eastern Europe (Meyer 1970).

[35] Mouré (2002, chapter 5).

[36] Mouré (1996) describes the thought process behind choosing the rate.

steady the rate and recruited Charles Cariguel, a banker with experience in London and Paris, to handle operations in 1927.[37] By the time France formally established the franc Poincaré through a June 1928 law creating a gold bullion standard, holdings of foreign exchange were roughly half the BdF's international reserves and totaled nearly £220 million.[38]

But the French did not subscribe to the gold-exchange standard philosophy: They had accumulated foreign exchange out of necessity rather than conviction. Moving forward, the BdF had no intention of adding to its foreign exchange assets and hoped to rebalance its reserves toward gold, a preference that at times tested its relations with London since large conversions of sterling into gold threatened to wreak havoc on the BoE's balance sheet. Often, the two sides worked out amicable arrangements, the French understanding that selling too much sterling too quickly could be self-defeating.[39] All in all, by the end of 1930, foreign exchange accounted for one-third of France's international reserves, reflecting sales of sterling and even greater purchases of gold.[40]

Beyond the coordinated effort to return to the gold standard, there were several other important developments in monetary cooperation. First, during the war, Strong and Norman had developed plans for earmarking gold with each other, whereby the BoE agreed to hold FRBNY gold in its vaults and vice versa.[41] The aim was to make the system more efficient: Having central banks store gold with one another would diminish the need for gold shipments, as a simple change of title would suffice. By the 1920s, earmarking was common practice. Second, central banks set up offices to handle international relations in recognition of their growing dealings with one another. Norman brought Harry Siepmann in to manage the BoE's efforts in 1926, with the title adviser to the governors (the plural referencing the governor and deputy governor).[42]

In addition, the Bank for International Settlements (BIS) opened in 1930. While its immediate purpose was to facilitate the payment of German reparations, it also had the statutory goal of "promot[ing] the co-operation of central banks."[43] Coming into life just as the gold standard system neared its collapse, the BIS failed to develop into the strong institution its founders had envisioned. It did not help that Washington, intent on disassociating itself from all matters related to reparations, prohibited the Federal Reserve from joining. But the monthly meetings in Basel of the

---

[37] Mouré (2002, 111).   [38] Mouré (1991, table 2.1).   [39] Clarke (1967, 116–23).
[40] Nurkse (1944, appendix II). See Accominotti (2009) for a study of France's reserve policy.
[41] Mouré (1992, 261–62).   [42] Sayers (1976, 2:620).
[43] See Toniolo (2005) for a history of the BIS.

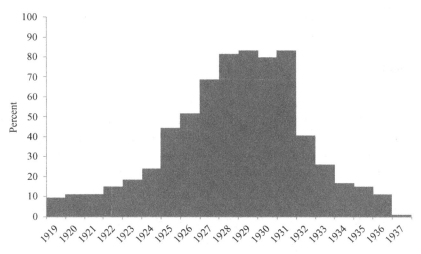

Figure 2.3 Share of countries on the gold standard, 1919–1937 (percent).
Source: Eichengreen (1992, table 7.1)

central bank governors comprising its board provided an opportunity for policymakers to build relationships, discuss issues, and air grievances. And despite the Federal Reserve's absence, H. Merle Cochran, a US diplomat in Basel and later Paris, who served as de facto financial attaché to the continent, attended the board meetings each month for informal discussions, earning respect as an "honorary central banker."[44]

By the end of the 1920s, the world was back on gold. Figure 2.3 depicts the share of fifty-four countries on gold from the end of the war through the Great Depression; by 1929, all but nine were on some form of the gold standard. But the world was not on gold in the way it previously had been. Gold coin circulation was appreciable only in the United States. Foreign exchange was an increasingly important component in the reserves of many central banks. For some policymakers, the moves to economize gold were improvements to the system; for others, they marked its fatal flaws. For all, the system's existence would be short-lived.

SECRET STASH OF CASH

The global economy seemed to be doing quite well in the mid-1920s. Exchange rates were stabilized, trade was increasing, and capital was

---

[44] Cobbold to Sayers, October 24, 1974, BoE ADM33/25.

flowing. But trouble lurked below the surface – from the burden of reparations and war debts to the disparities in competitiveness and the rise in leverage. The reconstituted gold standard operated in a world far different from that of its predecessor, an environment that sapped it of its credibility. Much of the British public, having sacrificed in countless ways during the war and its aftermath, questioned why maintaining parity was worth higher interest rates, deflation, and slower growth. Should push come to shove, it was not clear that authorities in a democracy could or would continue to subordinate internal conditions to external ones.[45]

There were other issues with the gold standard. Despite all the talk about the rules of the game, practice did not follow principle. Sterilization of capital flows was common. Britain tended to offset reserve losses through open market purchases of securities. On the other hand, France and the United States sterilized gold inflows through open market sales of government securities, thereby hitting the brakes on expansion.[46] The decision not to expand resulted in the acquisition of idle gold stocks in the two countries that contributed to a suboptimal distribution of gold. By 1929, the United States held 38 percent of the world's gold reserves and France 16 percent; Britain had just 7 percent.[47] New York and Paris could continue to gain gold, but London could lose only so much before something had to give.[48]

Indeed, doubts about sterling began swirling around as the decade came to an end and Britain's balance of payments deteriorated. Wall Street, in the midst of a spectacular boom, inhaled capital from London, adding to the pound's woes. The BoE's gold reserves peaked in September 1928 at £174 million and then started to decline, as Figure 2.4 shows. Election of the Labour Government under Ramsay MacDonald in the summer of 1929 did not reassure investors, nor did the worsening budget deficit. Reserves fell to £134 million that autumn, well below the £150 million minimum suggested by the Cunliffe Committee.

In fact, the gold losses did not fully reflect the severity of the situation, for the BoE was also losing foreign exchange reserves.[49] Unbeknownst to

---

[45] This description follows Eichengreen (1992), who also argues that the system failed due to a lack of cooperation. Cooperation actually went far beyond what had occurred during the days of the classical gold standard; it just was not enough.

[46] Meltzer (2003, 139–40); Eichengreen (1992, 256).   [47] Eichengreen (2008, table 3.1).

[48] Concern about the distribution of gold and operation of the gold standard led to the convening, through the League of Nations, of the Gold Delegation to study the problems in 1929. See Clavin (2013, 51–71).

[49] Moggridge (1972, chapter 8) is the seminal work on this topic.

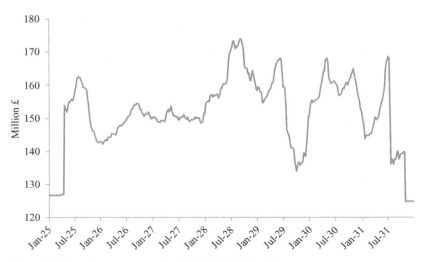

Figure 2.4 Issue Department gold, 1925–1931 (million £).
Source: Huang and Thomas (2016)

the public, Threadneedle Street had been intervening in exchange markets since 1925. It already had some experience with intervention, having operated in the market to peg the pound during the war. Politicization of Bank Rate in the postwar period pushed the BoE to once again intervene systematically. While the BoE had regained much of its formal independence in setting rates by the end of the decade – in February 1929, the Cabinet concluded that "His Majesty's Government has no responsibility for the movement of the Bank Rate and does not control the policy of the Bank of England" – official recognition in theory did not always play out in practice. The Treasury made clear its dislike of higher rates, often resorting to informal persuasion to prevent hikes.[50] Jawboning did not always work, but it naturally affected the BoE's willingness to alter rates and made exchange intervention appear more attractive.[51]

The BoE thus started accumulating dollars shortly before returning to gold in 1925, creating an Exchange Section in 1926 to handle the growing

---

[50] Cabinet minutes, February 7, 1929, CAB 23/60. The BoE was reluctant to increase Bank Rate, according to Cairncross and Eichengreen (1983, 63), "owing to concern for the state of industry, out of sensitivity to political pressure, and because of doubts that a higher discount rate would succeed in stemming the gold outflow."

[51] Moggridge (1972, 162).

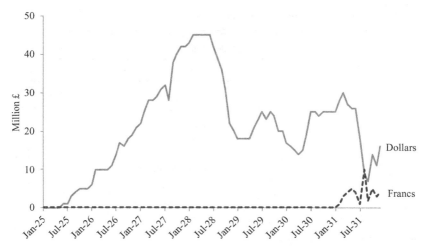

Figure 2.5 BoE foreign exchange holdings, 1925–1931 (million £).
Source: Huang and Thomas (2016)

operations. It continued to buy dollars when times were good, believing that they would one day come in handy.[52] Once the tide turned against sterling in 1928, they did. Selling foreign exchange could keep the exchange rate from reaching gold export point and thus reduce the outflow of gold without having to resort to politically sensitive interest rate hikes. The BoE still sold gold and raised rates, but exchange intervention provided a new dimension on which to work.[53] Figure 2.5 depicts monthly foreign exchange reserves, which were primarily dollars and peaked at £46 million in June 1928, accounting for 22 percent of the BoE's international reserves. They then fell in half as markets turned against sterling in the latter months of 1928.

The BoE insisted on conducting these interventions secretly. This emphasis on confidentiality was in line with traditional BoE practice. In addition, disclosing foreign exchange holdings would have required detailing gains as well as losses, the former likely to increase pressure to reduce interest rates and the latter liable to set off capital outflows as faith in the parity plummeted. Better to keep the information closely held.

---

[52] Hennessy (1992, 83). Much of the foreign exchange had been purchased off-market through transactions with central banks; for example, the Netherlands Bank exchanged some of its dollar assets for sterling as it rebalanced its portfolio (Moggridge 1972, 181).

[53] Norman aimed to split the loss of reserves evenly between gold and foreign exchange (Moggridge 1972, 186).

Table 2.1 *BoE return, January 2, 1929*

Issue Department			
Liabilities		**Assets**	
(million £)		(million £)	
Notes issued	413.1	Gold coin and bullion	153.1
		Fiduciary issue	
		Silver coin	5.2
		Government securities	244.6
		Other securities	10.2
	413.1		*413.1*
Banking Department			
Liabilities		**Assets**	
(million £)		(million £)	
Capital	18.0	Government securities	62.6
Public deposits	22.3	Other securities	64.7
Other deposits	122.1	Notes	34.8
		Gold and silver coin	0.2
	162.4		*162.4*

Note: Items may not add due to rounding.
Source: Huang and Thomas (2016)

The BoE was so discreet that only in 1928 did it start sharing partial information with the Treasury.[54]

Camouflaging interventions required some work, as the BoE had to release a statement detailing its general position every week. Table 2.1 reproduces the statement from January 2, 1929. The return summarized the position of the Issue Department, which handled the note issue, and the Banking Department, which conducted the BoE's business as a banker.[55] Profits from the Issue Department accrued to the government while those from the Banking Department went to the BoE. Newspapers analyzed the return from all angles to get a sense of where monetary policy

---

[54] Ibid., 160–61 and 184. The Currency and Bank Notes Act of 1928 required the BoE to provide the Treasury with information regarding securities in the Issue Department.

[55] The separation between the departments existed only in an accounting sense, and the Macmillan report in 1931 recommended merging them: "On more general grounds we see no advantage in the separation of the departments. It is confusing and misleading to anyone who is not an expert.... It is inconceivable that anyone settling the matter afresh to-day would devise the present form of statutory return." Committee on Finance and Industry, "Report," June 1931, T 200/7/144.

was headed. At some level, notes were notes, gold was gold, and there was not much room to conceal information in these statements.

But the return was not completely transparent. The BoE had wide latitude in choosing which assets to place in "Other Securities" in both the Issue and Banking Departments. In fact, it could even place government securities in that category, despite a separate listing for them.[56] When it started buying dollars in 1925 to build up a buffer, it therefore had the perfect place to hide them, a conveniently vague listing inscrutable to the outside world. Moreover, because the BoE sterilized these operations – selling sterling securities when buying dollars and vice versa – the "Other Securities" entry did not change with intervention, asset sales balancing purchases and leaving the total unaffected.[57] Even if market operators suspected official intervention, the weekly statement obscured purchases and sales.[58] Secrecy and sterilization became the hallmarks of British intervention.

This foray into exchange intervention was not enough to keep sterling on gold. The tide against sterling swamped the ammunition provided by the secret stash of dollars. In hindsight, the episode marked the faint beginnings of a new era of intervention that would truly start with the establishment of the Exchange Equalisation Account in 1932. In the moment, however, intervention merely succeeded in giving policymakers some space. It could do no more. Time was now running out.

"END OF AN EPOCH"

The world economy entered a downturn in 1929 that soon became a depression, unleashing an unprecedented period of economic deprivation. Though many countries would start recovering after a few years, the Great Depression cast a shadow over the entire decade. In Germany, Hitler played on the anger and despair to gain power. In France, a succession of governments failed to reinvigorate the economy, fueling the very polarization and radicalization that made handling the crisis that much more difficult. In America, serious questions about the legitimacy of democratic

---

[56] Sayers (1976, 1:24). As Ernest Harvey, the BoE's deputy governor, testified to the Macmillan Committee, the division between "Government Securities" and "Other Securities" was "entirely within the discretion of the Bank." Committee on Finance and Industry, "Minutes of Evidence: Volume I," 1931, T 200/8/12.

[57] Clay (1957, 255).

[58] Brown (1940, 1108–10) discusses market suspicion of intervention in 1931 and 1932 when the BoE did not confine operations to "Other Securities."

capitalism arose, questions that eventually found an answer in a New Deal that saved the system from itself. In Britain, the economic decline was not as severe as elsewhere, in part because growth in the 1920s, while a respectable 3 percent per year, did not reach the soaring heights common in other countries. But the 1930s were lean years nonetheless. Export volumes fell over 30 percent from 1929 to 1932 and did not reach their 1929 level until after the Second World War. The unemployment rate more than doubled from 8 percent in 1929 to 17 percent in 1932, remaining above 10 percent until 1937.

While all of the pressures on the British economy fed into the stress on sterling, the pound's terminal crisis was actually set in motion by events in Germany.[59] In the summer of 1931, budgetary and financial troubles in Berlin imperiled Germany's financial system and thus the world's. US President Herbert Hoover declared a one-year moratorium on intergovernmental debts in June 1931 in an attempt to free Germany, temporarily, from the burden of reparations. The BIS, BoE, BdF, and FRBNY also provided a £20 million credit to the Reichsbank to keep the crumbling financial system afloat, but the moves were not enough. In mid-July, Berlin ordered a banking holiday and imposed capital controls as the crisis spun out of control.

The conflagration immediately threatened London's financial system, which had substantial sums invested in Germany that could no longer be repatriated. In just two weeks in July, the BoE lost one quarter of its gold and foreign exchange reserves as investors bailed from sterling.[60] Confidence in sterling also fell with publication of the Macmillan Committee report, which included alarming details on the extent of short-term sterling liabilities, and the May report, which called for strict economies to bring the deficit under control. The controversy over how best to handle the situation led to the collapse of the Labour Government and the installation, still under Prime Minister Ramsay MacDonald, of a National Government dominated by Conservative forces.[61]

With foreign exchange and gold sales accelerating, the BoE raised Bank Rate from 2.5 percent to 3.5 percent at the end of July and then 4.5 percent one week later. France and America also came to Britain's aid. To increase

---

[59] Straumann (2019) provides an excellent discussion of the German crisis.

[60] Clarke (1967, 202).

[61] See Cairncross and Eichengreen (1983), Kunz (1987), and Morrison (2015) for narratives of these events.

the BoE's firepower in the foreign exchange markets, the FRBNY and the BdF each granted £25 million credits, payable in dollars and francs, respectively. The British Treasury also received £40 million loans both in New York and Paris, again payable in the respective currency. These credits represented genuine attempts to help Britain maintain parity.[62] The FRBNY's George Harrison, who took over the governorship after Strong's death in 1928, was in constant contact with the BoE, as were the French. Everyone wanted to save Britain from suspending convertibility, a fearsome outcome with unknowable consequences.

But the credits did not last long and the onslaught on Britain's reserves continued. Planning for suspension proceeded. In August, the BoE's Siepmann prepared detailed notes on leaving gold. He hoped to stay on "at all costs," but if suspension became necessary, the gold reserves would have to be "conserved," because "there is no practicable alternative to returning, sooner or later, to the gold standard."[63] As the situation worsened over the following weeks, the BoE's leaders delivered more and more pessimistic news to the Cabinet. The roughly £135 million of gold remaining in mid-September was just enough to cover the above credits and other commitments.

Though the epicenter of the crisis was in London, where investors sold sterling and ministers and officials huddled in conferences, developments up north fueled the flames. On September 15, hundreds of miles away in Invergordon, a harbor at the northern tip of Scotland, sailors started protesting. They considered recently announced cuts to their pay, part of the austerity measures enacted to balance the budget, unfair and draconian. Such protests in a military setting amounted to mutiny – even if the reality was for the most part tame, with sailors remaining respectful and largely confining their actions to refusing to work – and concern spread that the revolt could grow. To prevent escalation, the Admiralty cancelled upcoming maneuvers, and the protests resolved peacefully the next day. But the damage to confidence was done, the government's control over the budget and the entire apparatus of state put into question.[64] Britain's prestige hinged on the Navy and sterling: shock about the state of the former now added to doubts about the latter.

On September 17, the Treasury produced draft legislation for suspending convertibility.[65] A secret memorandum written by Major Harry

---

[62] Sayers (1976, 3:257–63) provides details on the credits.

[63] Siepmann, "Going off the Gold Standard," August 19, 1931, BoE G1/459.

[64] Williamson (1992, 402–03).

[65] Phillips, Untitled memo, September 17, 1931, BoE G1/459.

Nathan, member of Parliament, set out the necessity for preparing a "War Book," outlining the steps to take should suspension occur. Since Britain imported the majority of its food and a lower exchange rate would make such purchases more expensive, the memorandum warned of "the risk of starvation." Nathan, likely influenced by events in Invergordon, went on to declare the "maintenance of public order" an issue that "may become of the first importance."[66] Alarmist, perhaps, but then again, leaving the gold standard during peacetime had been unthinkable only weeks earlier. The potential ramifications seemed unbounded.

On Friday, September 18, the BoE concluded that time for suspension had come and informed the prime minister, effectively presenting the government with a fait accompli.[67] On Saturday, Ernest Harvey, the BoE's deputy governor and acting head (Norman was on exhaustion leave in Canada) wrote a letter to MacDonald and Chancellor of the Exchequer Philip Snowden, formally requesting that the BoE be "relieved of their obligation to sell gold" under the 1925 statute.[68] MacDonald assented. Only a tight circle knew of the decision until, on Sunday, MacDonald briefed the Cabinet.[69] Later that night, the government issued a statement informing the public, and Parliament formalized the decision by passing the Gold Standard (Amendment) Act of 1931 on Monday, September 21.

By week's end, sterling was below \$4.00; by year's end, it was under \$3.40. The BoE would never again sell gold – in coin, bullion, or any form – to all comers at a fixed price. Central banks with foreign exchange immediately sought to offload it. While some peripheral countries had left gold earlier, Britain's departure was the earthquake that shattered the international monetary system and sowed the destruction of the gold standard so arduously installed just a few years earlier. The decision also made evident, to anyone who was not yet convinced, the finality of Britain's fall from a century of economic hegemony.

The immediate reaction abroad was shock. Morgan et Cie, the Paris outpost of the House of Morgan, cabled to New York that "everyone seems

---

[66] Nathan, "Memorandum on Measures to Meet a Break in Sterling," September 17, 1931, BoE G1/459; Richardson (2019, 159). O. M. W. Sprague, an American economist advising the BoE, was likewise concerned about food imports and wanted the BoE to retain enough gold to finance such imports if necessary. "Committee on Foreign Exchange," September 18, 1931, BoE C43/98.

[67] Williamson (1992, 413) writes, "in a last exercise of its traditional independence," the BoE "unilaterally decided that the gold standard should no longer be defended."

[68] Harvey to MacDonald and Snowden, September 19, 1931, BoE G1/459.

[69] "Conclusions," September 20, 1931, CAB 23/68/13.

dazed."[70] Officials and bankers tried to exude confidence and prevent the panic from spreading. Clément Moret, governor of the BdF, assured the public, "The position of the franc is absolutely unassailable. Our money is secure and we can remain calm. Our holdings consist partly in gold, partly in dollars deposited in New York, which can from day to day be converted into gold."[71] He conveniently neglected to mention sterling holdings of £62 million, which plummeted in value as the pound depreciated.[72] One banker in the United States thought it was "like the end of the world."[73] Others were cautiously optimistic that this move would lead to a quick realignment of parities. Russell Leffingwell, a former US Treasury official, thought that, given the circumstances, the "National Government did everything in its power to prevent the collapse of the pound and to maintain the gold standard." "We have been living," he continued, "in the midst of dreams, political and economic, during the last seventeen years. We are now beginning, just beginning, to face reality."[74] These generally sanguine reactions would turn decidedly more hostile as the consequences of suspension – notably the repercussions on currency values and sterling holdings – sunk in.

Feelings in Britain ranged from depression to optimism, resignation to vindication. Norman, having been away during these crucial weeks, was livid upon his return, his grand dream smashed to pieces. He was, a colleague recalled, "profoundly depressed and for a time his temper showed it."[75] Sir Otto Niemeyer of the BoE considered suspension "a very great disaster, the full dangers of which we are as yet far from realising."[76] *The Economist*, bemoaning "The End of an Epoch," was a bit more subdued. Suspension was "not a deliberate act of policy, but the acceptance of the inevitable." Indeed, it was widely believed in Britain that the country had been forced off gold: It had fought as long as it could and had no option but to surrender. The newspaper went on to argue that it was far too early to render a verdict on the move; all that could be said was that "[t]he new situation with which we are confronted is such as to occasion neither alarm nor satisfaction."[77] And then there was the press baron Lord Beaverbrook, who had long campaigned against the gold standard. He

---

[70] Telegram to Whitney, September 21, 1931, ML ARC1221/31/1.
[71] "Paris Bourse Calm Amid Wide Decline," *The New York Times*, September 22, 1931.
[72] Mouré (1991, 70).   [73] Quoted in Kunz (1987, 113).
[74] Leffingwell to deSanchez, October 2, 1931, ML ARC1221/31/1.   [75] Clay (1957, 399).
[76] Niemeyer, Untitled memo, September 26, 1931, BoE G1/459.
[77] "The End of an Epoch," *The Economist*, September 26, 1931.

reveled in the moment, his *Daily Express* crowing, "Nothing more heartening has happened in years."[78]

But most of all, Britons – save for Norman and Niemeyer's cohort – experienced a feeling of cautious relief, a belief that while hard times might be ahead, the trajectory was at last pointing in the right direction. As the *Financial Times* proclaimed, "Now that all doubts have been resolved, the country will settle down cheerfully, despite its tightened belt, to pull through again to industrial prosperity based upon economic progress."[79] The demon of suspension had finally been confronted and, at first glance, did not actually look all that scary.[80]

Just over a month later, Keynes published a brief pamphlet, *Essays in Persuasion*. Looking at recent events through a wide frame, he observed that Britain was currently in "a lull in our affairs." The nation was:

in a quiet pool between two waterfalls. The main point is that we have regained our freedom of choice. Scarcely any one in England now believes in the Treaty of Versailles or in the pre-war Gold Standard or in the Policy of Deflation. These battles have been won – mainly by the irresistible pressure of events and only secondarily by the slow undermining of old prejudices. But most of us have, as yet, only a vague idea of what we are going to do next, of how we are going to use our regained freedom of choice.[81]

Suspending the gold standard was not the end of the drama; it was the beginning. Precisely because the move resulted from "the irresistible pressure of events," there was little sense of what would come next. Perhaps Britain would swiftly return to the gold standard; maybe it would sever all ties with the metal. How to use its "regained freedom of choice" would occupy policymakers for the rest of the decade. And as other nations reclaimed their freedom as well, the potential for monetary conflict would only grow.

---

[78] Quoted in Ahamed (2009, 431).

[79] "United the Nation Stands," *Financial Times*, September 22, 1931.

[80] Some in the press incorrectly believed suspension would be limited to six months. In part, this interpretation might have reflected a misreading of the legislation suspending the gold standard, which also gave the government powers to regulate exchange markets for six months as discussed in Chapter 3. "Gold Exports Suspended," *The Times* (London), September 21, 1931.

[81] Keynes (2010, xix).

3

Hostilities Commence, 1931–1933

On October 7, 1931, Sir Frederick Leith-Ross, a veteran Treasury diplomat with round wire glasses and a stern gaze, was in Paris. It was a little over two weeks since Britain had suspended convertibility, and the pound was now down 20 percent. Leith-Ross hoped to clear up some issues with France and met with Clément Moret, governor of the Banque de France (BdF). The discussion did not go well. Holders of sterling around the world were understandably unhappy, and the BdF, with £62 million of sterling assets, was downright apoplectic. The BdF's paper loss on sterling exceeded its capital; if it was not made whole, it risked insolvency. Moret thought it only fair that the British honor the original gold parity and compensate accordingly. With the Bank of England (BoE) refusing to do so, Moret turned to the British government.[1]

Leith-Ross replied that, while the British appreciated French support during the crisis, compensation was not justified and would never happen. No British government would dare submit such a proposal to Parliament. "M. Moret interrupted me at this point," Leith-Ross recorded, "and said that if this question could not be satisfactorily solved, it would not be possible for the Bank of France in future to co-operate with the Bank of England." Leith-Ross was taken aback by the pronouncement, which "sounded almost like a declaration of war." Matters did not improve when Leith-Ross disclosed that there were no immediate plans to return to gold. Moret "threw up his hands" in frustration. It was not an auspicious start to post-suspension relations.[2]

---

[1] Mouré (1991, 71–72).

[2] Leith-Ross, "Note of an Interview with Monsieur Moret," October 9, 1931, BoE G1/459. Leith-Ross' report was not sensationalized. Moret recounted the conversation similarly, saying that he had told Leith-Ross, "We are asking the British Government to weigh

51

The spirit of cooperation from the summer, when Britain, France, and America had jointly tried to uphold the system, was no more. As shock at Britain's suspension wore away, anger and dissention slowly took its place. The monetary battle had begun. Paris and Washington viewed London's policies with increasing suspicion. The pound continued to fall, and it seemed as if, far from entering a period of penance, Britain was reaping a windfall at the world's expense. Its goods became more competitive, and its economy began to recover in 1932. Yet, at the time, countries sticking with gold did not see in Britain's policies a potential roadmap for themselves; rather, they saw actions unbecoming of a true power. Goodwill dissipated. Nations turned inward, determined to protect themselves at all costs. Many central banks raced to sell their foreign exchange holdings, hoping to find safety in gold.

While countries committed to gold could retreat to orthodoxy, Britain had a more complex task. There was no precedent – surely nothing from the past 200 years during which it was either on the gold standard or attempting to return – to guide policy. Britain no longer operated under the convertibility constraint, but it did not yet know under what constraints it should operate. Should it return to the gold standard? Should it pick a new rate at which to peg sterling? Should it allow market forces to determine the rate? The BoE and Treasury had to find their way through this untrodden terrain. The Treasury, taking control of monetary policy, soon decided that returning to gold would be the (heavily caveated) long-run goal, at least for public consumption. In the meantime, frequent exchange intervention would be necessary, not to repeg the pound but to exert some influence on its value. In 1932, after several months of getting by through ad hoc arrangements, the government created one of the great monetary innovations of the decade, the Exchange Equalisation Account (EEA). The fund provided a means for large-scale intervention that respected the Treasury's new primacy and the BoE's technical expertise. But its size and secrecy naturally bred mistrust abroad, further hampering any attempts at cooperation.

This chapter traces the evolution of the international monetary system and the management of sterling from Britain's suspension of convertibility in September 1931 to the eve of Franklin Roosevelt's inauguration in March 1933. In the aftermath of suspension, the world splintered into monetary blocs: Many countries followed sterling's lead, some

carefully the consequences of an intransigent attitude on this question." Quoted in Mouré (1991, 72).

recommitted to gold, and others found refuge in exchange controls. This division, coupled with sterling's depreciation, the secrecy with which London managed the pound, and the increasing tendency of all to view policy in zero-sum terms, led to much bad blood between the powers. The establishment of the EEA further inflamed tensions, as it appeared to be nothing more than a weapon to obtain advantage. But the EEA was more than that. It offered a path forward for managing rates without a fixed point and would soon become a model – suspicion leading to imitation – as more countries sought monetary freedom.

THE WORLD FRAGMENTS

During the autumn of 1931, the French were not the only ones indignant at London's refusal to provide compensation for losses on sterling. A couple of weeks before Britain suspended convertibility, the President of the Netherlands Bank, Gerard Vissering, had been so concerned about the pound that he asked the BoE to cover his sterling holdings in gold. The BoE turned down the request but intimated that there was nothing to worry about.[3] The Dutch believed the reassurances, making them all the more furious when their fears materialized just one month later. They demanded compensation but to no avail: London felt it had been forced off gold and owed nobody anything. Vissering resigned at the beginning of October, ostensibly because of health issues, but many observers thought the political fallout from the loss on sterling played a role.[4] His successor, L. J. Trip, continued the fight. The Netherlands Bank soon issued a statement criticizing the BoE for not being "inclined to acknowledge the claims which the Netherlands Bank considers it was reasonably entitled to make."[5] Such was the bitterness that the Netherlands Bank at one point even considered turning to the International Court of Justice in The Hague for restitution.[6]

With Britain refusing to offer compensation, the French and Dutch governments ultimately provided financial support to their central banks. The Belgian government did so as well (the Swiss National Bank did not

---

[3] Sayers (1976, 2:414–15).

[4] "Netherlands Bank Policy," *Financial Times*, October 8, 1931. As Vanthoor (2005, 143) concludes, "Although Vissering's health was not perfect, the British decision was the push he needed to withdraw from active life."

[5] "Holland," *The Economist*, December 5, 1931. See also Trip to Norman, October 27, 1931, BoE G14/260.

[6] Vanthoor (2005, 143).

require funds, as it had sold much of its sterling prior to suspension.)[7] While these measures put an end to any worries of technical insolvency, the central banks did not enjoy going hat in hand to their governments, nor did the governments take pleasure in bailing out the central banks. Relations with London suffered as a result. The French had made their stance clear enough to Leith-Ross, even if their bluster was in part for show. As for the Dutch, "we could count on the Netherlands Bank until 1931," the BoE's Harry Siepmann later recalled. "But they never got over their losses from the devaluation of sterling," and it took years for them to ease up on their "aggrieved attitude."[8] In fact, more than three decades later, William McChesney Martin, chairman of the Federal Reserve Board of Governors, remarked, "To this day, the French, Belgian, and Netherlands central banks have not forgotten that the 1931 devaluation of sterling wiped out their capital."[9]

It was now evident that sterling was not as good as gold. The question was whether the other key reserve currency, the dollar, still was. Central banks did not wish to wait and see how the situation evolved. The BdF contacted the Federal Reserve Bank of New York (FRBNY) the day after sterling's suspension to arrange the conversion of dollars into gold; Belgium, the Netherlands, and Switzerland started selling as well. The United States lost record amounts of gold.[10] The scale of losses shocked Americans, and the banking system seized, throwing the country deeper into depression. President Herbert Hoover was convinced Europeans were conspiring in a nefarious attack on the dollar.[11]

Central bankers were aware that converting too many dollars into gold too quickly could precipitate a collapse of the currency, so they liquidated the balances in stages, working with the FRBNY to mitigate the damage. But there was no going back. The BdF converted most of its dollars into gold by the middle of 1932; sterling took more time to sell given its instability, but it was effectively out of the portfolio by the end of 1933.[12] Belgium, the Netherlands, and Switzerland similarly moved toward gold. Figure 3.1 depicts the dramatic fall in foreign exchange reserves.

After September 1931, central banks still talked to one another, if only to coordinate liquidation of foreign exchange reserves. But these conversations, as well as those between finance ministries, did not lead to

---

[7] At suspension, Belgium held £12.6 million, the Netherlands £11 million, and Switzerland £3.5 million. Straumann (2010, 100–03); Mouré (1991, 70–73); Vanthoor (2005, 141–45).

[8] Siepmann, "Central Bank Co-operation," July 19, 1943, BoE G14/33.

[9] Martin (1965, 10).   [10] Chandler (1971, 167–68); Mouré (1991, 74–77).

[11] Boyce (2009, 386–87).   [12] Accominotti (2009, figures 3 and 4).

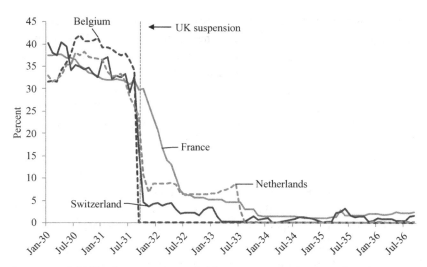

Figure 3.1 Gold bloc foreign exchange holdings, 1930–1936 (percent of total reserves).
Source: Board of Governors of the Federal Reserve System (1930–1936)

any cooperative plan to fix the monetary system, for there were too many land mines surrounding what little common ground remained, especially as governments became more involved in monetary policy (and thus intergovernmental problems infected monetary discussions).[13] Paris thought the key to world recovery involved the strengthening of the gold standard; London had no interest in a speedy return, determined not to repeat what it now considered the fiasco of 1925. Both believed a reduction in war debts imperative to unshackle the global economy; Washington did not agree. Of course, the three had disagreed on much long before September 1931. But the fallout from suspension made it even harder to work together. As Kunz (1987, 187) explains, "on all sides the dénouement of the [sterling] crisis produced bitterness and ill feeling," resulting in "the triumph of competition over cooperation. Increasingly an attitude of autarchy dominated the sphere of international monetary relations."

In this perilous environment, some countries insisted on maintaining parities and upholding classical principles. The most important members of this incipient gold bloc were France, Belgium, the Netherlands, Switzerland, and (for the time being) the United States.[14] The decision to

---

[13] Mouré (1992).

[14] After the World Economic Conference in 1933, a slightly more formalized gold bloc would emerge, consisting of France, Belgium, the Netherlands, Switzerland, Italy, and Poland. See Chapter 4.

double down on gold had several implications. First, liquidation of foreign exchange reserves reduced international liquidity and led to a counter-productive ratcheting up of discount rates to attract gold. Economic conditions therefore continued to deteriorate in these countries. Second, because maintaining their gold parities resulted in the appreciation of their exchange rates, they sought to level the playing field by imposing trade barriers.[15] For instance, in November 1931 France levied a surtax of 15 percent on goods from Britain and other devaluers.[16] Quotas – quantitative restrictions on imports, often implemented in a discriminatory manner against different suppliers – proliferated.

Even countries that had left the gold standard erected trade barriers. Britain reversed its long-standing policy of free trade by enacting a general tariff in early 1932. It then implemented a system of imperial preference, whereby trade within the Empire was favored, at the Imperial Economic Conference in Ottawa that summer, a gathering of delegates from across the Empire to discuss economic cooperation.[17] The race to get gold and the retreat to the supposed safety of tariffs and quotas unsurprisingly increased international animosity, making cooperation all the more difficult.

Not every country stuck with gold, however. The financial crisis in the summer of 1931 made Germany's gold parity untenable. Scarred by the postwar hyperinflation, Berlin's policymakers considered devaluation inseparable from inflation and a nonstarter. They therefore imposed exchange controls that turned the Reichsmark's connection to gold into a charade. All international transactions, capital and current, went through the government: Authorities regulated capital flows, exporters had to surrender the foreign exchange they obtained, and importers had to request what they needed. In time, the controls developed into a series of clearing arrangements, whereby Germany organized trade with other countries to effect bilateral balances. This centralized system was a convenient point of economic leverage that the Nazis exploited upon assuming power to expand Germany's influence in the east and south.[18] To the Western democracies, this system – particularly the restrictions on current transactions – was abhorrent. It went against the liberal philosophy of freedom of exchange that they still clung to, even if their resort to trade barriers raised doubts about their commitment. Exchange controls soon became associated with totalitarianism, a connection that raised the

---

[15] Eichengreen (1992, 289–91).   [16] Albers (2020).   [17] See Boyce (2009, chapter 7).
[18] The degree to which the Germans employed these clearing arrangements to exploit other countries remains debated. Ritschl (2001).

political stakes of economic policy and further burdened international relations.[19]

Other countries followed Britain. Breaking their gold parities, they pegged their currencies to and held the preponderance of their reserves in sterling, forming the Sterling Area. While it remained informal throughout the 1930s – there was no official membership or institutionalization – the Sterling Area encompassed a large part of the globe, accounting for more than one-fifth of the world's population.[20] Much of the Empire joined, as did Britain's oldest ally, Portugal; by 1933, so had Scandinavia. Britain was the biggest market for many of these countries and officials in Scandinavia and elsewhere thought it essential for trading purposes to prevent a sharp appreciation against the pound and maintain a steady exchange rate. By choosing sterling as a new anchor, they obtained a degree of stability during otherwise unsettled times. And unlike countries that doubled down on holding gold as reserves, members of the Sterling Area felt that holding sterling made the most sense given the importance of their exchange rates with the pound.

A bit ironically, then, Britain's retreat from the gold standard in some ways enhanced sterling's geopolitical importance. Just days after suspension, the BoE's Sir Otto Niemeyer, distraught over what he considered Britain's moral transgression, found in these political aspects some reason for cheer: "If we can now ... form a considerable sterling block, the position of the gold holding countries, i.e. France and America, will become more and more unenviable and their fears greater and greater."[21] The two countries would have no choice but to parley with Britain about war debts, tariffs, the structure of the monetary system, and all the world's economic ills.

But that was a long-run goal. British policymakers faced a much more immediate issue. Namely, what to do about sterling? "Clearly the urgent thing," Niemeyer enjoined, "is to show signs of having a policy."[22]

---

[19] Bloomfield (1966, 186).

[20] Aldcroft (2004, 35). See also Nurkse (1944, chapter 3). The Sterling Area became much more defined during the Second World War as exchange control regulations differentiated countries within and without, but during the 1930s it remained informal. One BoE official noted, "We have always avoided making any statement of the countries to be regarded as in the Sterling Area because the definition is not clear and the choice does not depend upon us. For working purposes we are accustomed to include the British Empire except Canada, Newfoundland and Hongkong; Scandinavia and Iceland; Finland, Estonia, Portugal and possessions, Egypt, Iraq, Siam, Argentina; and since the autumn of 1936 Latvia and Greece." Mynors, Untitled memo, June 23, 1937, BoE OV48/11.

[21] Niemeyer, Untitled memo, September 26, 1931, BoE G1/459.   [22] Ibid.

The implication was that they had no policy to speak of. They needed to devise one fast.

EARLY MONTHS

Though the decision to suspend convertibility was momentous, there had been no agreement on what exactly should follow. Back in August, Siepmann thought that any suspension would be temporary and that Britain would eventually return to gold. But he was sure that resumption would occur at a much-reduced rate: "I do not believe there is any power on earth which could get sterling back to 4.86 2/3 once the country has experienced the blessed relief of depreciation to $4.00."[23] Siepmann's colleague, Niemeyer, seemed at the end of September to consider $4.40 as a benchmark for policy, based on a presumed overvaluation of sterling of 10 percent.[24] Others thought the currency required a 30 percent depreciation to $3.40.[25]

However, these speculations were of little import for the time being. That stabilization of the exchange rate at some level and a return to gold in some form would happen were widely assumed – with a provisional stabilization of the rate likely preceding resumption of convertibility. But authorities quickly realized that neither would occur for some time. As a memorandum to the chancellor made clear, the "ultimate level of the £" was a question "less immediate" than the pressing daily matters at hand.[26] The unavoidable truth was that Britain had sacrificed a substantial portion of its reserves in its failed attempt to support the pound and now had just enough gold to cover forward commitments and the credits from the United States and France. Moreover, autumn was generally a time of seasonal weakness for sterling, making the picture even bleaker. The political situation was also unclear: An election seemed inevitable, but whether the National Government would continue in power was anybody's guess. And not to be forgotten was the massive dollar-denominated war debt Britain owed to the United States, payment of which was only temporarily suspended by the Hoover moratorium.

---

[23] Siepmann, "Going off the Gold Standard," August 19, 1931, BoE G1/459.

[24] Niemeyer, Untitled memo, September 26, 1931, BoE G1/459.

[25] Peden (2000, 255). See Howson (1975, 82–86 and appendix 4) for a synopsis of Treasury discussions on sterling in the months after suspension.

[26] Fisher, Untitled memo, September 30, 1931, BoE G1/459.

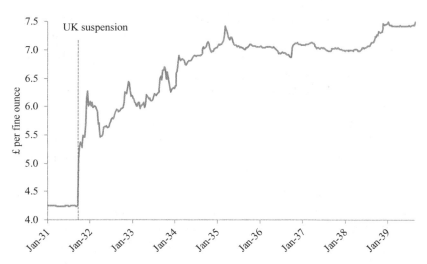

Figure 3.2 Market price of gold, 1931–1939 (£ per fine ounce).
Source: *Financial Times*

The first task was to formalize suspension with the Gold Standard (Amendment) Act of 1931. Passed on September 21, the legislation was bare bones.[27] It freed the BoE from the obligation to pay out gold bullion at £3. 17s. 10½d. per ounce, indemnified the BoE for not having done so during the previous weekend, and authorized the Treasury to regulate exchange transactions as necessary for up to six months. The Act did not, however, alter the official price of gold. The metal thus remained in the BoE's books at £3. 17s. 10½d. per standard ounce even as the market price jumped some 40 percent in sterling terms by the end of the year, as shown in Figure 3.2. Nor did the Act remove the gold cover requirements for the note issue. Convertibility was gone, then, but the metal still constituted the vast bulk of reserves and served as the basis for much of the monetary system. The Act simply took care of the first order of business and left all other decisions on the system's architecture for the future.

These decisions would not be made at Threadneedle Street. With suspension, monetary policy shifted into the government's hands. It could be no other way. The BoE, led by Norman, had championed the return to gold at $4.86; that policy was a failure. Though Norman remained governor for another twelve and a half years, his influence was never again as great as it

---

[27] Gold Standard (Amendment) Act, 1931, 21 and 22 Geo. 5. c. 46.

had been. In the wake of the unsuccessful attempt to maintain parity, interest rates and exchange rates became fully political after years of heading in that direction. The Treasury thus became the primary monetary authority, the BoE no longer able to act on matters of policy without its concurrence.[28] To be sure, the relationship was cooperative, not antagonistic. Whitehall valued the BoE's expertise, often deferring to its judgment. The exact division of responsibility changed with time and depended as much on trust as statute. And the BoE remained privately owned. But Norman's dream of central bank independence perished alongside the gold standard.

In the early weeks after suspension, the predominant fear was inflation.[29] It may seem odd that, with millions unemployed and prices still falling, the potential for inflation appeared to be a scourge and not a godsend. This mindset derived in large part from the experience of the previous decade, when Germany, Austria, and others suffered through devaluation and inflation concurrently and in large doses; it was too easy to imagine suspension leading to a loss of credibility and a dramatic or even unstoppable rise in prices. So while Britain had liberated itself from the convertibility constraint, it proactively sought to check rather than pump liquidity into the system, accompanying suspension with a hike in Bank Rate from 4.5 percent to 6 percent. The Treasury also forbade purchases of foreign exchange – save for what was required for trade, fulfillment of preexisting contracts, and travel purposes – by British residents in an attempt to gain some control over markets and limit domestic liquidation of the pound. These exchange restrictions were crisis measures, and unlike in Germany, temporary, eventually ending in March.[30]

With these safeguards in place, focus turned to sterling's rate. The BoE's Foreign Exchange Committee, formed in the second week of September before suspension to better handle the mounting crisis, worried, at first glance counterintuitively, that the pound had not fallen enough. For several days after suspension, sterling remained above $4.00, which policymakers viewed as a psychological benchmark that needed to be breached. If sterling did not drop sufficiently and began to rise too soon, there was a risk of an uncontrollable crash later. A delicate balance needed to be

---

[28] Peden (2000, 253). Of course, the government had always retained ultimate control over the exchange rate, but in the past, it had restricted itself to setting a fixed value for sterling and then entrusted the BoE to maintain it.

[29] Sayers (1976, 2:423).

[30] Ibid., 3:293–302 contains official statements and orders on restrictions.

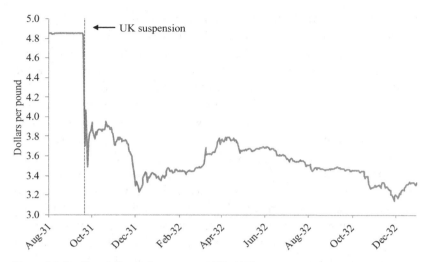

Figure 3.3 Sterling-dollar exchange rate, 1931–1932.
Source: Global Financial Data

maintained between letting sterling fall enough to reflect the new reality –
so that thereafter investors would feel safe placing funds in Britain –
without falling so much as to induce another crisis. For this reason, and
with the Treasury's support, the BoE began purchasing dollars, both to
nudge the rate down and build up reserves.[31] By September 30, sterling was
down to $3.87. Figure 3.3 shows the sterling-dollar rate in the months
after suspension.

Beyond this disposition to let sterling fall now rather than later, there
were several additional factors guiding policy. A BoE memorandum at the
end of September laid them out:

The exchange position seems to be dependent on the following main problems: (1)
The maintenance of the service of the old debts payable in dollars. (2) The
repayment of the Bank of England credit £50,000,000. (3) The repayment of the
Government credit, say, £80,000,000. (4) The building up of a foreign currency
reserve so as to prevent undue fluctuations in exchange and a substantial cushion
for the final stabilization of sterling at whatever rate is determined, say
$250,000,000.[32]

In short, the British needed resources to repay their debts and needed
reserves to impart some order on exchange markets. London amassed
enough foreign exchange (in conjunction with a fair amount of BoE gold)

---

[31] Ibid., 2:409–19.   [32] Untitled memo, September 29, 1931, BoE C43/98.

to pay off the central bank credits by February 1932 and the government credits by the following September.[33] As for market intervention, the goal was to counter "undue fluctuations" in the rate, a term that would later reappear as the EEA's principal mandate. The idea was not to buck the market trend but to smooth the transition – though at the time the BoE was actively pushing sterling down. It is also clear from this memorandum that "the final stabilisation of sterling" was taken for granted. The rate at which it would occur was a question for another day, but the fact that it would occur was axiomatic. This assumption that stabilization was inevitable and desirable would fade only as policymakers gained more experience with a floating exchange rate and realized that tying the pound to an increasingly unsettled international system was hardly a path to prosperity.

Prime Minister Ramsay MacDonald expressed the government's view on stabilization in November 1931 at the annual Lord Mayor's Banquet, a centuries-old tradition held in the medieval splendor of the City's Guildhall. To the white-tied attendees seated in the cavernous hall, MacDonald declared that the government would work diligently "to stabilize the pound on a definite basis," though he hastened to qualify the statement by noting that the time would have to wait for unspecified factors to work themselves out.[34] MacDonald's speech occurred just weeks after the general election, which resulted in the National Government coalition winning 554 out of 615 seats in the House of Commons, an unprecedented margin.[35] For MacDonald, his overwhelming victory was bittersweet, the joy of winning tempered by the anguish of defeating his once beloved Labour Party, but for the country it promised a much-needed period of political stability. Indeed, the National Government would rule through the end of the decade.

In the post-election Cabinet reshuffling, Neville Chamberlain, a member of the Conservative Party, became chancellor of the exchequer. While Chamberlain's reputation will forever be tied up with umbrellas and Munich, he had a long career in government predating his rule at the top. Scion of a political dynasty – his father and half-brother both served in Cabinet – Chamberlain first worked in the business world and then began his political ascent, becoming Lord Mayor of Birmingham in 1915 and entering Parliament in 1918. He served briefly as chancellor of the exchequer in 1923, an appointment for which he felt unprepared.[36]

---

[33] "Repayment of Bank and Treasury Credits 1931/1932," February 21, 1935, BoE C43/296.
[34] "The Guildhall Banquet," *The Times* (London), November 10, 1931.
[35] See Thorpe (1991) for a history of the election.   [36] Peden (2000, 137).

His second try, nearly a decade later, went better. According to Peden (2000, 249), "Treasury officials regarded him as the most competent Chancellor since [William] Gladstone," the towering politician who held the post four times over a span of thirty years in the second half of the nineteenth century.

Chamberlain's strong work ethic and dominating personality served him well in a Cabinet where, as he wrote in his diary in 1935, "I am more and more carrying this government on my back." MacDonald "is ill and tired," and Stanley Baldwin, the leading Conservative and lord president, "is tired and won't apply his mind to problems."[37] For these reasons, he became, and thought it only natural that he should become, the central figure in government. Authority over sterling policy rested with him, and while he progressively delegated this power as the situation calmed and the economy recovered, he jealously guarded the flexibility granted by suspension throughout his tenure.

In the weeks after Chamberlain's ascension, it was clear that exchange intervention would be imperative for the time being. But the current institutional setup was lacking. The Foreign Exchange Committee, while "strengthened" in December so as to better incorporate Treasury officials, still seemed too informal.[38] The BoE was a private corporation, and if it held foreign exchange in the Banking Department, it stood to gain from any profit or suffer from any loss on the portfolio. Back when sterling was pegged to gold, there was little concern about valuation effects, but now that the pound was floating, the possibility of large private impacts resulting from public policy seemed inappropriate. The BoE could manage the reserves through the Issue Department so that the Treasury received net profits, but the obvious focus on the BoE's every return now made such intervention more difficult to conceal. Moreover, the sheer uncertainty of the situation and the ever-present fear of volatile capital flows meant that the BoE's resources might not be sufficient for the task. After sterling fell sharply to \$3.25 in December, capital started flowing in with the new year, and there was concern that the BoE did not have enough sterling on its books to prevent a large appreciation of sterling.[39] Prompted by these considerations, the Treasury and BoE set about in search of a solution.

---

[37] Quoted in Crozier (2018).
[38] "Exchange Committee," December 28, 1931, BoE C43/98.   [39] Howson (1980, 7–8).

FIRST IN THE WORLD

The EEA was the brainchild of Sir Frederick Phillips. After graduating from Cambridge and ranking first on the civil service exam in 1908, Phillips entered the Treasury, where he worked for the next three and a half decades. Responsible for domestic and international finance as undersecretary from 1932, he was a consummate civil servant. But he was also somewhat of an eccentric. Famously gruff, Phillips had no interest in small talk. In John Maynard Keynes' telling, "His laconic manner, or, more exactly, his grunts of assent or dispute, were as well known and as well understood in Washington or Ottawa as in Whitehall; at Geneva he could be silent in several languages."[40] When working, he was apparently most productive with the heater blasting and music blaring. No doubt a character, Phillips was nevertheless widely respected, one of the Treasury's brightest minds and its key expert on monetary matters.[41]

In the early months of 1932, with bullish forces pushing sterling up, Phillips believed it essential that the pound not appreciate too much. By this time, the Treasury had shifted from fearing inflation to favoring it. Higher prices would make the vast domestic debt from the war, which was exacting a substantial toll on the budget, more affordable. Reflation would also promote recovery generally. As Phillips saw it, "The question of our own price level is the fundamental matter" in determining the policy for sterling: "A (relatively) low value of the pound is desirable – not because that is a good thing in itself but because it seems the only way to prevent sterling prices following gold prices down."[42] In March, he drafted proposals for a new account that would increase Britain's firepower in exchange markets to counter any inflow, as well as solve the aforementioned problems of responsibility and liability. The Treasury and the BoE then hashed out the final plan.[43]

The result – the EEA, often referred to as the exchange account or fund – marked the institutionalization of exchange rate management. Proposed to Parliament in April, it entered law as part of the Finance Act in June and began operations in July. The legislation set the EEA's goal as "checking undue fluctuations in the exchange value of sterling" and permitted it to deal in gold, foreign exchange, and sterling to that end.

---

[40] Quoted in Skidelsky (2001, 146).   [41] Peden (2000, 250–51).

[42] Phillips, Untitled memo, March 31, 1932, T 188/48.

[43] This section follows Howson (1980, 7–9) and Sayers (1976, 2:425–30). For other references on the EEA, see Waight (1939), Pumphrey (1942), and Bank of England (1968).

In time, the Treasury settled on slightly more detail in its public statements about objectives. Chamberlain told Parliament in 1933 that "we want the Exchange Account for smoothing out the variations in exchange caused by three sets of phenomena—first, the seasonal fluctuations; secondly, the operations of speculators, which increase those seasonal fluctuations, and other fluctuations, too; and thirdly, this special flight of capital from other countries for the sake of finding a safer place to stop in for a time."[44] Even under this more precise description, there was plainly little the Treasury and BoE could do that would run afoul of the mandate. As Siepmann later remarked, "the purpose assigned to it [the EEA] by the Act is so comprehensive as to include almost anything imaginable."[45]

The EEA was a public account placed under the control of the Treasury, which then appointed the BoE as its agent in managing the fund. The Treasury, and thus the chancellor, had the final say on exchange policy, reflecting a dramatic shift in power from the pre-suspension era, when the BoE intervened in exchange markets without Whitehall's knowledge. In the EEA's early years, the chancellor, with the governor's counsel, set overall goals – often a specific exchange rate target against the dollar or franc – and the BoE intervened to accomplish the objective. However, as time went on, the Treasury allowed the BoE to operate with more autonomy on day-to-day management. Norman summarized the relationship at a conference of Empire central bankers in May 1937:

I am proud to think that I am a Central Banker talking to Central Bankers; but I would also ask you to remember that I am an instrument of the Treasury. The two are, of course, not incompatible, especially in these days, and I would not say that I am in any way embarrassed by divided loyalties. But the money in the Exchange Equalisation Account is public money, and those who administer the account are responsible primarily to the Treasury.... In managing the Exchange Equalisation Account, we are given an extraordinarily free hand.... [W]e are not called upon to explain our interventions or our failure to intervene, nor to justify the complete discretion which the Treasury allow us in matters of day to day practice.[46]

While the notion of the BoE as an "instrument of the Treasury" would have been abhorrent to the Norman of the 1920s, he seemed to be making the best of the situation and, at least with respect to daily operations, could celebrate considerable autonomy.

---

[44] 277 Parl. Deb. H.C. (5th ser.) (1933) col. 1038–39.
[45] Siepmann, "E.E.A.: Law and Fact," May 4, 1938, BoE C43/26.
[46] "Introductory Remarks," May 26, 1937, BoE C43/25.

The Finance Act endowed the EEA with £150 million of sterling. An old Treasury account used to accumulate dollars for repaying the war debt was also rolled into the EEA, bringing the total to £171 million (4.1 percent of GDP).[47] In 1933 and 1937, Parliament augmented the account with another £200 million of sterling each time, making the total £571 million (10.7 percent of GDP).[48] Most of the sterling assets held by the EEA were Treasury bills. Officials favored this funding mechanism since it resulted in sterilized intervention, following the precedent from the 1920s. When purchasing foreign exchange, the BoE sold Treasury bills to obtain the necessary cash; when selling foreign exchange, the BoE used the sterling proceeds to purchase Treasury bills. In both cases, the monetary base remained unchanged, helping to insulate domestic conditions from international capital flows. The sterilization process was not entirely automatic or complete, but it was nearly so.[49]

Another carryover from the 1920s was the emphasis on secrecy. The public owned the EEA, but the government provided no information about the account's holdings until 1937. Even then disclosures were merely twice-a-year statements on aggregate reserves with a lag.[50] To be sure, the market picked up on intervention trends throughout the decade – sometimes it was obvious when the only buyer or seller was the government – but for the most part, the EEA's portfolio remained a

---

[47] "Exchange Account: 31st March 1932 to closing date 25th June 1932," undated, BoE C43/22.

[48] The entire capital was not always available for intervention, however. Because London had suspended gold convertibility without altering the statutory price of gold, there was now a gap of roughly 30 percent between the market price of gold and the price carried in the BoE's books. Anytime the BoE purchased gold for the Issue Department to increase the note issue, it incurred a large book loss as a result. The Finance Act fixed this problem by making the EEA bear the difference between the market and statutory prices for BoE purchases and sales of gold. Thus, when the BoE bought gold, the EEA took a paper loss. Another implication of this accounting scheme was that all gold transactions for the Issue Department now went through the EEA.

[49] Howson (1980, 10–11) argues that "sterilization was substantial" but incomplete. If the EEA completely sterilized its purchases and sales of foreign exchange, sterling assets would have consisted entirely of Treasury bills (no cash). Data on the division of sterling assets exists for November 1934 to the end of 1936. During this period, cash was on average 11 percent of sterling assets and Treasury bills were 89 percent. This split seems consistent with sterilization being the default, with cash largely held as working balances. Estimates calculated from the statements in T 175/87.

[50] Parliament's Public Accounts Committee received a strictly limited snapshot of holdings once a year. See BoE C43/65 for the disclosure of information to the Public Accounts Committee and T 233/1038 for disclosure to the public beginning in 1937.

mystery.[51] The exchange of information between central banks was more complicated. The BoE shared some details on intervention with its counterparts in New York and Paris during the EEA's first months, as it had back in the 1920s. But as relations deteriorated and governments assumed more monetary power in the following years, the BoE started to keep mum, especially in its (less and less frequent) conversations with New York. In a monetary war, exchange reserves were a state secret of the utmost sensitivity. Unsurprisingly, London's refusal to share information only intensified mistrust among the powers.[52]

As for personnel, there were a handful of key officials and exchange experts advising Chamberlain and Norman. From the Treasury, the most important were Phillips; Sir Richard Hopkins, senior to Phillips and the second-ranking civil servant; and Sigismund "Sigi" Waley of the overseas finance division.[53] From the BoE, Siepmann was the leading adviser on exchange matters and became formally responsible for the EEA in 1936. George Bolton, a banker who had been at the BoE since 1933, handled interventions.[54] The Foreign Exchange Committee, consisting of both BoE and Treasury officials, also met weekly to provide advice to the chancellor and governor.[55] The EEA operated under such secrecy that not only was the public unaware of its purchases and sales, but there appears to have been little knowledge about who was even running it. The *Financial Times*, for example, connected Siepmann to the account only once during the 1930s.[56]

---

[51] Exchange managers even discussed ways to "bamboozle the public" to prevent market participants from using public data to reverse engineer the EEA's holdings. Untitled memo, August 20, 1934, T 160/565.

[52] See Chapter 5 for a discussion on sharing information on exchange intervention.

[53] Waley's original surname was Schloss, which he changed to Waley as a result of anti-German hysteria in the run-up to World War I (decades later, he changed his given name to David.) Waley, like Siepmann, insisted on serving in the war. As his friend Arnold Toynbee recalled, Waley's Treasury superior "told him that it was his duty to go on being useful to him in Whitehall. Waley nearly quarreled with the Minister in his insistence on going to the front. He won his battle and eventually came back to Whitehall wounded and satisfied." "Sir David Waley," *The Times* (London), January 5, 1962; "Sir David Waley," *The Times* (London), January 9, 1962.

[54] Robert Kay, as head of the Foreign Exchange section, handled operations in the EEA's early years until his unexpected death in 1936. Other officials involved included Charles Hambro, an executive director until 1933, and Basil G. Catterns, chief cashier and later deputy governor.

[55] Records of the Committee's meetings end in November 1933, and it is unclear if it continued to meet regularly thereafter. The files from 1931 to 1933 can be found in BoE C43/96-98.

[56] "City Men and Matters," *Financial Times*, September 26, 1938.

Many observers around the world, even if they did not know which official handled what paperwork, were convinced they understood the EEA's true intentions. They viewed the account as a smokescreen, interpreting its seemingly anodyne mandate as code for lowering the pound's value. The EEA's early months seemed to prove them right: The pound fell from $3.57 in July 1932 to $3.14 in late November. Frank Vanderlip, former US Treasury official, testified before Congress some time later that the EEA "is a manipulative fund in the hands of an economic general, and is operated solely in the interests of England. . . . I regard it as dangerous as military airplanes crossing our borders without any aircraft guns to meet them."[57] Critics were to some extent justified in their suspicion. Though Whitehall insisted that the fund was created to iron out fluctuations and not to push sterling down, internal discussions show otherwise. In a note to Chamberlain in April 1932, Hopkins explained that the reason Britain needed the EEA was "the desire to keep *down* the pound. We cannot however put it quite as bluntly as that."[58] Preventing an appreciation of sterling was without doubt one of the motivations for creating the account.

Empirical analysis also lends some support to the concerns of Vanderlip and others. One way economists assess intent in exchange intervention is to determine whether transactions are consistent with "leaning against the wind": selling reserves when the exchange rate falls and buying when it rises. Such a strategy would tend to moderate exchange rate fluctuations. If Britain, however, was trying to push sterling down, it would buy reserves when the rate fell – in other words, lean with the wind. Using data on Britain's reserves for November 1932 to April 1936, Cairncross and Eichengreen (1983, 90) find "no evidence of leaning against the wind." Rather, London tended to push the pound down, "interven[ing] so as to reinforce exchange rate movements." London thus appears to have acted with at least some beggar-thy-neighbor intent.

But it was not the only motivation. The fund was a slab of clay, and its managers could mold it as they saw fit, repurposing it toward different ends as circumstances changed and their thinking evolved. Even during the period studied by Cairncross and Eichengreen (1983), there were episodes when London expended reserves to slow down depreciation.[59] It should

---

[57] Gold Reserve Act of 1934: Hearings on S. 2366, Day 2, Before the Senate Committee on Banking and Currency, 73rd Cong. 174 (1934) (Frank A. Vanderlip).

[58] Hopkins, "Exchange Equalisation Account Proposals," April 6, 1932, T 188/48.

[59] For instance, in September 1932, a meeting of the Foreign Exchange Committee reported, "We have lost exchange every day this week in keeping the rate over 3.45." "Meeting of the Exchange Committee," September 30, 1932, BoE C43/96.

not be surprising that in a decade as fluid as the 1930s, the motives behind exchange intervention were fluid as well. They reflected a host of factors discussed throughout this book: equilibrium estimates, political pressures, competitive advantage, precautionary reserves, dollar debts, international stability, and so on. At times, then, the secrecy of the EEA made the account appear more malign than it was. And while competitive motivations played a role in early years, under the Tripartite Agreement of 1936, London would follow a policy consistent with leaning against the wind, as examined in Chapter 6.

The EEA's launch was not the only significant monetary development in the summer of 1932. In June, the BoE lowered Bank Rate to 2 percent, matching the lowest level on record. It would remain at this level until August 1939. Save for a few occasions, there was little discussion about altering Bank Rate during these seven years.[60] Chamberlain extolled the benefits of "cheap and abundant supplies of money," and "cheap money" became the decade's monetary motto.[61] As part of this policy, the Treasury, with the BoE's assistance, undertook a massive conversion of World War I bonds into a new security at a lower interest rate, thereby easing the government's financing and supporting growth.[62] And the economy, fueled by low interest rates, started to recover.

The fear of inflation that had prevented expansive action in the early post-suspension days was now gone. In fact, at the Ottawa conference in the summer of 1932, Britain and the other imperial delegations explicitly called for a "rise throughout the world in the general levels of wholesale prices." The declaration also set "the ultimate aim of monetary policy" as "the restoration of a satisfactory international monetary standard" – that is, the gold standard – once a sufficient rise in prices had occurred and there had been "an adjustment of the factors political, economic, financial and monetary, which have caused the breakdown of the gold standard in many countries."[63] The long list of caveats signaled that the resumption of convertibility was drifting ever further into the future. Whitehall nevertheless cited the Ottawa declaration throughout the decade as proof of its bona fide desire to return to gold. Many policymakers truly did want to go back on gold at some point: The Finance Act even detailed instructions for how to wind up and liquidate the EEA, presumably once sterling was formally stabilized. There was a vision, common in government and BoE circles, of a

---

[60] In early 1939, Norman wanted to raise Bank Rate, but the Treasury convinced him otherwise. Sayers (1976, 2:565–66).
[61] Quoted in Boyce (2009, 523).   [62] Sayers (1976, 2:430–47).   [63] Ibid., 3:273–74.

future where sterling would once again be as good as gold and the EEA would no longer exist. But that day never came, and with Bank Rate already down to its lowest level in history, the EEA was now the center of action.

DOLLARS AND FRANCS

The EEA began intervening in July 1932. At the time, the international monetary system was a mixture of change and continuity. Many countries had joined or would soon join the sterling bloc, while Germany was refining its regime of exchange control. But the United States and France, along with Belgium, the Netherlands, Switzerland, and several others, clung to gold, even as they sank further into depression. The EEA's managers thus had to operate in a delicate situation, keeping in mind that it could change on any given day. Authorized to deal in foreign exchange and gold, they chose to concentrate on dollars and francs. By February 1933, foreign exchange comprised the majority of the EEA's assets. But this portfolio allocation was dangerous, for it risked imposing on Britain the very lesson France and others had already learned in September 1931: Currencies were as good as gold until, suddenly, they were not.

By time the EEA started intervening in July, the capital inflow that had propelled the account's establishment had turned into an outflow. From a monthly average of $3.64 in June 1932, the pound fell to $3.27 by December, before rising to $3.42 in February 1933. Much of the pound's weakness was due to the shift to record low interest rates.[64] The EEA's managers sought, as a Treasury memo detailed, "to smooth out, but not to alter the downward trend," while also being mindful of maintaining sufficient reserves.[65] To do so, they set targets for the exchange rate, in terms of the dollar, which they successively lowered as capital continued to leave. That is, the British spent some reserves to soften the fall at some times.[66] By November, however, the EEA stopped providing support altogether, and soon thereafter began accumulating reserves as capital started flowing back in. With the new year, policymakers concluded that "the interests of industry would be best served by keeping sterling about where it is ($3.35)

---

[64] Howson (1980, 15–17).   [65] Waley, "Exchange Committee," August 5, 1932, T 175/71.
[66] In mid-October, the British were selling roughly $3 million a day to steady markets. "Meeting of the Exchange Committee," October 14, 1932, BoE C43/96.

and in any event by not letting it rise either now or later as high as $3.50," and sold sterling to that end.[67]

This early intervention to slow the pound's fall and then build up reserves involved transactions in two currencies: dollars and francs. The continued links between gold and the dollar and franc simplified the decision-making process as to which currencies to deal in. So long as neither currency depreciated, their values would remain steady in terms of gold, which was the international safe asset. The currencies were also convertible into gold on demand. In 1932, despite all that had happened, it was still possible to believe that the United States and France, holding over 60 percent of the world's gold reserves, would weather the storm and maintain parity.[68] These two currencies were therefore ideal vehicles for British intervention.[69]

But the EEA's managers could also intervene by buying and selling gold. London was the world's gold market: Production from all over the globe made its way to London, where dealers bought, sold, and then shipped it around the world. There was no better place to transact in the metal. The market was wrapped in tradition, most notably the daily "fixing." Every morning at 11 a.m., six bullion dealers met in the offices of N. M. Rothschild and Sons, matching their various orders from clients to find a price that balanced supply and demand. With a price reached, calls of "Fixed!" made their way through every corner of the City. Cables immediately went out informing all the major financial capitals of the price.[70] No event was more important in the market day, even if its "rather archaic mechanism" left Siepmann and others a bit embarrassed.[71]

Exchange managers considered gold to have several advantages to foreign exchange. First, gold was the preeminent reserve asset. If the British were one day to reinstate gold convertibility, it made sense to begin acquiring gold. The metal was also free of foreign exchange risk – countries were devaluing against gold, not revaluing against it. On the other hand, gold earned nothing, had transportation and storage costs, and, if held

---

[67] Hopkins to Chamberlain, January 21, 1933, T 175/71.

[68] Eichengreen (2008, table 3.1).

[69] As Howson (1980, 36) explains, in 1935 the EEA branched out to dealing in Dutch guilders and Swiss francs in small amounts. After the Tripartite Agreement, the EEA began operating in belgas as well. In the last years of the decade there were also small transactions in Swedish kronor, Norwegian kroner, Canadian dollars, Argentine pesos, and Indian rupees.

[70] Balogh (1947, 219).

[71] Siepmann, "Gold: The Mechanism of E.E.A. Dealings," April 22, 1938, BoE C43/26.

overseas, could be blocked from export or confiscated in the event of war or regulatory changes. And quaint as the gold fixing was, it had the disadvantage that the price of gold was not quoted continuously, whereas exchange rates were. As a result, buying or selling gold in the afternoon would not affect that day's quoted price but doing so for dollars would, an important factor given that one of the primary goals of intervention was to impact prices.

The effects of intervention in gold and exchange markets were not identical either. True, changes in the sterling price for gold resulted in equivalent changes in the exchange rate with gold standard countries: From October 1931 until the dollar began depreciating in March 1933, the correlations between the monthly changes in the dollar and franc rates and the gold value of sterling were 0.99. But there were significant differences in the gold flows resulting from foreign exchange as opposed to gold transactions. All else equal, when the EEA worked toward increasing the sterling price of gold by direct purchases of the metal, it attracted gold from the rest of the world through arbitrage transactions: The incoming gold was sold for sterling, which was then sold for foreign currencies, and eventually the depreciation of sterling made the transaction in gold no longer profitable. On the other hand, when the EEA purchased and held foreign currencies, the depreciation of sterling against those currencies made it profitable to buy gold in London, sell it in the gold standard country, and convert the proceeds back into sterling. Once the sterling price of gold increased enough to match the depreciation, the transaction was no longer profitable. The former method brought gold from the rest of the world to London; the latter moved gold from London to the rest of the world. In sum, purchasing gold directly could increase pressure on gold standard countries, while purchasing and holding foreign exchange could ease pressure on them.

There were thus many variables to consider. Archival evidence suggests that policymakers wanted to focus on foreign exchange, not gold. The government's reaction to the attempt by some members of Parliament to restrict the EEA's powers provides insight into its thinking. A proposed amendment to the Finance Act sought to rid the EEA of the ability to deal in gold entirely.[72] The fear underpinning the proposal was that the account had sufficient resources to increase the sterling price of gold through direct

---

[72] Another amendment sought to allow the EEA to purchase silver. Officials made sure this power was not included, for silver "in the absence of international agreement is not money and a store of silver is really no more useful for the purposes of the Exchange

purchases of the metal, and this increase could drain gold from the rest of the world, reducing prices abroad and worsening the downturn. Treasury officials shared this concern: Howson (1980, 18) writes that "they did not want to be gold hoarders," sucking up the world's gold and exacerbating deflationary tendencies abroad. And while they successfully fought the amendment – few administrators desire a reduction in policy tools – their reasoning suggests that they nevertheless favored intervention through foreign exchange. An internal memo opposing the amendment explained:

When you are dealing with foreign exchange on a large scale it is essential to have power to buy and sell gold as well as to buy or sell foreign exchange. Sometimes the only method of acquiring holdings of a particular currency or of moving balances from one financial centre to another is by a shipment of gold and it is not in the interests of this country that the operation of the new Account should be robbed of all flexibility by a quite unnecessary squeamishness in the matter of buying or selling gold occasionally.[73]

The point then was that gold transactions were necessary to operate in exchange markets efficiently, but they were most useful to the extent that they supported those operations. Dealing in gold would be necessary only "occasionally."

This early concentration on foreign exchange is evident in the data. In the EEA's first months, foreign exchange reserves were large and at times significantly greater than gold reserves. Figure 3.4 shows gold and foreign exchange assets (at cost). As the EEA ramped up operations in the autumn of 1932, foreign exchange holdings became dominant. By the end of the year, they were 27 percent greater than gold holdings. By the middle of February 1933, they were double gold and reached their peak at £77 million.[74] The breakdown between dollars and francs varied, but at this point, dollars accounted for 70 percent (£55 million) and francs made up the rest (£22 million).[75]

Equalisation Account than a store of tin or rubber or wool or any other primary product." Treasury notes on amendments, May 23, 1932, BoE C43/22.
[73] Ibid. [74] Weekly data on exchange holdings are from various statements in T 175/72.
[75] Technically, the EEA held 23 million Reichsmarks (carried in the books at roughly £1.5 million) that were a legacy asset from the creation of the BIS. As Phillips explained, they were "an historical accident, due to the EE A/C when set up taking over some ancient assets of the former Exchange Account. The money is not foreign currency in any ordinary sense of the words." Untitled memo, June 11, 1938, T 233/1038; Howson (1980, 60).

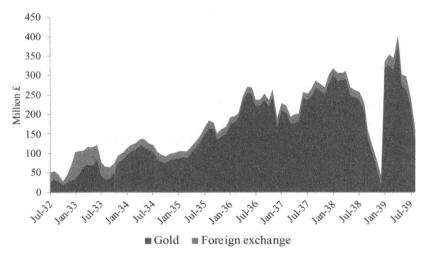

Figure 3.4 EEA holdings, 1932–1939 (million £, at cost).
Source: BoE C160/78

It is surprising that after depreciating the pound by so much, the British were willing to maintain large long positions in foreign exchange.[76] Three factors seemed to be at play: an attempt to be cooperative by not redirecting gold to London, optimism that the mighty Americans and gold-rich French would not devalue, and confidence that the EEA's experts could unwind the position quickly if trouble loomed. Indeed, as late as January 1933, Phillips wrote that "the prospect of either the dollar or the franc being forced off gold is still very remote," and thought that "[f]rom the point of view of general world interests we should hold a good amount of dollars and francs and not too much gold."[77]

But Phillips also recognized that "there is more risk to us in holding dollars or francs."[78] Taking precautions seemed prudent, even if the likelihood of America leaving the gold standard was small. And the FRBNY, fearful that Britain could amass large dollar reserves and then suddenly demand conversion into gold at an inopportune time, wanted the BoE to reduce its holdings.[79] The Foreign Exchange Committee

[76] A BoE report in 1939 made the curious claim that "the E.E.A. converted into gold automatically and at once all or nearly all the foreign currencies purchased" during the previous seven years, a statement that seems not to take account of the substantial buildup of foreign currencies in 1932 and early 1933. Bolton, "The Exchange Equalisation Account," undated, BoE C160/78.

[77] Phillips, Untitled memo, January 28, 1933, T 175/71.   [78] Ibid.

[79] Howson (1980, 18); Phillips, Untitled memo, January 28, 1933, T 175/71.

recommended at the end of January, with the chancellor's concurrence, to lower franc and dollar reserves to no more than £28 million each. "The rest of our foreign resources must be in the form of gold."[80] The EEA's managers did in fact reduce franc reserves, bringing them down from £22 million in February to under £1 million the following month. Yet dollar reserves continued to exceed £40 million as March began.

Thus, in the EEA's first eight months, London bought and sold dollars, francs, and gold, preferring dollars the most. Total reserves (EEA plus Issue Department) increased substantially, from £262 million to £332 million when measured in current prices. And, to Whitehall's delight, the pound ended the period lower than it had started. Management was not easy: There were difficult questions about how to balance holdings of foreign exchange and gold, not to mention the usual tactical issues with intervention relating to timing and force. Exchange managers nevertheless seemed well-equipped to continue on with little drama so long as the situation continued as it was. It did not. When the clocks in Washington struck noon on March 4, 1933, a new, unpredictable state of affairs commenced that would radically alter exchange dynamics.

---

[80] Hopkins to Hambro, January 31, 1933, BoE C43/97. The recommendation was to reduce liquid holdings to £28 million and to consider holding some US government securities in addition as a way to lessen FRBNY fears of quick conversion.

4

Washington Declares War, 1933–1935

Back in 1931, when Harry Siepmann, adviser at the Bank of England (BoE), doubted that there was "any power on earth which could get sterling back to 4.86 2/3 once the country has experienced the blessed relief of depreciation to $4.00," he had not accounted for Franklin Roosevelt.[1] At the time, Roosevelt was merely the governor of New York, but in little over a year he was elected president. In his inaugural address on March 4, 1933, he asserted that the economic emergency facing the United States was tantamount to war and necessitated a response commensurate to the danger. While Roosevelt had kept mostly mum on monetary policy through the campaign, it soon became clear that he would not permit traditional thinking on the subject to continue to paralyze Washington. He was a dynamo, seeking action on any promising front and willing to burst through restraints as he saw fit. Roosevelt jettisoned the gold standard and embarked on a program of gold purchases to increase the price of gold and depreciate the dollar. Before year's end, sterling was back not just to $4.86 but well past $5, Siepmann's prediction one of many proven wrong by a president intent on "bold, persistent experimentation."[2]

Roosevelt was singularly focused on the domestic situation. Once he found the tactic of depreciating the dollar to raise prices and spur recovery sensible, he believed it essential. He did not want to waste time dithering, worrying about legal technicalities or diplomatic delicacies. Domestically, this resolution – and the pursuit of other heterodoxies – cost him the service of many economic advisers, who saw his policies as precipitating

---

[1] Siepmann's statement referred in particular to the possibility of the British government reinstituting the gold standard at the old parity. Siepmann, "Going off the Gold Standard," August 19, 1931, BoE G1/459.

[2] Roosevelt, Oglethorpe University Commencement Address, May 22, 1932, RMSF 476.

"the end of Western civilization," in the histrionic words of one.[3] The financial establishment shared this concern, which likely only strengthened Roosevelt's faith in his instincts.

Internationally, his conduct made him out to be a monetary madman. Europeans found the new president and his policies inscrutable and unpredictable. The British always asserted that they had had no choice but to suspend convertibility, a plausible claim given the months-long fight to maintain parity; the world found Roosevelt's gold maneuvers, on the other hand, to be willful, a first choice rather than the last resort. As Chancellor of the Exchequer Neville Chamberlain noted in a meeting days after Roosevelt announced a complete embargo of gold exports, "The deliberate abandonment of the gold standard by the United States had thrown Europe into chaos and created mistrust and unsettlement everywhere."[4]

Roosevelt, of course, faced a crisis of epic proportions and wanted to leave no stone unturned. But the manner in which he implemented his policies, beyond the policies themselves, contributed to the sense of "mistrust and unsettlement." The process of leaving gold and depreciating the dollar was prolonged and mysterious; the president's closest advisers, including Secretary of the Treasury Henry Morgenthau, Jr., seemed out of their depth. Roosevelt acted with little regard for the concerns of other countries, one minute appearing open to cooperative efforts and the next turning around and spurning them. After visiting the United States in December 1933, the BoE's Henry Clay reported that the president's policies were largely a combination of "ignorance" and "irresponsibility," and "it would be unwise for other countries to enter into any long-term commitments to America, whether of exchange stabilisation or any other economic arrangement."[5] Indeed, for the next three years, the democratic powers not only failed to reach agreement on how to restore order to the system but, for the most part, stopped even attempting to do so.

These then were the dark years of international monetary relations, with the monetary war at its worst. The United States followed its own course, determined to fix the economy and negate any advantage Britain had gained since 1931, even creating an exchange fund in 1934 with the express purpose of countering London's. Britain, for its part, was pleased with its

---

[3] Quoted in Rauchway (2015, 65).

[4] "Interview between the Chancellor, the Deputy Governor and Mr. Hambro," April 22, 1933, BoE G1/303.

[5] Clay, "U.S.A.—November 1933," December 6, 1933, BoE G1/139.

strengthening recovery but guarded its monetary flexibility ever more vigilantly, convinced that the United States was not a potential partner but a threat. All the while, France and the rest of the gold bloc held on to the metal, remaining stuck in depression as they blamed their ills on monetary heresies abroad. Central bankers continued to talk to one another but more often to keep in touch, express displeasure with governmental policies, or commiserate about the state of the world than to work together on anything of much substance. In Britain and even more so in the United States, power was in the hands of the Treasuries, and they saw little room and had less desire for compromise.

This chapter describes the monetary antagonism that pervaded the world from Roosevelt's inauguration in 1933 to the development of an uneasy ceasefire by the middle of 1935. Roosevelt's policies fundamentally changed the monetary system, and the way in which he enacted them, given that the system was already fragmented and devastated by depression, ensured that there would be no meeting of the minds on international stabilization and reform. Instead, suspicion festered in the great capitals of the world. Once Roosevelt officially devalued the dollar in January 1934 and returned the country to a limited gold standard, Britain and France were clueless as to what, if anything, America would do next; America and France were furious as Britain refused to stabilize the pound; and the world watched France flounder as its currency increasingly came under pressure. By the middle of 1935, Britain and the United States were largely content with their rebounding economies. A suspension of monetary hostilities – neither negotiated nor announced – took hold, where both sides remained heavily armed but neither desired to resume firing first. The precariousness of the franc, however, meant that this superficial stability was liable to crumble at any moment.

HURLING BOMBS

Roosevelt's monetary program cannot be understood without first grasping the severity of the economic crisis plaguing the country. The depression in the United States was far worse than in Britain, France, and all other major powers save Germany. From 1929 to 1932, industrial production plummeted 46 percent in the United States, as compared to 31 percent in France and 17 percent in Britain. One-quarter of the workforce was unemployed. Whereas Britain and France managed to avoid systemic banking crises, the United States suffered through a series of them. The meltdown greeting Roosevelt was the worst yet: As he took the oath of office, more than half of the states had already closed banks.[6] The nation's farmers, devastated by the cruel one-two punch of falling prices for their crops and high nominal debts on their mortgages, were in a wretched state, with resentment threatening to boil into outright revolt.[7]

In this environment, Roosevelt had no option but to act and to act quickly. Inevitably, the administration would make mistakes, officials would misread situations, and foreign governments would misinterpret actions. The scholarly consensus is overwhelming that Roosevelt was correct in devaluing, as were all other countries that did so: Freedom from the old parity helped stimulate – though did not guarantee – recovery. This book in no way dissents from this view. But the secondary matter of how governments carried out devaluations – as no two devaluations are ever precisely the same – is critically important for understanding how countries interpreted the move and responded. Roosevelt, leader of the largest economy and creditor in the world, did not simply downplay international monetary diplomacy but gratuitously condemned it, adding fuel to a fire that was already burning out of control.

In the early weeks of Roosevelt's administration, there was no time to chart a long-term monetary plan: The crisis at hand was all-consuming.[8] To get some breathing space, Roosevelt announced a national bank holiday and a ban on gold exports (except for gold already held on earmark by governments and central banks) on March 6, freezing the financial system in place. On March 12, the night before banks were to begin reopening, he plainly and brilliantly explained the banking system's dependence on confidence to a weary nation in his first Fireside Chat. With his peroration, "[t]ogether we cannot fail," he exhibited the infectious optimism for which he was famous.[9] The next morning, deposits flowed back as the gears of finance started to move again. But gold, which remained the base of the system, was not returning quickly. People continued to hoard it, finding in the metal a bit of safety and certainty in an otherwise dangerous and volatile world.

To remedy this problem, Roosevelt issued an executive order in early April that forever changed the role of gold in American life. The First World War had brought an end to gold circulation in most countries, but it

---

[6] Silber (2009).   [7] Rauchway (2015, 55–57).

[8] The following discussion on Roosevelt's monetary policy relies heavily on Edwards (2018), Friedman and Schwartz (1963, chapter 8), Meltzer (2003, chapter 6), and Rauchway (2015, chapters 3–5).

[9] Roosevelt, Fireside Chat, March 12, 1933, RMSF 616a.

had not done so in the United States; as late as 1932, gold coin and certificates accounted for one-sixth of the currency.[10] The quickest way to increase gold in the government's vaults was to tap into holdings stored under mattresses and in safe-deposit boxes. The president's executive order required individuals and businesses to turn over all such monetary gold in excess of $100. By nationalizing gold, Roosevelt put an end to domestic convertibility of the dollar. But the executive order permitted licenses for the export of gold, leaving open the possibility of maintaining the gold standard's international component.

Whether or not and to what extent the dollar would remain convertible internationally at its statutory parity of $20.67 was uncertain, both in Roosevelt's mind and to the world at large. After all, everything was a whirl during these weeks. Few in Washington knew what to expect on any given day. And the further from Washington, the fuzzier things were. The Federal Reserve Bank of New York (FRBNY) was lost – Governor George Harrison complained to the British of being "completely in the dark" – though it tried to share what information it had with the BoE and the Banque de France (BdF).[11]

During this time, Roosevelt remained open to international efforts to combat the Depression. Back in the summer of 1932, governments had called for a World Economic Conference to discuss how best to bring about recovery. With the Conference set to convene in London in June, Roosevelt invited foreign delegations to visit Washington for preliminary discussions.[12] The prospect of significant agreement at the upcoming Conference was always small: Navigating through the thicket of war debts, trade restrictions, and exchange rates was a daunting task. The French had defaulted on their war debts in December 1932, the British considered a final settlement essential to recovery, and the United States planned to ignore the topic. Imperial preferences, quotas, and tariffs were bitterly contentious. On exchange rates, the French remained steadfast exponents of the traditional gold standard and believed stabilization of exchange rates was critical for recovery. The British were open to short-term stabilization efforts to maximize the chances for progress on other issues but refused to consider permanently repegging sterling to gold. The United States had no set policy. These were just a few of the innumerable hurdles, but the

---

[10] Friedman and Schwartz (1963, table 21). Gold certificates were legal tender notes redeemable for gold held by the Treasury.
[11] Quoted in Clavin (1996, 111).   [12] See Ibid. for a history of the Conference.

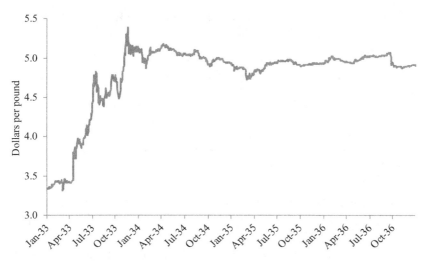

Figure 4.1 Sterling-dollar exchange rate, 1933–1936.
Source: Global Financial Data

invitation by the new American leader nevertheless offered some reason for optimism.

Hopes, however, deflated before the talks even began. On April 19, 1933, as the British and French delegations were crossing the Atlantic en route to Washington, Roosevelt casually told reporters gathered in his office that the administration would no longer grant licenses for gold exports, thereby ending the international component of the gold standard. The dollar plummeted, with the sterling-dollar rate going from $3.47 on April 18 to $3.87 on April 24 as shown in Figure 4.1. Roosevelt was by this point convinced that some inflation was urgent – "the whole problem before us is to raise commodity prices," he explained to the press – and so he thought it best to free the country from the constraint posed by gold exportation.[13] Indeed, he had just decided to support the Thomas Amendment, partially modified to his liking, which, when passed as part of the Agricultural Adjustment Act in May, provided the president an array of options to spur inflation, including the right to devalue the dollar by up to 50 percent against gold.[14]

The decision to prohibit the export of gold caught the world off guard. The FRBNY first heard of it from press reports.[15] Sir Frederick Leith-Ross

---

[13] Roosevelt press conference, April 19, 1933, RPC 13.   [14] Rauchway (2015, 64–67).
[15] Crane conversation with Cariguel, April 19, 1933, FRBNY C261.

was on board the SS *Berengaria* with Prime Minister Ramsay MacDonald when the news came. Decades later he recalled the British reaction:

We were approaching New York when, on 19th April, we heard that the President had suspended the sale of gold which meant that the dollar had gone off the gold standard.... [T]his was a surprise, indeed a shock to us. Unlike the United Kingdom, the U.S.A. had ample gold reserves and could undoubtedly have maintained its parity with a comparatively small loss of gold. It looked as if they aimed at a competitive depreciation of the dollar with the pound. However, the dollar gold parity was the anchor on which all the schemes for currency stabilisation had been fixed and the sudden abandonment of gold by America threw everything into the melting pot.[16]

Leith-Ross wondered whether, on disembarkment in New York, the British should simply board another ship and head home, "as the American action made nonsense of all the plans for the Conference."[17] MacDonald would not hear of it and held out hopes of a productive visit, but the timing of the announcement did not augur well for the meetings. Members of the French delegation heading to Washington were likewise enraged.[18]

Talks began on April 21. Just four days later, on April 25, Chamberlain, who remained in London, upped the ante by requesting parliamentary authority to increase the capital of the Exchange Equalisation Account (EEA) by £200 million, more than doubling its size to £371 million. The account's sterling resources had been running low for some time as its stock of gold and foreign exchange increased. Without more sterling, the British would not be able to purchase any more reserves, a disturbing possibility at a time when they acutely felt the need to be prepared for any eventuality. Chamberlain stressed publicly that there was "no connection whatever between the American action and the increase in the Exchange Equalisation Fund, which was decided upon long before we had any conception that the American Government might go off the Gold Standard."[19] The decision for an increase had indeed been made weeks before, with discussion of boosting the EEA's firepower having begun as early as January.[20] But Roosevelt's termination of gold exports appears to have influenced Chamberlain into augmenting his request from £150 million to £200 million. He wanted all the ammunition he could get, and

---

[16] Leith-Ross (1968, 160).   [17] Ibid.
[18] Sayers interview with Mönick, May 7, 1969, BoE ADM33/32.
[19] 277 Parl. Deb. H.C. (5th ser.) (1933) col. 46.
[20] By March 5, officials seem to have decided that an increase in capital would become necessary. "Exchange Equalisation Fund," January 25, 1933, BoE C43/23; Hopkins to Chancellor, March 5, 1933, T 175/71.

as he had told BoE officials on April 22, "politically speaking ... the present situation in America made the increase even more necessary."[21]

Chamberlain's move to refill the fund's coffers appeared to many American observers to be retaliation, a feeling likely intensified by the constant protestations of innocence. Sterling depreciated from $3.87 on April 24 to $3.72 on April 27, and as the *New York Herald Tribune* observed, the action "was seen as a challenge to President Roosevelt's present tactical advantage in the currency restabilization situation."[22] The EEA was, of course, already viewed warily by American and French officials. Even before the increase, Leith-Ross reported back home that, in the nonstop negotiations in Washington, he had "taken every opportunity to dispel misunderstandings about [the] equalisation fund."[23] Suspicion only heightened after the capital injection. The BoE's deputy governor, Ernest Harvey, attempted to allay fears in a phone call to Harrison, who "said that he was glad to hear about this as there was a good deal of criticism in America that this action had been taken as a reprisal."[24] The head of the British Library of Information in New York – a Foreign Office outpost designed to improve American understanding of British policy – wrote to London of the "fuss" and requested additional information on the EEA, due to "growing apprehension" about the fund.[25] The optics of vastly increasing the EEA's capital just days after the United States suspended the gold standard were not exactly conducive to fostering goodwill. It looked more like a monetary arms race.

In Washington, the conversations, intended to reach a preliminary understanding prior to the World Economic Conference, unsurprisingly made little headway. Everyone knew that ultimate authority lay with Roosevelt, but nobody knew which of his representatives actually spoke for him. "Amid this welter of ideas and with the inchoate Administration in Washington," a frustrated Leith-Ross informed London, "it was extremely difficult to get any effective discussion as to the dollar policy."[26] In a separate memorandum, he noted, "There is no one at the Treasury responsible for exchanges. The Federal Reserve Board is practically not

---

[21] "Interview between the Chancellor, the Deputy Governor and Mr. Hambro," April 22, 1933, BoE G1/303.

[22] "British Match U.S. Inflation by Big Fund," *New York Herald Tribune*, April 26, 1933.

[23] Leith-Ross telegram to Hopkins, April 24, 1933, T 188/78.

[24] Harvey conversation with Harrison, April 27, 1933, BoE G1/139.

[25] Fletcher to Leeper, May 4, 1933, T 160/730.

[26] Leith-Ross, "Discussions at Washington on the Dollar Exchange," May 15, 1933, BoE G1/139.

functioning and the Federal Reserve Banks are discredited at Washington."[27] It did not help that Secretary of the Treasury William Woodin was enfeebled with what appeared to be a sore throat but was in fact the cancer that would take his life in little more than a year. The meetings were adjourned with the prospects for the Conference as uncertain as ever.

So much hinged on what Roosevelt's next step would be. The dollar was no longer on the gold standard, but the official price remained $20.67 per ounce. Would Roosevelt formally devalue the dollar and then allow the resumption of gold exports? Would he float the dollar? Would he maintain the $20.67 price and install permanent exchange controls and clearing arrangements?

One stumbling block to altering the price of gold was the prevalence of clauses in public and private contracts that committed the debtor to repay in dollars defined by the $20.67 gold parity. An increase in the dollar price of gold would increase the number of dollars required to clear debts, throwing many debtors into bankruptcy. The administration considered these gold clauses a threat to recovery and requested the Congress to repeal them, which it duly did in the beginning of June.[28]

By this time, Morgenthau, officially the governor of the Federal Farm Board but, as a close friend of Roosevelt's, much more, had shown the president charts prepared by George F. Warren, an agricultural economist at Cornell. Warren's figures suggested that, historically, higher gold prices were associated with higher commodity prices. As Edwards (2018, 70) summarizes, Warren went on to argue that, "if the government raised the price of gold, higher prices for cotton, wheat, corn, rye, barley, eggs, hogs, and other products would increase almost immediately and in the same proportion as the increase in the price of gold." The theory had many holes, but Roosevelt found the charts appealing and, as spring turned to summer, he became captivated by the prospect of boosting commodity prices by increasing the dollar price of gold.[29]

By time the World Economic Conference convened in June 1933, the three powers had agreed to hold parallel talks – in London but separate from the formal deliberations – to negotiate a short-term stabilization of exchange rates for the Conference's duration.[30] The hope was that this

---

[27] Leith-Ross, "Report by Sir F. Leith-Ross on Conversations at Washington and New York," May 12, 1933, BoE G1/139.

[28] See Edwards (2018) and Dam (1983).   [29] Wicker (1971, 875–76).

[30] See Edwards (2018, chapter 8), Clavin (1996, chapter 6), and Nichols (1951).

monetary truce (in addition to a tariff truce) would make the atmosphere more propitious by removing fears that heated conversation in the morning would lead to retaliation in the afternoon. The representatives in London reached a tentative plan for holding exchange rates in check, but as rumors of potential stabilization spread, the dollar appreciated and US equity and commodity prices declined. Roosevelt concluded that the plan was more likely to hurt than help his recovery program, so he instructed his team in London to reject the terms. The negotiators, trying to salvage the situation, then made headway in drafting a statement that committed countries to nothing but mentioned the benefits of reducing currency speculation and proclaimed the return to an international gold standard as a universal goal; substance was sacrificed in an effort to find some area of agreement that could build trust.

But the document incurred Roosevelt's wrath. On board the USS *Indianapolis* as he headed back to Washington from a vacation, Roosevelt cabled his infamous response on July 3. The United States, he made clear, would not fall into the trap set by the "old fetishes of so-called international bankers":

I would regard it as a catastrophe amounting to a world tragedy if the great Conference of nations ... should ... allow itself to be diverted by the proposal of a purely artificial and temporary experiment affecting the monetary exchange of a few nations only....

The world will not long be lulled by the specious fallacy of achieving a temporary and probably an artificial stability in foreign exchange on the part of a few large countries only. The sound internal economic system of a nation is a greater factor in its well being than the price of its currency in changing terms of the currencies of other nations.[31]

This denunciation of stabilization talks doomed the Conference. And this failure, Toniolo (2005, 136) writes, "taking place at such a critical time for the world economy, dispelled whatever hopes were still nurtured about multilateral coordination in general and on monetary matters in particular." Delegates continued to meet for several more weeks, largely for show, until proceedings concluded on July 27. Chamberlain thought "there has never been a case of a Conference being so completely smashed by one of the participants."[32] No doubt this episode contributed to what one British

---

[31] "World Conference: The Monetary Declarations," *The Economist*, July 8, 1933.
[32] Neville to Ida Chamberlain, July 15, 1933, in Chamberlain (2002, 398).

diplomat later characterized as the chancellor's "almost instinctive contempt for the Americans."[33]

It would, of course, be foolish to think that, but for Roosevelt's "bombshell" message, the Conference would have reached a grand deal on the myriad issues besetting the world economy. The president might merely have expedited an inevitable result. After all, in the run-up to the Conference, disagreements on war debts had continued to bedevil negotiators. When the year's first installment came due on June 15, Britain made a token payment to avoid default, with US acquiescence, but the French again refused to pay anything, a decision that did not endear them, or their insistence on stabilization, to Roosevelt. And even though the United States insisted that war debts not appear on the Conference's agenda, MacDonald's opening address stressed the importance of a settlement. The US ambassador to Britain found MacDonald's remarks "inexcusable and unwise," believing that "MacDonald had wrecked the conference, unless the President should save it."[34] But the president did not save it, nor did he particularly try to. "The rivalry and mutual incomprehension between Britain and the United States," Skidelsky (2001, 184–85) writes, "now exploded into full-blown economic warfare." And the shellshock from Roosevelt's message, disparaging so much of what had been worked on, would linger for years, making peace that much harder to reach.

The international monetary system further fragmented. Hours after Roosevelt's message, France, Belgium, the Netherlands, Switzerland, Italy, and Poland issued a joint declaration "confirm[ing] their intention to maintain the free functioning of the gold standard in their respective countries at the existing gold parities and within the framework of existing monetary laws."[35] The gold bloc, as the group was known, stood firm against the heterodoxies engulfing the world.[36] At the same time, the vow to maintain existing parities fastened its members to a policy of deflation, exacerbating economic distress and sowing social discord. On the other side of the monetary spectrum, representatives of the British Empire issued a declaration at the Conference's conclusion that reaffirmed the Ottawa resolutions from the previous year, calling for a continued rise in prices and an eventual return to gold, this latter goal appropriately caveated so that it did not impinge on current policy.[37]

---

[33] The comment was from Sir Alexander Cadogan. Quoted in Self (2007, 311).
[34] Quoted in Clavin (1996, 120).
[35] "World Conference: The Monetary Declarations," *The Economist*, July 8, 1933.
[36] Mouré (2002, 205).   [37] "Empire Currency Policy," *The Economist*, August 5, 1933.

A little over a week after ending the stabilization talks, Roosevelt, perhaps feeling that he had gone a bit too far, authorized the FRBNY to sell up to $20 million of gold to the BoE to prevent the dollar's depreciation beyond the old parity of $4.86. The arrangement lasted for two weeks, but it was not renewed, and soon enough the dollar passed $4.86.[38] This half-hearted attempt to stem the tide was the last act of monetary cooperation between the two countries for more than two years.[39] In the aftermath of the Conference's collapse, the BoE's George Bolton recalled nearly four decades later, "there was a complete break in relations on the technical level with the Americans."[40] Central bankers, while remaining on mostly friendly terms, did not have the space to cooperate, as the governments were now in control. And even though both governments shared a desire for higher prices and repudiated the gold standard's strictures, they saw each other more as rivals than allies.

In the months after the Conference, Roosevelt was dismayed that commodity prices were not increasing as swiftly as he desired. In October 1933, he settled on a scheme to give them a jolt by purchasing gold at rising prices in line with Warren's recommendations.[41] Each morning, several aides came to his bedroom where the president, eating breakfast, chose the day's price. One morning he decided to up the price by 21 cents because it was three times seven, a lucky number. Even Morgenthau, who supported the general policy, privately worried, "If anybody ever knew how we really set the gold price through a combination of lucky numbers, etc., I think that they really would be frightened."[42]

Though observers did not know the mechanics of the process, they certainly perceived the randomness. Montagu Norman, governor of the BoE, expressed his concern repeatedly to Harrison, warning that the program could "bring about complete currency and exchange chaos in Europe. . . . [T]he great danger of the policy was that no one knew how far it would be carried, what amounts of gold would be bought, or how low Washington wished to depress the dollar."[43] There was a feeling that Roosevelt was putting the cart of higher prices before the horse of economic recovery, focusing too much on manipulating prices up rather than

---

[38] See BoE C43/307 and Meltzer (2003, 450–51).

[39] In late 1933, the administration asked the FRBNY to sound out the BoE on a joint devaluation against gold, but the British were not interested. Meltzer (2003, 455); Norman conversation with Harrison, December 1, 1933, BoE C43/312.

[40] Sayers interview with Bolton, January 20, 1971, BoE ADM33/25.

[41] See Edwards (2018, chapter 10).   [42] Dictation, November 5, 1933, MD 00/96.

[43] Harrison conversation with Norman, November 2, 1933, FRBNY C261.

creating a fertile environment for growth. And to add to the bewilderment, Roosevelt, in large part due to pressures from the silver lobby, began purchasing silver to increase its price too, a policy that drained countries on the silver standard of the metal and caused head scratching in Whitehall.[44]

London's response to the dollar's fall was multilayered. Policymakers first had to figure out what to do about the EEA's dollar holdings. Just as sterling's depreciation in 1931 had wrecked the balance sheets of several central banks, the dollar's departure from the gold standard in 1933 threatened the EEA's. The account's managers decided to stop purchasing dollars and to run down the balance methodically. The EEA had roughly $190 million in dollar assets when Roosevelt embargoed gold exports in April; at the end of the year, it held less than $3 million.[45] The sales resulted in a book loss of more than £14 million, putting the EEA in the red. The strict secrecy surrounding the account prevented any embarrassment that would have come had the balance sheet been public. In fact, it even provided cover for Chamberlain to claim erroneously that the account was profitable, a matter of some importance to the public and members of Parliament, concerned as they were about the fiscal costs of this new fund.[46]

By getting out of dollars, however, London could no longer orient its exchange policy around the dollar. And even if the British had been willing to continue operating in dollars, such a policy would now seem especially provocative. As the Treasury's Sir Richard Hopkins warned days after Roosevelt's bombshell, pegging the sterling-dollar rate could be seen by Roosevelt "as a declaration of war" and set off further retaliation.[47]

One option was to exit foreign exchange markets altogether and deal in gold only.[48] The BoE considered this possibility, but experts concluded that intervention in exchange markets was essential for proper management.[49] Britain instead turned to the franc, setting targets for sterling in terms of the franc and buying and selling francs to reach those targets. During the World Economic Conference, London held sterling to around 85 francs,

---

[44] China, in particular, experienced wrenching deflation (Friedman 1992).

[45] "A Review of the Exchange Equalisation Account," April 11, 1934, BoE C43/23; various statements in T 175/72.

[46] "Exchange Equalisation Account," March 3, 1939, BoE C43/683; "Financial Notes," *The Economist*, April 21, 1934.

[47] Hopkins, Untitled memo, July 7, 1933, T 175/71.

[48] See BoE C43/243 for the relevant files.

[49] Catterns, "Exchange Equalisation Account," November 24, 1933, BoE C43/23.

though by September the rate was down to 80 (some 35 percent below the previous parity of 124).[50]

Importantly, however, Britain did not accumulate francs. The dollar's depreciation made clear the dangers of building up a long position in currencies, leading the EEA's managers to rebalance the account from foreign exchange to gold. Foreign exchange went from two-thirds of the EEA's reserve assets at the beginning of 1933 to less than 1 percent by year's end. Intervening in francs without holding any was possible by virtue of the franc's convertibility. When London bought francs in the market, it converted them into gold at the BdF; when it needed to sell francs, it obtained them by selling gold to the BdF. The EEA's earlier practice of amassing foreign exchange reserves, let alone favoring them over gold, was over. Even though Britain was no longer on the gold standard, it joined the ranks of France, Switzerland, and other gold bloc members in viewing the metal as the reserve asset par excellence.

DEFYING DESCRIPTION

As 1933 ended, Roosevelt was growing tired of his gold-purchase program. The market price of gold was now above $30 per ounce and the sterling-dollar rate was well above $5, but the program seemed to be running out of steam. In an open letter to Roosevelt, John Maynard Keynes complained that the "gyrations of the dollar" seemed to be "more like a gold standard on the booze than the ideal managed currency of my dreams."[51] The time had come to end the program and formally devalue the dollar. A higher statutory price for gold would increase the dollar value of the US gold stock, providing a nice profit, as well as cement the dollar's depreciation against gold. However, repegging the dollar would rob the United States of the initiative in the monetary battle, leaving it vulnerable to the possibility that other countries – most notably Britain – would depreciate further against gold and the dollar. For these reasons, Roosevelt wanted to stabilize without full stabilization, to get all the benefits of a higher statutory price of gold without forfeiting the ability to respond to any perceived attack.

---

[50] "Meeting of the Exchange Committee," June 9, 1933, BoE C43/97. The EEA expended significant reserves holding the target during the summer. Bolton, "The Exchange Equalisation Account," undated, BoE C160/78.

[51] Quoted in Edwards (2017, 210).

The Gold Reserve Act of 1934, signed into law on January 30, did just that.[52] A milestone in US monetary history, the Act set the course for the rest of the decade and left a legacy that remains to this day. The Thomas Amendment already granted the president the power to devalue the dollar by up to 50 percent. The Gold Reserve Act required that any such devaluation be at least 40 percent, so that the new price of gold could be as low as $34.45 or as high as $41.34.[53] On January 31, Roosevelt announced a 41 percent devaluation to $35 an ounce. He thus kept in his back pocket the power to devalue up to $41.34 (or, should he desire, to revalue to $34.45). This license to devalue at will was new, as gold standard parities had previously been under the domain of legislatures, not executives. It armed the United States, in Morgenthau's words, with a "weapon in reserve."[54] While Roosevelt never altered the $35 price, the fact that the president – particularly this president – could change it on a whim always lurked in the background, putting foreign governments and market operators on notice.

Whereas the British did not choose a new price for gold and thus did not get to write up the value of their existing gold stock, the Americans reaped a paper profit of $2.8 billion when increasing the price from $20.67 to $35. Roosevelt made sure the Act transferred the Federal Reserve's gold, which accounted for the majority of the nation's reserves, to the Treasury, giving the government the profit and leaving no doubt that the Treasury was now predominant in monetary affairs.[55] The Act then set aside $2 billion from the devaluation profits to endow the Exchange Stabilization Fund (ESF), a tool for managing the dollar day-to-day that was far more agile than the clunky power of altering the official gold price.[56] The ESF had "the purpose of stabilizing the exchange value of the dollar," following the EEA's

---

[52] See US Treasury (1934, 189–94) for the text. Friedman and Schwartz (1963, section 8.2) discuss the Act in detail.

[53] Additionally, the secretary could buy and sell gold at whatever price he liked – the official price would not change but the effective one would. According to the Act, the secretary, with the approval of the president, could buy and sell gold "at such rates and upon such terms and conditions as he may deem most advantageous to the public interest."

[54] Treasury telegram to London embassy, February 28, 1939, MD 166/251.

[55] Meltzer (2003, 456–58).

[56] For histories of the ESF, see Schwartz (1997), Henning (1999), and Bordo, Humpage, and Schwartz (2015). Of the $2 billion endowment, $1.8 billion went into an inactive account, leaving $200 million immediately available. Ultimately, when Congress ratified the Bretton Woods Agreement in 1945, it directed that the $1.8 billion in inactive funds go toward the US subscription to the IMF. In addition to intervening in the 1930s, the ESF also loaned funds to countries in financial distress, such as Mexico and China (Bordo, Humpage, and Schwartz 2015, 108–11).

precedent of setting vague, hard-to-argue-with objectives. And the fund's activities were to be secret, operating "under the exclusive control of the Secretary of the Treasury, with the approval of the President."[57]

Washington considered the ESF indispensable, the key to reaching parity in the monetary arms race with London.[58] The House Majority Report on the Act praised the proposed fund as "equally effective in attack and defense. The reason for its establishment in this case is to defend the American dollar and our gold stocks against the invasion of similar funds operated by competitor nations." The report blasted the EEA for having been "so effective in driving our dollar up that we were forced off the gold standard."[59] A closed-door meeting of officials and bankers convened by Morgenthau to discuss the legislation likewise concluded that "the only way we can keep the £ from going down is thru an equalization fund."[60]

London, having introduced the exchange fund, now had to contend against one. Sir Ronald Lindsay, the British Ambassador, warned the Foreign Office that "both parties [in Congress] regarded the fund as a necessary weapon in the international currency struggle, Great Britain being the principal country against which such a weapon of defence is required."[61] He was unsure how big of a threat the ESF was – whether Roosevelt would employ it for defensive or offensive purposes – but there was no doubt that both sides saw the two funds as antagonistic, their operators staring each other down across the Atlantic, always on alert.

Beyond setting limits for devaluation and establishing the ESF, the legislation granted the secretary of the Treasury broad authority to regulate the new system. The secretary imposed handling charges of 0.25 percent for gold transactions, so that the Treasury bought at $34.91 and sold at

---

[57] There was concern that giving control of the ESF to one person was dangerous. The Minority Report in the House argued that it was "contrary to every true principle of American Government. We believe that it is economically unwise to place this power in the hands of any one man thereby depending upon the judgment of one person." H.R. Rep. No. 73-292 part 2, at 4 (1934).

[58] The ESF and the authority to devalue were originally subject to periodic reapproval by Congress. In 1945, Congress made the ESF permanent, though two years earlier it had stopped granting the power to alter the gold parity. Friedman and Schwartz (1963, 509); Henning (1999, 15).

[59] H.R. Rep. No. 73-292, at 2–3 (1934).   [60] Dictation, January 19, 1934, MD 1/6.

[61] Lindsay to Simon, January 25, 1934, T 188/78. Lindsay suspected that Roosevelt wanted the ESF to increase his leverage in future negotiations, not to further devalue the dollar. Lindsay to Simon, February 8, 1934, T 188/78.

$35.09 per ounce, but he could alter these charges as desired and thereby change the effective price of gold.[62] The Treasury would buy gold from anybody bringing the metal to a specified mint or assay office. The Treasury would sell gold, however, only to central banks that were on the gold standard and would do so only once the dollar was at gold export point. That is, central banks could not convert dollars into gold on demand but had to wait until the dollar had fallen sufficiently, at which point arbitrageurs could apply for licenses to ship gold on consignment to the purchasing central bank.[63] Since Britain was not on the gold standard, it could not turn dollars into gold ever, no matter what the exchange rate; this prohibition angered London and cemented its decision to abstain from intervening in dollars. The dollar was therefore still connected to gold, with the fixed price keeping it in line with other gold currencies, but the relationship was far from the textbook model. The jumble of regulations created a new monetary system that defied simple categorization – Brown (1940, 1303) terms it an "administrative international gold bullion standard" – but that plainly placed immense power in the hands of the president and secretary.

That Morgenthau, an apple farmer from the Hudson Valley, would wield much of this power struck many as absurd. Emmanuel Mönick, a French financial diplomat, expressed the elite's disdain decades later: Morgenthau "was [the] son of a v[ery] intelligent & bright man who had been Ambassador to Turkey, who thought nothing of his son & made him a farmer."[64] In fact, the younger Morgenthau's love for agriculture developed in 1911 while recuperating from typhoid in Texas, and he hoped farming would allow him to prove his worth independently of his father – though he first needed his father's support to purchase the farm. Roosevelt, neighbors and friends with Morgenthau since 1915, brought him to Washington in 1933 to head the Federal Farm Board. The president then moved him to the Treasury in November as the replacement for Dean Acheson, who as undersecretary had been carrying out the ailing Woodin's

---

[62] While the large spread widened the gold points, Brown (1942, 5) suggests that the reasoning behind it was "solely for revenue purposes."

[63] US Treasury (1934, 201). Refusing to sell gold to central banks not on the gold standard likely reflected an attempt to protect the US gold stock from countries that might seek to out-depreciate the dollar. In addition, the Federal Reserve could deal in gold when, "in the judgment of the Secretary of the Treasury," it was "necessary to settle international balances or to maintain the equal purchasing power of every kind of currency of the United States." "Provisional Regulations," January 31, 1934, MD 1/8.

[64] Sayers interview with Mönick, May 7, 1969, BoE ADM33/32.

duties and whose fierce opposition to the gold-purchase program made him persona non grata.[65] The appointment to undersecretary was a prelude to the top job given Woodin's declining health, and Morgenthau ascended to the cabinet post on New Year's Day 1934.

A profile in 1939 by Washington columnists Joseph Alsop and Robert Kintner – for which Morgenthau cooperated – opened: "Henry Morgenthau, Jr., is probably the least imposing of the great officers of the government. A tall, heavy, ungainly man, he has a nervous smile, small, nervous eyes behind pince-nez, and a high, nervous voice. He is slow-thinking and slow-speaking.... He is self-conscious without self-confidence, a born worrier and inclined to be suspicious. Indeed, at first acquaintance, a doglike devotion to the President seems to be his only affirmative trait." One strains to imagine how they would have begun their portrayal had Morgenthau not cooperated. There was simply no getting around the fact that he was ill-prepared for his position as the nation's chief financial officer at a time of depression.

But the operative phrase in the profile was "at first acquaintance." As the writers noted, "the world's estimate of Henry Morgenthau is curiously wrong." He was "sure, pretty shrewd and obstinately determined to understand his job.... Doggedly pertinacious, incredibly hardworking, he uses work as a substitute for religion, and will sacrifice anything to it, even himself."[66] Morgenthau threw himself into his job and surrounded himself with talented staff.[67] On international affairs, he was more perceptive than most in the administration, grasping, from an early date, the threat posed by Germany, Italy, and Japan. He served for over eleven years – a tenure

---

[65] Blum (1959, 5–12); Elinor Morgenthau, Untitled note, undated, MD 1/83; Schlesinger (2003, 241–43).

[66] "'Henny Penny' Farmer at the Treasury," *The Saturday Evening Post*, April 1, 1939. Morgenthau sat down with the reporters and also provided them access to his staff. Kintner to Morgenthau, March 24, 1939, MD 171/13–14. The profile had three parts: the second article was "The Great World Money Play," dated April 8, and the third article was "The Secret Finale," dated April 15. The second and third articles dealt in the main with the negotiations leading to the Tripartite Agreement. The British did not know what to make of the articles. Given the many behind-the-scenes details revealed, the financial attaché in Washington was sure Morgenthau provided the reporters information – "a highly improper performance on Mr. Morgenthau's part to reveal international negotiations in this way after so short a lapse of time." Back in London, Waley thought there was no way Morgenthau could have been directly involved, for the "references to him are so unflattering." Bewley to Waley, April 14, 1939, T 160/840/8; Waley to Balfour, April 24, 1939, T 160/840/8.

[67] Morgenthau also sought advice from world-class experts, including Jacob Viner of the University of Chicago and John Williams of Harvard.

second only to that of Albert Gallatin, who had led the Treasury under both Thomas Jefferson and James Madison – helping to finance recovery from depression and then finance victory over fascism. No doubt many people on paper appeared more suited for the job, but few would have lasted as long. As Schlesinger (2003, 244) aptly concludes, Morgenthau "chose good people, used them effectively, ran tight organizations, got results, and kept his mouth shut."

Among the best of these "good people" Morgenthau recruited was Archie Lochhead, president of the Foreign Exchange Club of New York.[68] Lochhead provided the expertise on foreign exchange that Morgenthau desperately needed and became the ESF's manager. His title, technical assistant to the secretary, belied his importance, for he was a top adviser not only on day-to-day intervention but also grander monetary strategy. Respected within the Treasury for his calm, methodical manner – balancing out the often-excitable secretary – he stood watch over the dollar, always on call in case developments half a world away impacted markets. Though he preferred to stay out of the limelight, widespread interest in the ESF's secretive operations made it impossible for him to escape attention, and he became a subject of fascination in the press. He was the Treasury's "mystery man," the "gold kitty's watchdog," a "wizard" who held "$2,000,000,000 in blue chips in the world's greatest poker game."[69] He was, as the Treasury's undersecretary endearingly called him, the "jovial Scotchman with all the money."[70]

To put this money to work, Lochhead needed the FRBNY's assistance. Just as the British placed the EEA under the Treasury's control and assigned the BoE as agent, the Americans put the ESF under the Treasury's control and assigned the FRBNY as agent. Jay Crane, deputy governor and manager of the Foreign Department at the FRBNY, handled interventions on the Treasury's behalf until 1935, at which point L. Werner Knoke took over. But whereas Whitehall left tactical decisions to the BoE, Washington maintained a tight grip on operations. Lochhead was in contact with New York every day, giving orders for intervention,

---

[68] "Archie Lochhead is Dead at 78," *The New York Times*, January 16, 1971.

[69] "$2,000,000 in Blue Chips Lochhead's Ante in U.S. World Currency Stabilization Gamble," *The Washington Post*, September 30, 1936; "Gold Kitty's Watchdog Has to Be an Early Bird," *Associated Press*, February 15, 1935; "Sun Never Sets on Job Held by Money Expert," *Associated Press*, November 14, 1935.

[70] Magill to Lochhead, September 13, 1938, personal collection of Cameron Lochhead.

sometimes direct from Morgenthau.[71] With time, the administration grew to value the FRBNY's expertise and delegated more authority, but it remained too suspicious of bankers to step back as much as the British Treasury did.[72]

Washington now had $2 billion with which to play. But during the ESF's first months, far from going on an all-out attack, the Treasury did not even intervene in exchange markets.[73] There just did not seem to be much of a reason to. While the ESF involved discretionary intervention, the Treasury's gold buying policy was automatic, and the massive devaluation of the dollar, by overvaluing gold, attracted the metal to the United States in record amounts. Arbitrageurs profited by taking gold from Europe, transporting it across the Atlantic, selling it for $34.91 an ounce, and then converting the dollars back into the original currency – or simply holding onto dollars now that the situation in America was improving vis-à-vis Europe. So large was the movement of gold, Brown (1940, 1306) writes, that ships of all kinds "were pressed into service as bullion carriers." In 1934, US gold reserves rose 21 percent by weight (104 percent in dollar terms given the rise in the gold price), and the gain accounted for 89 percent of the world's increase in visible reserves. The money supply thus increased, aiding the incipient recovery. Wholesale prices jumped nearly 14 percent in 1934. And the sterling-dollar rate was above $5. Everything seemed to be working out. The ESF was at the ready if needed, but after months of incessant worry on the exchange situation, Roosevelt and Morgenthau could finally take a breath.

"PADDLE OUR OWN CANOE"

Across the Atlantic, the British were not as happy with the Gold Reserve Act. They struggled to make sense of the "obscure" regulations; years later they were still confused as to exactly how much discretion the secretary

---

[71] See, for example, Dictation, January 15, 1935, MD 3/104; Dictation, January 24, 1936, MD 16/43; Treasury meeting, October 5, 1936, MD 37/202.

[72] The Washington-based Federal Reserve Board of Governors was uninvolved in these matters – though not by choice. Morgenthau developed intense animus toward the chairman, Marriner Eccles, and refused to share information. Moreover, the FRBNY was unable to inform the Board about its activities with the ESF due to its confidential relationship as agent. The Board often became frustrated with this state of affairs. "Matters to be discussed with the Treasury," October 12, 1936, MEP B49F3.

[73] The first intervention was in September 1934 (Bordo, Humpage, and Schwartz 2015, 68–69).

had in setting the price of gold.[74] Ministers and officials believed that Roosevelt's devaluation was shamelessly excessive, and they were not even sure he was done. "As regards dollar stabilisation," the Treasury's Sigi Waley wrote in early February 1934, "I think that our main reactions are, (1) that so long as the dollar is under-valued, and therefore on an artificial level, the American policy may do a good deal of harm to the rest of the world; and (2) that our policy remains as it has always been, namely, that we are anxious to return to the Gold Standard when the necessary conditions exist, but not till then."[75]

The second point was the standard mantra that meant less and less as the months went by. The British had no intention of re-subjecting their economy to the straitjacket of the gold standard. This principle hardened into a refusal to countenance any commitments on exchange rates or even to discuss exchange rate policy as a means to soothe tensions (that is, to stabilize monetary relations). Not that London's disinterest held back any rapprochement with America: Tempers were still too hot for either country to consider coming to terms with the other. It certainly did not help that Britain defaulted on its war debt in June 1934, nor that the US Congress passed the Johnson Act forbidding American citizens from lending to governments in default.[76] At a meeting that December between Morgenthau and George Schuster, a well-connected British banker, the secretary remarked, "I think it is absolutely hopeless to get together with England," to which Schuster replied, "Our people feel exactly the same way."[77]

The pound went from $3.41 in Roosevelt's first month in office to $5.09 a year later, a matter of deep concern to Whitehall. A stronger pound relative to the dollar elicited complaints from industry. An undervalued dollar also led to a gold outflow from Europe. But because London and Washington had both devalued against gold and pursued expansionary monetary policies, the sterling-dollar exchange rate was no longer a matter of life and death. A rate near the old parity was far less constricting in 1934 than it had been in 1931. The British economy was recovering and the gold position was strong, with the EEA holding £121 million in reserves in February 1934, up from £66 million the previous September. The British did not think the dollar's devaluation justified, worried about America draining gold from the rest of the world, and remained

---

[74] Hawtrey, Untitled memo, April 12, 1937, T 177/35.
[75] Waley to Pinsent, February 8, 1934, T 160/949.   [76] Clavin (1996, 177–81).
[77] Morgenthau conversation with Schuster, December 17, 1934, MD 2/315–16.

apprehensive about further shocks. They did not trust Roosevelt and had no interest in dealing with him. But they did not believe that the situation merited a direct counterattack to push the pound down against the dollar, in part because the response from America, still in the infancy of its recovery, could be devastating.

The British were also concerned about the impact on the gold bloc. Sir Frederick Phillips, writing in February 1934, argued that the gold bloc was on borrowed time and thought that its members should undertake a coordinated devaluation of 10 to 15 percent. But until that occurred, he urged that the well-being of the bloc be borne in mind when crafting policy: "While the gold bloc remains on gold we ought not to strive to drive the pound down, merely for the purpose of keeping it say at the old par $4.86 2/3." Doing so would "greatly intensify the strain on France" by attracting gold from Paris.[78] London recognized that depreciation harmed the gold bloc and should not be a deliberate goal. And so, for the first few months of 1934, the pound stayed above $5 and above 77 francs. But while the British no longer felt it prudent to actively push the pound down, they did not much worry when market forces did. As the usual autumnal weakness set in, Britain was fine seeing sterling fall, ending 1934 under $5 and below 75 francs.

Then, in the beginning of 1935, the US Supreme Court nearly forced Roosevelt to reverse his monetary policies.[79] Not every American had accepted the abrogation of the gold clause in June 1933, and the Court began hearings on the matter in early January. If the Court found the repeal unconstitutional, debts subject to the clause would be repayable in dollars at the old gold parity, leading to mass bankruptcy. Most observers believed Roosevelt would have to restore the dollar to the $20.67 parity to mitigate the fallout, and the dollar began appreciating as a result. The dollar's rise vis-à-vis the franc should have triggered gold arbitrage, with gold moving from Paris to New York, but operators refrained from shipping gold for fear that a steep cut in the US price while the metal was in transit would decimate the transaction's profitability.[80] The dollar thus continued to appreciate, heightening the sense of alarm in the White House.

Morgenthau and Roosevelt were not going to let the judiciary endanger all the progress they had made. As Morgenthau exclaimed, "I don't care *what* the Supreme Court says. The Supreme Court can't tell the United

---

[78] Phillips, "Future Exchange Problems," February 15, 1934, T 188/78.
[79] See Edwards (2018).   [80] Bordo, Humpage, and Schwartz (2015, 70–72).

States Treasury what they can pay for the price of gold."[81] On January 14, Roosevelt even suggested to Morgenthau that he employ the ESF to "keep things on an unsettled basis," the idea being that greater market volatility would make the consequences of an adverse ruling more vivid to the Court, but Morgenthau refused to play such a role.[82] Roosevelt backed down, and Morgenthau intervened instead to check the turmoil. To counter the dollar's appreciation, he purchased sterling and francs and also provided the BdF dollars against gold in Paris as a substitute for private arbitrage. To the administration's glee, the Court ruled in its favor in a 5-4 decision on February 18 that, while notorious for its opaque reasoning and hair-splitting legalisms, quashed a serious threat to recovery.

With the dollar's position now secure, Morgenthau felt vindicated, and he drafted a speech in the spring to explain the administration's policy to the American people and the world. "In going off gold, we were not the first, we were the thirty-first," he declared on May 13, 1935, in a nationally broadcast radio address. The devaluation was necessary to save the economy, and since January 1934, "we have enjoyed the soundest currency in the world." In addition to providing a defense of the past, Morgenthau sought to shed light on the future. The critical section was the concluding paragraph on the prospects for stabilization:

The world should know that when it is ready to seek foreign exchange stabilization, Washington will not be an obstacle. Our position was that of an innocent bystander who suffered untold loss in a fight that he did not start, and from which he could not escape. Why should we be singled out and admonished that the moral duty to restore order is primarily ours? Before we make any commitments, we must be sure that we will not lose what we have just regained. We are not unwilling to stabilize. However, if the great trading nations elect to continue under the present absence of rules we are no longer at a disadvantage. We revalued our currency no more than was necessary and we can go either way. Our hands are untied.[83]

It would be difficult to craft a more inscrutable statement. Morgenthau was at once generous and self-pitying, offering to work together on stabilization and castigating the rest of the world for the perceived slights of the past. And then there was that last sentence: "Our hands are untied." Harry Dexter White, a rising official in the Treasury, found it "ominous."[84] It was

---

[81] Morgenthau conversation with Crane, January 16, 1935, MD 3/138.

[82] Morgenthau conversation with Roosevelt, January 14, 1935, MD 3/98.

[83] Morgenthau, "The American Dollar," May 13, 1935, MD 5/88B.

[84] White, "Recovery Program: The International Monetary Aspect," March 15, 1935, HDWP B3F13. While the file is dated March 15, 1935, White clearly wrote parts of the memorandum after Morgenthau's speech in May.

actually restrained compared to earlier drafts, one of which included a line reading, "There will be no stabilization until we see the whites of their eyes," a reference to William Prescott's immortal battle cry at Bunker Hill.[85]

Foreign governments naturally did not find much to like. Leith-Ross told Mönick, the French financial attaché in London, that "if it was an offer, it was no good." Mönick was similarly incredulous: "How can they, after doing untold damage to every country in the world, first by their gold policy, now by their silver policy, claim that they are not responsible."[86] Phillips informed the prime minister that the speech "holds out no hope that an early resumption of international discussions on monetary matters would be attended by valuable results."[87] At best, the speech changed nothing; at worst, it reaffirmed the deepest suspicions about Morgenthau and Roosevelt. What is most perplexing is that Morgenthau was in fact beginning to favor international cooperation. As he was delivering his address, White was in London, under the secretary's orders, trying to feel out British opinion on an agreement of some sort.[88] Perhaps Morgenthau's strategy was to put on a stern face for public consumption while acting more agreeable behind the scenes. But the gambit did not work. Morgenthau was not yet set on reaching an understanding with Britain, the president remained dubious, and the British were not interested in any dialogue.

The world thus entered the summer of 1935 in a stalemate. The sterling-dollar rate was remarkably calm, staying within 2 percent of the $4.86 benchmark for the rest of the year. But this stability was not the product of any démarche. Both countries continued to view the other warily. The problem was that, however placid the exchange situation seemed on the

---

[85] "Complete History of the Radio Address," undated, MD 5/43.

[86] Leith-Ross, "Note of an Interview with M. Mönick," May 17, 1935, T 188/116. Some policymakers viewed the speech in a more positive light. Jacques Rueff of the French Treasury was "very interested" in Morgenthau's speech and thought it offered an opportunity. Quoted in Jackson (1985, 178).

[87] Phillips, "Note by Sir F. Phillips for the P.M.," May 16, 1935, T 188/116.

[88] For a summary of White's trip, see Steil (2013, 30–32). In March 1935, White drafted a lengthy paper on monetary issues and hit on the governance philosophy that would later animate the Tripartite Agreement: "The inescapable conclusion is that at least agreement on the essential points should be arrived at informally and secretly. Nor need the agreement be binding. It might well become merely the policy of the respective Treasury Departments so as to avoid the need for Congressional or Parliamentary action." White, "Recovery Program: The International Monetary Aspect," March 15, 1935, HDWP B3F13.

surface, latent dangers rendered it combustible. In March, Belgium, unable to maintain its parity, defected from the gold bloc and devalued. The other members survived the ensuing turmoil in the markets, and Belgium was a small enough country that its exchange policy did not seriously impact Britain or the United States. France was a different story, however. If it devalued, the rest of the gold bloc would almost certainly do so as well. The franc was also a much more important currency than the belga, and how London and Washington would respond to its depreciation was anybody's guess. The international monetary system was therefore at a way station. That it would move from its current position was clear; where it would end was not. So, for the time being, all that the British could do was, in Leith-Ross' words, to continue to "paddle our own canoe as well as we can into the rapids which loom ahead."[89]

[89] Leith-Ross to Bewley, May 14, 1935, T 188/116.

5

Negotiating Peace, 1935–1936

In 1935, after some two years of managing the dollar with little concern for others, Washington started to pivot, slowly, toward a more cooperative policy. In a sense, the turn was lubricated with liquor – not a glass or two but boatloads of it. The French island of St. Pierre, located just off the coast of Newfoundland, had been a smuggling entrepôt for Canadian spirits making their way to the United States during Prohibition. Even with the repeal of the 18th amendment in 1933, bootlegging from St. Pierre continued, as high taxes on alcohol kept the illegal trade profitable. In January 1935, *The New York Times* published an exposé on the "rum runners," and the US Treasury, responsible for tax evasion, resolved to end the practice.[1]

So determined was Secretary of the Treasury Henry Morgenthau that, after no success going through regular diplomatic channels, he asked Jay Crane of the Federal Reserve Bank of New York (FRBNY) to get in touch with the Banque de France (BdF) and see if it could persuade the French government to act. Morgenthau had been providing dollars to the BdF against gold in Paris as part of his effort to counter the appreciation of the dollar, and thus depreciation of the franc, during the turmoil induced by the gold clause cases; he knew the BdF wanted these transactions to continue and would therefore likely try to assist, even though the matter went well beyond its purview. The BdF's governor, Jean Tannery, discussed the issue with the Ministry of Foreign Affairs, and the French government soon clamped down on smuggling.[2]

---

[1] "Rum-Runners Again Challenge the Law," *The New York Times*, January 13, 1935; Blum (1959, 109).

[2] Crane conversation with Morgenthau, January 18, 1935, FRBNY C261; Crane conversations with Cariguel, January 18 and 22, 1935, FRBNY C261; Morgenthau conversation with de Laboulaye, April 19, 1935, MD 4/162.

Morgenthau was ecstatic. In April, he sent word to Paris that he was "delighted at the outcome and wants the French to know how he feels about it and that he is anxious to cooperate closely with them."[3] Privately, Morgenthau told Crane that he now planned "to cultivate the French." "Let's forget about the British," he continued. "[I]f we work very closely together, the British will have to come to us – it's a three-pointed triangle and if the French and ourselves stick together, then the British have to come to us."[4]

Putting an end to the monetary war would not be so simple. For one, Morgenthau's budding internationalism was still tempered by his (and the president's) suspicion of Europe: Only a month after sending his thanks, he put the world on notice that America's "hands are untied" on currency policy. Washington was thus slow to change its attitude. Moreover, while Paris was eager to cooperate, its foremost goal was to defend the franc Poincaré, a commitment that became more and more untenable as the BdF's reserves fell ever lower.

Rather than Paris and Washington uniting to pull London in, the key to monetary peace was a rapprochement between London and Washington that could provide support for an orderly devaluation of the franc. But the British expressed little interest in coming to terms with an administration that it neither respected nor trusted. Exchange rate commitments were out of the question: In October 1935, Chancellor of the Exchequer Neville Chamberlain parroted Morgenthau, declaring that the time was not yet ripe to "venture to tie our hands."[5] Nor did Britain care for other initiatives to "stabilize" the situation short of actually stabilizing rates – such as increasing transparency on exchange intervention, discussing market developments, or crafting a framework for consultation. London merely wished to tend to its, and the Empire's, business and, as a result, adopted a standoffish posture toward Washington.

But, in a flurry of activity during the summer of 1936, everything changed. The anti-fascist Popular Front coalition in France won elections and formed a government under the socialist Léon Blum. Though hesitant to devalue, Blum started to accept that there might be no other option. In Washington, Morgenthau realized that his plan to cultivate France in isolation would not work and that there was no good alternative but to deal with Britain directly to try to prevent any crisis from spinning out of

---

[3] Crane conversation with Cariguel, April 9, 1935, FRBNY C261.
[4] Morgenthau conversation with Crane, April 9, 1935, MD 4/164–68.
[5] Foreign Office telegram to Osborne, October 3, 1935, T 160/840/3.

control. In London, policymakers concluded that it was better to come to terms with Morgenthau than spurn his overtures and risk retaliation. Soon, each country determined that a joint arrangement supporting devaluation and promising to work together offered the best path forward, thereby making the French devaluation a turning point for monetary peace rather than allowing it to open up another front in the war. After innumerable discussions and cables, the parties arrived at the Tripartite Agreement in the early hours of September 26, 1936, Paris time.

This chapter narrates the twists and turns in monetary relations that culminated in the Tripartite Agreement.[6] After discussing the franc's deteriorating position from the spring of 1935 and the implications for Britain's management of the pound, it turns to the pivotal Anglo-American relationship. Distrust was pervasive, but the two sides eventually came to an understanding, assuring each other that they would not further depreciate their currencies in response to a fall in the franc. With London and Washington talking again, there was now space for an agreement to facilitate French devaluation. The parties differed in their motivations for negotiating the accord, with France and America most enthusiastic for the political aspects of binding the democracies together, while Britain focused on the short-term objective of making the devaluation as smooth as possible and hesitated at first to assign too much importance to the politics. With time, the Agreement – informal and vague, unconventional and pathbreaking – would turn the page on the chaos of earlier years and redefine the international monetary landscape.

"RELIGION OF THE FRANC"

In the mid-1930s, France was not in a good place. Though the Depression was less severe there than elsewhere, the French economy, pulled down by an overvalued currency, continued to contract even as others started to recover. The political situation was a tinderbox: The left feared a fascist takeover, the right feared a communist one, and the future of parliamentary democracy seemed at stake. Governing coalitions formed only to fall. From the beginning of 1933 to the end of 1936, the premiership changed hands some ten times. On the international front, tensions with Germany were rising. Hitler announced the introduction of conscription and enlargement of the army – violations of the Treaty of Versailles – on

---

[6] This chapter builds on Blum (1959, chapter 4), Clarke (1977), Drummond (1981, chapters 8–9), and Mouré (1991, chapters 6–7).

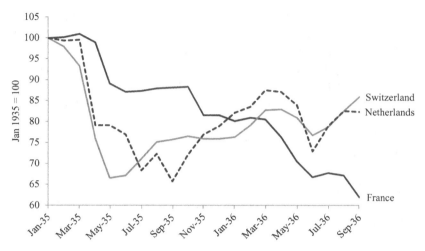

Figure 5.1 Gold bloc reserves, 1935–1936 (January 1935 = 100).
Source: Board of Governors of the Federal Reserve System (1935–1936)

March 16, 1935. It was only two days later that Belgium imposed capital controls after a prolonged run on the belga and then enacted a provisional devaluation of 28 percent at the end of the month (in March 1936, the government made the devaluation official and removed the controls.)[7]

Belgium's move was a blow to confidence, but the rump of the gold bloc managed to hold on for another eighteen months. To do so, central banks disgorged vast sums of gold in the weeks after Belgium's devaluation. By the end of May, the Swiss National Bank had lost almost 30 percent of its reserves, the Netherlands Bank over 20 percent, and the BdF more than 10 percent relative to the start of the year. But as shown in Figure 5.1, the BdF's reserves kept falling with only occasional breathing spells, while the other central banks eventually recouped some of the losses. Investors, speculators, anybody with movable funds wanted to know which country would capitulate next, and France seemed a fair bet.

When assessing the likelihood of devaluation, many French citizens spoke with their money – converting their francs into gold or other currencies and thereby hastening the event – even as they spoke from their hearts when attacking the notion of devaluation as immoral and unpatriotic. Defending the franc was a point of pride. In April 1935, the nationalist newspaper *Le Matin* declared, "the religion of the franc is none other than the religion of France."[8] After the First World War, Paris had devalued by

---

[7] Straumann (2010, 164–66).   [8] Quoted in Mouré (1991, 212).

80 percent; to do so again, especially after so short a time, would destroy the nation's credibility.

Anyway, politicians, experts, and business leaders did not believe devaluation would be beneficial. The French economy was not suffering because the franc remained fastened to gold at an unchanged parity, the thinking went, but because other countries had left gold, unleashed exchange instability, and imposed trade barriers. Some rather impressive mental gymnastics were involved in contrasting the recovery in countries that had left gold to the stagnation in those that had not and then insisting that salvation lay with persistence. But this was the consensus. The path to recovery, then, involved stabilization of the world's currencies and a general return to gold.

There were a few lone voices preaching the benefits of devaluation. Paul Reynaud, a former finance minister, began calling for one in the summer of 1934.[9] As the most prominent advocate, Reynaud was the target of countless screeds and even some death threats. Indeed, opposition to Reynaud's plans was one of the few points of unity in the bitterly divided country. "This was no party issue," Jackson (1985, 187) explains: "Devaluation was condemned by all political parties from the Action française to the Communist Party; by economists; by publicists ... by governments; by Chambers of Commerce; and by all leading representatives of the employers." Governments differed in how they planned to maintain parity – during the first half of 1935, Premier Pierre Flandin thought some reflation could boost growth and get France out of its rut; during the second half, Premier Pierre Laval favored full-scale deflation – but that defending the franc was the ultimate goal went without question.

The BdF was committed to upholding the franc's parity, increasing the discount rate and yielding gold to that end. Though gold arbitrage was at the heart of the system, sometimes pressure on the franc was so strong that the private sector did not have the wherewithal to bring the franc into line. There was only so much shipping capacity and so much gold that banks were willing to purchase. These limitations became binding at the beginning of 1935. As the US Supreme Court considered the gold clause cases, operators thought an adverse ruling would force the administration to lower the dollar price of gold. Many arbitrageurs refused to engage, since any gold crossing the Atlantic risked a massive hit to its value.[10] With gold

---

[9] Ibid., 196–204.   [10] Brown (1942, 54).

stuck in France despite the franc being at gold export point, the currency weakened, intensifying doubts about its parity.

In these circumstances, the BdF was willing to enter the market directly and sell dollars to support the franc – even though it generally found such intervention an artificial interference. Since it no longer held foreign exchange, its best source for dollars was the US Treasury, which promised to purchase gold in New York at $35 per ounce from anyone. This option worked well when the BdF held gold on earmark at the FRBNY. But when it did not, the Treasury policy was of no immediate help, since the French first had to replenish their US stock by shipping gold across the Atlantic. For this reason, in January 1935 the BdF asked if the US Treasury would purchase gold in Paris against dollars, thereby providing dollars for instant use. Morgenthau, who was already using the Exchange Stabilization Fund (ESF) to buy francs and counter the dollar's appreciation, authorized limited purchases of gold in Paris for a couple weeks, and the situation soon eased with the Supreme Court's decision confirming the abrogation of the gold clauses.[11]

Nevertheless, the franc was once again in distress in late May, as the aftershocks from Belgium's devaluation continued to reverberate and the Flandin government teetered toward its eventual collapse at the month's end. Of the banks that normally engaged in arbitrage, all but one stopped due to fears of a devaluation or embargo. The head of the BdF's foreign exchange department, Charles Cariguel, requested the United States to renew the dollar orders but now on a much larger scale. Morgenthau, with Roosevelt's approval, agreed on May 30 to purchase up to $150 million of gold as part of his effort to cultivate the French.[12]

Upon hearing the news that night, Cariguel was able to get some sleep for the first time in several days. Not that he had been debilitated by worry: He would not have survived nearly two decades managing the franc had panic overtaken him during every crisis. He just understood the stakes and worked tirelessly. H. Merle Cochran, the financial attaché at the US Embassy in Paris, knew Cariguel well and provided one of the few surviving sketches of the man to Morgenthau:

You have never met Cariguel. I should explain that he is not the high-strung nervous type of Frenchman. He is a strongly-built, red-faced, cool-headed Breton. He spent several years in London, where he studied economics and was employed

---

[11] Crane to Morgenthau, January 16, 1935, FRBNY C261; Crane, Untitled memo, January 16, 1935, FRBNY C261; Brown (1942, 63–66).

[12] Dictation, June 3, 1935, MD 5/176–77.

by a French bank.... His colleagues in Central Banking circles recognize Cariguel as an excellent technician and a dependable contact. Governor Tannery is said to depend upon him more than upon anyone in the Bank of France for matters of policy as well as technique. Cariguel is frank if he trusts one, but gifted in circumlocution and evasion if he is not convinced of the other's sincerity.[13]

George Bolton of the Bank of England (BoE) was similarly impressed by Cariguel, later recalling: "The Bank of France and Ministry of Finance régimes changed from time to time, but Cariguel remained the operator, and with increasing experience became the uncrowned king whatever the régime."[14] With new BdF governors in 1935, 1936, and 1937, and five different finance ministers during those years, he was a welcome source of stability – to colleagues at home and counterparts abroad – in chaotic times.

Armed with the power to sell up to $150 million, Cariguel got to work. As Cochran reported, "with the Treasury's 150 million dollars at his disposal he [Cariguel] went out to the exchange market on May 31, feeling like he had just won the grand lottery, told stories, joked with the traders, especially the well known big speculators, loafed around throughout the session, and successfully put over the impression of a man who did not have a worry in the world."[15] In combination with sharp increases in the discount rate from 2.5 percent on May 23 to 6 percent on May 28, dollar sales helped put an end to the crisis. A new cabinet under Laval took office on June 7, and reserve losses petered out.

This gold arrangement was significant because Morgenthau was under no obligation to purchase gold in Paris. Treasury regulations required only that he buy gold at select locations in the United States, so his approval of the French request was cooperative in the sense that he did something he did not have to. After all, acquiring gold abroad was riskier than doing so at home, and even though Morgenthau made sure the BdF "guaranteed" it as "free for export under any circumstances," holding gold thousands of miles away was not the same as having it on US soil.[16] Tannery released a statement thanking Morgenthau for his "broad understanding of the situation," which led the Americans to "constantly suppl[y] the market

---

[13] Cochran to Morgenthau, June 19, 1935, MD 7/80–81.

[14] Sayers interview with Bolton, January 20, 1971, BoE ADM33/25.

[15] Cochran to Morgenthau, June 19, 1935, MD 7/88–89.

[16] Knoke telegram to Cariguel, May 30, 1935, FRBNY C261; Brown (1942, 80–84). The arrangement was not, as Drummond (1981, 191) suggests, a loan. The BdF first had to earmark the gold before the FRBNY credited dollars to its account.

with dollars to prevent the dangerous consequences of any cession of gold purchases." Morgenthau told the press the purchases were simply "common decency among nations."[17] But since common decency had been lacking of late, it was at least a start.

The two sides did little, however, to build on this foundation. In November, French reserve losses recommenced, and the United States offered to once again purchase gold in Paris. The BdF gladly accepted the authorizations, though in the event made no use of them.[18] The central banks continued to talk on a fairly regular basis, sharing updates on market developments. But nothing much beyond that occurred since there was not much to do in the absence of a realignment of exchange rates, which the French were not yet ready to consider. Morgenthau's hopes of uniting with the French to pull the British in thus proved fruitless.

Through the rest of 1935 and much of 1936, Paris continued to fight for what it considered its monetary honor. The economy recovered a bit in 1935, but the problem of an overvalued exchange rate remained. Laval's premiership came to an end in January 1936 amid an outcry over his handling of the Abyssinian crisis, and a caretaker government took over to lead the country through elections in May.[19] The Popular Front, the anti-fascist coalition composed of Socialists, Communists, and Radical Socialists, emerged victorious. With Léon Blum's accession to the premiership in June 1936, nobody knew exactly how this coalition would govern: All that was certain was that change was in the air. Except, that is, with respect to the franc. The Popular Front had campaigned on a platform of "Neither deflation nor devaluation," and when presenting his government to the Chamber of Deputies on June 6, Blum reassured the public that the "country need not fear that one fine morning we will cover the walls with the white notices of a devaluation, the white notices of a monetary coup d'état."[20] The new government appeared as devoted as its predecessors to the religion of the franc.

---

[17] "U.S. Rescued Franc in Recent Crisis, Tannery Reveals," *The New York Times*, June 17, 1935; "Treasury Averted World Money War," *The New York Times*, June 18, 1935.

[18] FRBNY telegram to Cariguel, November 15, 1935, FRBNY C261; Knoke conversation with Cariguel, December 10, 1935, FRBNY C261.

[19] The controversy surrounded Laval's pact with Sir Samuel Hoare, Britain's foreign secretary, to cede much of Abyssinia to Mussolini. See Parker (1974) for a discussion of Anglo-French actions during the Abyssinian crisis.

[20] Quoted in Mouré (1991, 206 and 242).

MANAGING THE POUND

The British watched developments across the Channel in 1935 and 1936 with concern and exasperation. They were annoyed by French governments, viewing them as unwilling to take the steps necessary to get their house in order. An unstable France meant an unstable franc, complicating Britain's management of the pound; and an unstable franc meant an unstable France, worsening the politico-military situation on the continent. To keep markets from imploding, the BoE worked with the BdF on some technical management issues. But policymakers refused to get involved in matters of long-term policy. London did not even venture to suggest that devaluation could be beneficial.[21] While the British had little faith in the franc and were sure that devaluation was inevitable, they also considered the currency the best option on which to base the pound for the moment and did not want to hasten any alteration that could jeopardize that. Sterling policy thus aimed largely at maintaining the status quo.

The early months of 1935 had been a time of weakness for the pound, due in part to the uncertainty over the gold clauses. The pound fell from a monthly average of \$4.99 in November 1934 to \$4.77 in March 1935 – the drop below the old parity of \$4.86 causing "great nervousness" in Washington, according to the British ambassador – and from 75.7 francs to 72.0 francs.[22] Sterling's weakness troubled Paris and Washington, with the French suggesting to the United States that they offer Britain a joint credit to induce it to stabilize. But Morgenthau had no interest in approaching London and politely declined to participate, scotching the French initiative.[23]

London would not have been receptive anyway. Whitehall and Threadneedle Street were largely united in regarding stabilization as a nonstarter, despite proclaiming it as the eventual goal. Chamberlain declared in 1935: "While I look forward to the ultimate re-establishment of the gold standard, I do not think that conditions are yet sufficiently favourable to enable us to make so difficult an experiment."[24] Montagu Norman, the BoE's governor, thought that there were "very few hereabouts who deep down do not long for stabilisation" at an opportune

---

[21] As Waley argued, it was important that the government "hold studiously aloof from any devaluation controversy so that no country can claim later that they either stayed on gold or left gold as a result of suggestions from this side." Waley to Gwatkin, April 16, 1935, T 160/840/2.

[22] Lindsay telegram, March 13, 1935, T 188/116.   [23] Blum (1959, 131–32).

[24] Foreign Office telegram to Leith-Ross, October 3, 1935, T 160/840/3.

time – including himself – but he could only "guess" that the chancellor was of like mind.[25] Whether or not Chamberlain truly wanted to return to gold, he took no action moving in that direction.

There were three main arguments against tying the pound down. First, the moment never seemed propitious. The gold bloc's implosion always appeared on the horizon: The Treasury's Sigi Waley commented in 1935 that it would "clearly be absurd for us to go on to the gold standard just when everyone else is likely to go off."[26] Second, distrust of the Americans was universal. They had thrown the stabilization discussions at the World Economic Conference into disarray, and the British, spurned once, were hesitant to risk making it twice. Finally, and most fundamentally, stabilizing the pound would have implications for the handling of domestic monetary policy that the government was not willing to accept. Freedom of maneuver was nonnegotiable. London could not, Waley argued, peg the pound and then, if the balance of payments deteriorated, "have to choose between going back on our promise to stabilise or committing economic suicide by a policy of deflation."[27]

Stabilizing exchange rates, either by repegging to gold or announcing a provisional parity with the dollar, was not the only possible form of monetary cooperation. Sharing information on exchange fund interventions could improve relations. Consulting on market developments could as well, as could agreeing not to undertake certain actions, such as competitive depreciations or implementing exchange restrictions. Even stronger forms of cooperation included coordinating interventions, intervening on joint account, or lending to one another. While some in Whitehall were open to talking with the United States "as quietly as possible" to "explore the situation and to illustrate our difficulties," Chamberlain refused, "on the ground that such conversations would be futile and would cause a great deal of misunderstanding."[28]

Refusal to stabilize or cooperate did not mean that the British were against stable rates. They believed that lower exchange volatility boosted trade and confidence. On occasion, managers of the Exchange Equalisation Account (EEA) sold gold to cushion sterling's fall. Surely, fear of Morgenthau retaliating against a weak pound played a role: The British

---

[25] Norman to Towers, March 16, 1935, BoE G1/487.

[26] Waley, "Stabilisation," September 28, 1935, T 160/840/3.

[27] Waley to Pinsent, May 28, 1936, T 160/840/3.

[28] Leith-Ross to Bewley, May 14, 1935, T 188/116.

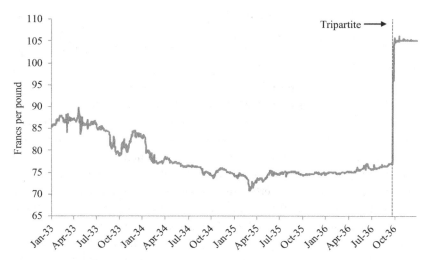

Figure 5.2 Sterling-franc exchange rate, 1933–1936.
Source: Global Financial Data

Treasury "did not want a tug of war between the two Equalisation Funds."[29] But while the EEA was not used solely to push the pound down, its reserve assets still rose dramatically on net over 1935, growing from £101 million to £167 million.

This intervention occurred not through the dollar – verboten since 1933 – but through the franc and, to a lesser extent, in the gold market. From June 1935 to April 1936, the British held the pound between 74 and 76 francs, as shown in Figure 5.2. Because the dollar and franc were linked through gold parities and flows, the sterling-dollar rate was relatively stable as a result, keeping within the range of $4.88 to $5.03 (see Figure 4.1).[30] But Anglo-American tensions did not ease; suspicion over each other's exchange funds continued unabated. In June, Oliver Sprague, Harvard economist and former adviser at the BoE, told his London friends that he was "seriously concerned by widespread popular distrust in the United States of the British Equalisation Account."[31] The stability in day-to-day rates merely masked the underlying forces pushing toward eventual upheaval.

---

[29] Leith-Ross, "Note of interview with Monsieur Rueff and Monsieur Mönick," undated, T 188/116.

[30] The EEA sometimes executed dollar orders on behalf of third parties such as central banks. Catterns to Phillips, June 4, 1935, BoE ADM23/1.

[31] Clay to Norman, June 6, 1935, BoE G1/487.

By the beginning of 1936, the policy of holding the sterling-franc rate had morphed de facto into one of supporting the franc. "[I]t is part of our present policy," the BoE's Harry Siepmann minuted, "not merely to control sterling exchange but, in the general interests of monetary order, to support the franc." The problem was that, with rising pressure on the franc, maintaining a steady sterling-franc rate required larger purchases of the currency by the EEA. Since the French were "fighting a losing battle," Siepmann thought the British needed to better protect themselves in these operations.[32] Converting francs into gold eliminated most of the risk in buying francs but not all. Francs purchased in the market were not credited and thus could not be converted into gold for two days, leaving the EEA on the hook should gold convertibility cease or the gold value of the franc change prior to settlement. To safeguard against these risks, the BoE worked out an arrangement with the BdF in March. When the BoE purchased francs, the BdF provided an immediate advance of francs to the BoE, which the BdF then converted into gold on the spot; once the francs purchased in the market were credited to the BoE's account, the proceeds cleared the advance.[33] Though the measure was simply a stopgap, it did help nurture the technical relationship between London and Paris.

Even with this protection, Siepmann, who became the EEA's manager in March 1936, remained uncomfortable, worrying that focus on supporting the franc was detracting from the task of managing the pound. The BoE began contingency planning for what would happen should the French go off the gold standard. For all the talk among policymakers of the danger of Britain returning to the gold standard, they desperately wanted France to remain on it. London hoped Paris would enact a clean devaluation – maintaining the promise to buy and sell gold at fixed prices – rather than float as it did or restrict convertibility to gold standard countries as Washington did. The British did not feel secure managing sterling against an inconvertible currency, and with the dollar off limits, the franc was all they had.

Should the franc become inconvertible, the BoE decided that it would cease dealing in foreign exchange and shift its operations to the gold market. "This was recognised to be an experimental and cumbersome method of doubtful efficacy," Siepmann recorded, but it seemed to be the best option. "We should still be concerned with the price of gold not for its

[32] Siepmann, "Exchange Equalisation Account and Risks of Franc Depreciation," January 23, 1936, BoE C43/24.
[33] See BoE C43/422 for the negotiations relating to this arrangement.

own sake but as providing a link between sterling and other currencies, and there would be no intention to maintain it, independently of currency relationships, within even a wide range."[34] The risk surrounding foreign exchange, hammered into policymakers' minds after the loss on the EEA's dollar assets in 1933, was too great to permit dealing in non-gold currencies. Gold intervention would have to suffice.[35] That is not to say that officials were interested in the metal as an anchor for the pound – there would be no fixed price nor publication of the policy – but rather that they saw it as the key reserve asset, a useful vehicle, and a safe investment.

In the end, London did not have to activate this plan. A warming of relations between Britain and America in the summer of 1936 opened up the path for a French devaluation and set in motion a new system of gold convertibility that allowed the EEA to deal not only in francs but, after nearly three years of nonintervention, in dollars as well.

ANGLO-AMERICAN DÉTENTE

It would not be easy for London and Washington to reach an understanding. For one, leaders had a visceral dislike for each other. Skidelsky (2001, 186) well summarizes Roosevelt and Morgenthau's early attitude toward London: "US economic policy was dominated by a grotesque overestimation of Britain's financial strength and a corresponding suspicion of Britain's motives. Vigilance against British Machiavellianism rather than the production of constructive ideas was the watchword of Morgenthau's Treasury, a tendency reinforced by British secretiveness." London considered the two men mercurial, irresponsible, and ignorant. Even those few officials supportive of coming to terms with Washington, such as Britain's ambassador, Ronald Lindsay, thought any communication with the Americans "ought to be couched in words of one syllable and written with insulting clarity."[36] It did not help that the two Treasuries had almost no contact with each other. T. K. Bewley, the British financial attaché posted in Washington from 1933, does not appear to have had a meeting with Morgenthau until November 1935. Similarly, W. Walton Butterworth, the

---

[34] Siepmann, "Policy," undated, BoE C14/1.

[35] Drummond (1981, 220) argues that exchange managers would have accepted the risk involved in dealing in foreign exchange, but the evidence is to the contrary.

[36] Quoted in Clarke (1977, 19).

US financial attaché in London, did not meet regularly with the British Treasury until 1936, three years into his assignment.[37]

Unsurprisingly, with Morgenthau focused on developing a Franco-American alliance, attempts at forging improved Anglo-American relations in early 1935 were sporadic and in vain. In February, Lindsay mooted to an official from the State Department the idea of sharing information on exchange interventions, as the funds were prime sources of suspicion. But London quickly quashed the conversations, instructing Lindsay to halt his personal initiative and confirming Washington's impression of the British as cool and uncompromising.[38] The issue reappeared in May. Again, there was no progress. Norman, who "shudder[ed] to think of Bewley sitting down with Morgenthau to play poker with the two Exchange Accounts as chips," was "against giving, and therefore against receiving, detailed information or confidences about these Accounts, mostly because of politics and personalities and leakiness in Washington."[39] The British Treasury concurred, and so mutual ignorance – and thus mistrust – continued unabated.

Here matters stood until November 1935, when the first constructive action in rebuilding technical relations took place. The impetus was not diplomatic initiative but internal politics. The flow of gold from Europe to America had begun to "disturb" Morgenthau and Roosevelt; they feared that, once conditions in Europe improved, a large outflow from America could set in with harmful political effects. Despite the massive increase in US gold holdings – in October 1935, they were up 148 percent in dollar terms and 47 percent by weight from March 1933 – the prospect of the metal suddenly fleeing back to Europe brought to mind the deflation at the worst of the Depression. If gold began flowing out as the election approached the following autumn, Morgenthau thought "politicians here would claim that it was moving out of this country because financial interests were worried that Roosevelt was going to be reelected."[40]

The secretary thus decided, with Roosevelt's support, to build up a gold stash in London. This gold would be held on the ESF's account: Purchases would not be published, and more important, neither would sales. The idea

---

[37] Bingham telegram to Treasury, May 30, 1935, MD 5/187; Morgenthau conversation with Bewley, November 7, 1935, MD 11/33; Bingham to Chamberlain, October 16, 1936, BoE C43/327.

[38] Lindsay telegram, March 12, 1935, T 188/116; Lindsay to Leith-Ross, March 29, 1935, T 188/116; Fisher, Untitled memo, May 25, 1935, T 188/116.

[39] Norman to Hopkins, May 27, 1935, BoE G1/140.

[40] Morgenthau conversation with Roosevelt, November 12, 1935, MD 11/141.

was that whenever the dollar-equivalent price of gold in London was low enough that it was profitable for arbitrageurs to purchase the metal, transport it, and sell it to the US Treasury, the BoE would purchase the gold instead for US account. The gold would stay in London, available for future European transactions or ready to be shipped to the United States when desired, and the FRBNY would credit the BoE with dollars. The BoE agreed to act as agent in this matter, and the FRBNY thereafter provided weekly orders, specifying a maximum amount of gold to be purchased and a maximum price of $34.77.[41]

This arrangement had advantages from Britain's perspective as well. The BoE, if it wished, could now create dollars on demand to sell into the market to strengthen the pound. That is, the standing order allowed the BoE to sell dollars without currently holding any and without having to limit itself to gold held on earmark in New York. As the BoE's Henry Clay explained, "the arrangement does make possible transactions in dollars from which we have abstained in the past. If sterling is weak owing to a demand for dollars and we wish to prevent it from falling, instead of meeting the demand for dollars as at present by selling francs or (as we have done occasionally) selling gold in the market, we could sell gold to the F[ederal].R[eserve].B[ank]. under the new proposal and use the dollar proceeds to meet the demand for dollars direct."[42] Though the BoE made little use of the arrangement at first, it would employ the facility with increasing frequency in later years.[43] The other half of the equation, of course, was to be able to convert dollars into gold. On this, Morgenthau was not yet ready to budge.

While the arrangement made both sides happy, nothing fundamental changed, and as 1936 progressed and expectations of a French devaluation heightened, Washington planned for a variety of contingencies. Devaluation of the franc per se was not of much concern, so long as it was in the range of roughly 20 to 30 percent. However, there was great anxiety about how the British would respond. "The crux of the situation," read a May 1936 memo to Morgenthau, "is the behavior of sterling." The report described the hope of reaching an understanding with Britain but argued that the United States could not sit idly by if the pound started to

---

[41] Harrison conversation with Norman, November 15, 1935, FRBNY C261; Harrison telegram to Harvey, November 19, 1935, FRBNY C261. See also the files in BoE C43/313 and Bordo, Humpage, and Schwartz (2015, 77–81).

[42] Clay, "Gold Purchases for the F.R.B.," November 21, 1935, BoE C43/313.

[43] Siepmann, Untitled memo, April 8, 1936, BoE C43/313.

sink. "If sterling declines below the level we feel is reasonable, the situation, so far as we are concerned, represents a state of monetary 'war,' and our plans must be evaluated in that light. We can always change our tactics, withdraw, or settle, but we cannot in justice to our own interests let England do what she pleases with the sterling price of gold."[44] Should London seek to depreciate the pound, Washington would have to consider purchasing sterling to offset the interventions in a tit-for-tat battle.

Morgenthau understood that this strategy was far from ideal, as it risked spiraling out of control through reprisals on any number of dimensions. He decided that he should at least try to come to terms with Britain. After all, his efforts with the French had amounted to nothing. More important, he sensed that the European situation was increasingly precarious and that the best hope involved getting France to devalue, for it needed to deal with its financial situation in order to project strength against its increasingly menacing neighbor. For France to devalue, it would at the very least need Anglo-American assurances that they would not retaliate. The prerequisite was that Britain and America give each other such assurances. Only in this way could they avoid a "smash-up" in Europe, which had become more combustible with Hitler's remilitarization of the Rhineland in March.[45]

Morgenthau thus devised a strategy for approaching London. He asked Roosevelt on April 29, 1936 – just days after the first round of the French election suggested a strong trend in favor of the left – for "permission . . . to open conversation with the British on stabilization." Roosevelt wanted Britain to move first, but Morgenthau persisted, his argument strengthened by the fact that the president could not confuse him for an Anglophile or so-called international banker with ulterior motives. Roosevelt relented, allowing Morgenthau to ask Bewley about a recent transaction under the gold arrangement as a means of testing Britain's interest in engagement.[46] The British did not bite, at which point Morgenthau upped the pressure. "If we were at war with each other," he scolded Bewley on May 18, "we could not be acting any differently." He continued: "This is my last attempt as a gesture. I will never do it again. Any further move will have to come from the British Treasury."[47]

This outburst seemed to do the trick. Lindsay cabled home, "Whatever blame lies for past events I cannot conceive that it can be to our advantage

---

[44] Haas, "French Devaluation," May 8, 1936, JVP B49F7.
[45] Morgenthau conversation with Bewley, June 4, 1936, MD 26/117.
[46] Morgenthau conversation with Roosevelt, April 29, 1936, MD 22/155.
[47] Morgenthau conversation with Bewley, May 18, 1936, MD 24/192–94.

needlessly to rebuff [the] strongest financial country in the world." One of Morgenthau's subordinates, playing the good cop to the secretary's bad cop, explained to Bewley that "the past was the past and it seemed to them to be nonsensical for the two Treasuries to remain at arms length from one another." The United States wanted a "statement of British monetary policy in the light of present French situation."[48] London thought Morgenthau's gambit of first asking about a gold transaction was clumsy and far from promising – much better to have been forthright from the get-go – but nonetheless agreed that some response was warranted.[49] Since the British believed a French devaluation to be merited, they had no plans to retaliate and felt secure relating that to the Americans. Bewley informed Morgenthau on June 1 that Chamberlain saw no reason why the sterling-dollar rate would change in the aftermath of a French move. Barring a steep drop in prices or uncontrollable outflows of gold from London, as long as the dollar kept steady against gold, "the parity between the pound and the dollar would remain unaltered."[50] Bewley also provided the secretary a note from the chancellor expressing the latter's desire for "the closest and most friendly contact between the two Treasuries."[51]

"I congratulate you," Undersecretary of State William Phillips enthused to Morgenthau the following day, "on the most important diplomatic step that has been taken. We have been working on this for three years."[52] That Bewley's measured response triggered such excitement from Phillips – a man who had seen much in his decades-long career at the State Department – underscores just how dismal relations had been. These two indispensable countries had been separated by a seemingly uncrossable chasm. Now they were finally willing to meet each other halfway and call

[48] Lindsay telegram, May 19, 1936, BoE G1/140; Lindsay telegram, May 16, 1936, BoE G1/140; Lindsay telegram, May 22, 1936, BoE G1/140.

[49] Instructions possibly for Bewley, undated, BoE G1/140.

[50] Morgenthau conversation with Bewley, June 1, 1936, MD 26/2. London told Bewley that, in the event of a franc devaluation, so long as prices did not fall, "we see no reason for any considerable change in exchange relations between dollar and sterling," language slightly more hedged than what Bewley told Morgenthau. Later, Chamberlain tried to emphasize the caveats in a meeting with an American official in London, leading to some uncertainty in Washington as to what the British were saying. But it soon became clear that the substance was as Bewley relayed, and Chamberlain merely wanted to avoid being locked into anything. Telegram to Lindsay, May 28, 1936, BoE G1/140; Morgenthau conversation with Bewley, June 18, 1936, MD 27/117; Morgenthau conversation with Bewley, June 24, 1936, MD 27/177.

[51] Morgenthau meeting with Bewley, June 1, 1936, MD 26/2A-2E; Lindsay to Morgenthau, May 29, 1936, MD 26/2F-2G.

[52] Morgenthau conversation with Phillips, June 2, 1936, MD 26/15.

an armistice. Morgenthau explained to Bewley that the United States would not push the dollar down either.[53] With assurances that neither intended to depreciate in the event of a French devaluation, they could now focus on the deteriorating situation in France without having to keep an eye on each other. Morgenthau was beaming and soon told Bewley that any suspicions he once had about Britain were now put to rest.[54]

To be sure, Bewley's brief statement that London did not plan deliberately to lower the pound merely made explicit a policy it already had in mind. Indeed, the British did not think they were committing to anything and did not even think they were suggesting anything new. They seem to have taken this step because there was little cost: It did not tie them down and it offered at least the potential for future dividends. For instance, Bewley asked Morgenthau to once again allow Britain to convert dollars into gold in the spirit of cooperation.[55] The British considered it "technically the one link required in order to establish contact between the currency policy of the two Treasuries."[56] While Morgenthau did not agree on the spot, he strongly hinted that he would be willing to do so at some time.[57] It must be stressed, however, that the British did not yet subscribe to any notion of an Anglo-American monetary partnership. They were glad to reduce suspicions, open up channels of communication, and gain some clarity on US policy, but they were not ready for proactive measures.

Morgenthau, then, was the driving force in this reconciliation, and the British felt it best not to slam the door in his face. Concurrent with the Treasury discussions, the two central banks began talking more frequently and sharing some information on intervention, which the BoE now considered "good cooperation, just what we need" given the uncertainty about the franc.[58] Much, no doubt, still remained to be figured out. The British preferred consultation to go predominantly through central banks, which were best equipped to communicate quickly and knowledgably about market developments; the Americans were insistent that Treasuries lead the effort and central banks provide support. Morgenthau was still an unread farmer to the British, Chamberlain a haughty imperialist to the Americans. They were far from allied on monetary matters, but Britain and

---

[53] Morgenthau conversation with Bewley, June 4, 1936, MD 26/117.
[54] Lindsay telegram, June 18, 1936, BoE G1/140.
[55] Morgenthau conversation with Bewley, June 3, 1936, MD 26/51.
[56] "Suggestions in Rough Draft," June 4, 1936, BoE G1/140.
[57] Morgenthau also drafted papers granting Britain access to gold, though he sat on them for the time being. Morgenthau conversation with Roosevelt, June 7, 1936, MD 26/152.
[58] Untitled note, May 28, 1936, BoE C43/92.

America were talking once more. And having come to an understanding between themselves, the dialogue now focused squarely on France. "Things have come to a pretty pass," the FRBNY's Vice President Allan Sproul wrote to Siepmann in early June, "when we must all spend our weekends waiting to see or hear what a Mr. Blum may do!"[59]

ROAD TO THE TRIPARTITE

To his supporters, Léon Blum was a devoted man, fighting for the just cause of a more equitable world. He was also wise, recognizing the threat posed by Germany and convinced of the need to build up the democracies by binding France to Britain and the United States. To his enemies – and he had many – Blum was two things: a Jew and a socialist. No combination was more unforgivable. In early 1936, fascist thugs nearly beat him to death. When Blum presented his government to the Chamber in June, a deputy rose to grieve that "this old Gallo-Roman country will be governed ... by a Jew."[60] The nation Blum took the helm of was coming apart at the seams, socially, politically, and economically.

He could not sit and stew about the hatred surrounding him; he had to act quickly to keep the country from collapsing. France was at a standstill due to a general strike, organized by workers convinced that their time for equality had finally arrived and eager to push the new government to action. Full-scale revolution, as well as counterrevolution, seemed possible. Blum negotiated an agreement with employers and unions that granted workers various rights and pay increases and passed legislation conferring a forty-hour work week and paid vacation.[61] The country soon got back to work and tensions eased somewhat. The new government also brought the BdF, which the left had long felt was of and for the "moneyed aristocracy," more firmly under its control.[62] Indeed, the government was so suspicious of the BdF (and vice versa) that Cariguel was convinced his phones were being tapped and instructed the BoE to refrain from discussing anything sensitive.[63] Soon enough, the government removed Governor Tannery, installed the trusted though unqualified Émile Labeyrie as head, and reformed the BdF's governance to make the institution more democratically accountable. The Spanish Civil War then broke out in July, opening up a frightening new front in the battle between fascism and democracy.

[59] Sproul to Siepmann, June 5, 1936, BoE C43/313.   [60] Quoted in Birnbaum (2015, 1).
[61] Jackson (1988) provides an excellent history of the Popular Front and its reforms.
[62] Boris (1936).   [63] Siepmann to Catterns, July 7, 1936, BoE OV45/86.

But through it all, the question of the franc remained. In fact, it was connected to France's confrontation with fascism. Paris was convinced that the Nazis were provoking runs on the currency to trigger crises, bleed the nation of its reserves, threaten its capacity to rearm, and generally cause chaos. German press talked down the franc constantly. Intelligence reports as early as 1933 even suggested that Hitler was behind the speculative attacks.[64] Should the continent descend into war, whatever was left of the gold stock would become the war chest. France thus had to get its currency situation under control not simply for economic reasons but for national security ones.

There were three methods to stop the outflow of gold: deflate, enact exchange controls, or devalue. As deflation was abhorrent to the party of the workers and had already inflicted much suffering, the government never considered it an option. Exchange controls, while more compatible with socialist economic ideology, were problematic for other members of the grand coalition and were considered "fascist" given their use in Germany and Japan.[65] Devaluation, on the other hand, could redress the payments imbalance without permanently interfering in the economy, but it was still deeply unpopular and might tar the government as betrayers of the national trust.

International political considerations hung over the decision. Blum met with Emmanuel Mönick, the financial attaché in London and a well-known proponent of devaluation, during the interregnum between the elections in May and the formation of his government in June. As Mouré (1991, 243) explains, "Mönick argued that defense of the franc" at its current parity "would require exchange controls and economic self-sufficiency, the route traveled by Germany; if France wished to ally itself with the great Western democracies, it was essential to align the franc with the dollar and the pound." Blum worried that London and Washington would retaliate to any devaluation, but Mönick suggested that there was room for an agreement.[66]

Indeed, on June 6, just two days after Blum presented his government, Morgenthau instructed Cochran to sound out Vincent Auriol, the new finance minister, as to "whether it would be helpful to the French if they could devalue knowing that the United States and England would not

---

[64] James (2001, 190).   [65] Mouré (1991, 243).
[66] Sayers interview with Mönick, May 7, 1969, BoE ADM33/32.

devalue further."[67] Morgenthau believed Blum might then be able to "save his country."[68] Auriol was not receptive at the moment, fearful that if word got out that he was even considering devaluation political pressure would force his resignation.

In mid-June, however, Blum sent Mönick to Washington on a secret mission to thank Morgenthau for his message and discuss the situation. Blum's choice of envoy hinted at his growing inclination for devaluation. Mönick was a well-known player on the international monetary scene. Though he did not have the best reputation – he was so self-assured that his counterparts struggled to know when he represented the views of his government rather than just himself – Washington was nevertheless keen on what he had to say.[69] Good that it was, for his trip set in motion three months of negotiations, at times contentious and far from linear, that would result in the Tripartite Agreement.

Mönick met with Morgenthau on several occasions, as well as with Roosevelt, and argued that France's best hope, politically and economically, lay with devaluation. To make devaluation acceptable to the public, Mönick believed it had to be part of an international agreement: "We must give the feeling in France that the battle is over, and that it is the beginning of monetary peace and some form of collaboration between the stable currencies."[70] Mönick shared with Morgenthau a proposal for devaluation and collaboration that he had drafted on his own authority. The British would hold the pound between $4.75 and $4.97 (the midpoint being the old parity of $4.86) and the French would hold the franc between $0.0475 and $0.0497 (corresponding to 100 francs to the pound as compared to the current rate around 76). In addition, none of the countries would resort to

---

[67] Auriol mooted a broader series of agreements that would have included the gold bloc; Cochran followed up on this idea in Basel but nothing came of it. Morgenthau conversation with Cochran, June 6, 1936, MD 26/148; Cochran telegram, June 6, 1936, MD 26/149; Cochran telegram, June 8, 1936, MD 26/154.

[68] Morgenthau conversation with Roosevelt, June 4, 1936, MD 26/121.

[69] In February 1938, Herbert Feis, the top economic official at the State Department, diplomatically described Mönick as follows: "I won't attest to his methods. As to his intelligence, watching him for a long, long time, he has always been to me one of the most intelligent one would meet. He has seen situations before the rest have and he has clear perspective and I, therefore, take seriously any initiative that Mr. Mönick pronounces, even if involved in that initiative might be a question of his personal position." Treasury meeting, February 23, 1938, MD 112/23–24.

[70] Morgenthau conversation with Mönick, June 24, 1936, MD 27/178G.

measures of "economic defense likely to hamper the revival of international trade" and all would seek to remove such barriers as already existed.[71] Morgenthau found the general idea attractive. Mönick suggested trilateral negotiations in Washington, but Roosevelt reminded him that British "amour propre" was not to be neglected, and the better method was to send any future messages to Washington and London simultaneously.[72]

By the time Mönick sailed to Paris at the end of June, the drain on the BdF's gold reserves had slowed, and there was less pressure to reach an agreement. Blum was also contending against colleagues who were outraged that he was considering devaluation. He thus did not send Mönick to run his draft by the British until the second half of July.[73] Of course, the suggestion that the British hold the pound between $4.75 and $4.97 was dead on arrival, as London would not commit to any range for sterling. After discussing the matter with Mönick, Waley nevertheless felt that some action would be necessary, concluding that "we cannot wisely offend President Roosevelt and Monsieur Léon Blum by rejecting the idea of co-operation outright and we shall have to attempt to find some formula which means very little."[74]

Blum visited London at the end of July to discuss a range of issues and met with Chamberlain. The two sides then decided to draft a letter to Blum in Chamberlain's name expressing support for devaluation and stating that London would not retaliate. The letter was to be sent, and if desired, publicized, in the event France took the plunge. That Chamberlain, the chancellor of the exchequer, was writing to Blum, the head of government, was somewhat odd, but Chamberlain was the driving force behind most of government during these years, especially after Stanley Baldwin replaced Ramsay MacDonald as prime minister in mid-1935. From then on, Chamberlain was prime minister-in-waiting.[75]

In the draft, Chamberlain wrote that he regarded the prospect of devaluation "with every sympathy," as long as it did not exceed 100 francs to the pound.[76] While he refused to hold the pound between fixed points, he assumed that the French plan was to establish a new gold price and maintain convertibility, not float. The British message did not reference

---

[71] Mönick, "Suggestions for tentative draft of a monetary accord between the United States, Great Britain and France," undated, MD 27/178P-Q.

[72] Phillips, Untitled memo, June 23, 1936, MD 27/176C.   [73] Sayers (1976, 2:477).

[74] Waley, Untitled memo, July 22, 1936, T 160/840/4.

[75] Baldwin often took a hands-off approach and was, moreover, recovering from a breakdown during the summer of 1936. Self (2006, 256).

[76] Phillips, Draft letter, July 30, 1936, T 160/840/4.

the United States, nor did London mention it to Washington. The French argued that cooperation between all three democracies was essential and drafted language to that end in their suggestions for the letter, but the British were not yet convinced. As Waley reported, Mönick "attached great importance to the reference to a French Exchange Equalisation Fund" – not yet in existence but likely part of any devaluation package – "and the collaboration between the British, French and American Equalisation Funds.... The Bank of England will have none of it. They know that no one can collaborate with Mr. Morgenthau."[77] British distrust of Morgenthau ran deep and would take time to ebb.

Little happened in the next few weeks, the draft letter filed away for safekeeping. As Blum recounted several years later, even though he and Auriol understood that devaluation was inevitable, "as slight as the chance was of avoiding it, we wished to take that chance to the very end."[78] But by the beginning of September it was clear that the terminal crisis had arrived. Auriol reopened conversations, sending a draft trilateral agreement to Washington and London. "The high contracting parties" were to cooperate toward maintaining their exchange rates within set limits (left unspecified in the draft) and to work toward "the final objective" of "the general return to the international gold standard."[79] None of this document survived the weeks of negotiating that followed, but it set everything in motion. Morgenthau took issue with the language on returning to gold – it was "not the Roosevelt philosophy" – and responded with the US position on the benefits of stability and cooperation as well as the need to always consider "internal prices and economic conditions." He suggested that the French and British could write "substantially similar" statements to his reply, which could then be "given simultaneous publication by all three Governments."[80]

London also considered the draft unrealistic, bordering on "hopeless," in the overwrought language of the Treasury common when dealing with Paris and Washington.[81] Any set of fixed points for sterling was nonnegotiable, even if, as in this plan, the commitment was not binding. There were also signs that the French would not devalue on gold, heightening concerns about how the British would manage the pound. The French,

---

[77] Waley, Untitled memo, July 25, 1936, T 160/840/4.   [78] Quoted in Mouré (1991, 249).

[79] Cochran telegram, September 9, 1936, MD 32/48–53.

[80] Treasury meeting, September 9, 1936, MD 32/54; Morgenthau telegram to Cochran, September 9, 1936, MD 32/78–80.

[81] Phillips, Untitled memo, September 10, 1936, T 160/840/4.

Chamberlain fumed, "have treated me very shabbily in this matter," and he responded that he could not exceed his July letter.[82]

But Whitehall began discussing the matter with the US Treasury, and the near-constant exchange of telegrams helped build a firmer basis for consultation. London informed Washington and Paris that the "maintenance by each country of the greatest possible stability in monetary relations and a due consideration at all times for the effect of its decisions upon other countries afford a more desirable as well as a more practical basis of cooperation at this stage than any formal convention."[83] The Americans were delighted by the message and were likeminded, favoring a "a gentleman's agreement."[84] Tripartite talks had now commenced. If the British were willing to go beyond their July letter by broadening to a three-party announcement and the French dropped their aims to pin down rates, a compromise was in reach.

The French relented on specifying exchange rates and shared a new draft on September 17. "[A]nxious to safeguard peace and liberty" and aiming "to the development of prosperity in the world and to the improvement of the standard of living of all social classes," the "undersigned governments" would work toward the "maximum of stability" in the monetary field and consider the impact of their decisions on others. The French would "proceed to the adjustment" of the franc to give the world the best chance for lasting stability, the Treasuries and central banks would "unite their efforts," and all would strive to reduce barriers to trade in an effort to champion liberal economic values.[85] The document did not receive a positive reception in Washington. Officials cringed at the thought of Americans referring to "social classes," did not want to mention central banks in an agreement between governments, were stunned that the sentence on returning to the international gold standard remained, and were concerned that the French had yet to inform them of the extent of their planned devaluation.[86]

---

[82] Phillips, Untitled memo, September 9, 1936, T 160/840/4.

[83] Foreign Office telegram to Mallet, September 14, 1936, T 160/840/4.

[84] Morgenthau meeting with Hull, September 9, 1936, MD 32/65.

[85] Cochran telegram to Morgenthau, September 17, 1936, MD 32/278–84.

[86] Treasury meeting, September 17, 1936, MD 32/289–95. Morgenthau did not even inform the FRBNY about the discussions until September 23. A Treasury adviser had suggested the previous week that the secretary bring Marriner Eccles, chairman of the Board of Governors, into his confidence, but Morgenthau did not trust Eccles and would not hear of it. He eventually informed Eccles just hours before the announcement. Dictation, September 23, 1936, MD 33/58; Treasury meeting, September 18, 1936, MD 33/8Q-S; Morgenthau conversation with Eccles, September 25, 1936, MD 34/96.

Morgenthau, determined to maintain monetary flexibility, insisted that the United States would not be part of a treaty and recommended that each government issue its own "nearly identical" statement. He sent a revised version written as a US communiqué, which became the basis for the final statements. Rather than mention central banks, the US draft referred to the governments "using appropriate available resources" – that is, exchange funds – to promote stability. It also included a line that the government "trusts that no country will attempt to obtain an unreasonable competitive exchange advantage."[87] Morgenthau was nervous that the fascist powers would try to undercut the agreement by out-devaluing France and thought the sentence would serve as "notice to Japan, Germany and Italy that we won't stand any monkey business."[88]

In London, Sir Richard Hopkins found Auriol's document "inconceivably French" and in need of much revision.[89] But having scuppered any reference to bounds for sterling, Whitehall was now less concerned about the wording of the document and more stressed about the future of the franc. The BoE's Cameron Cobbold went to the BdF to discuss French plans, and his dispatches contained two troubling reports. First, the French were considering devaluing to 110 francs to the pound. A rate of 110 as opposed to 100 was not a deal breaker, but it did cast doubt on French credibility after the discussions in July. More worrisome, Cobbold's interlocutor at the BdF thought Paris would not stay on the orthodox gold standard. Precisely what variant the French would choose was unclear: They might follow the American path by restricting gold convertibility to central banks on the gold standard or they might not convert at all.[90] Either way, Britain would be out of luck, its "halcyon days" of managing sterling against a gold-convertible currency over, Hopkins bemoaned.[91] Sir Frederick Phillips found the prospect unacceptable: "The Bank of England ought to get busy in impressing on the Bank of France that there are certain things we won't stand. One of the things we won't stand is an arrangement by which the French and Americans would buy and sell gold from each other, but not from us. If that is proposed there is no chance of British cooperation."[92]

[87] Morgenthau telegram to Cochran, September 19, 1936, MD 33/28L-O.
[88] Treasury meeting, September 18, 1936, MD 33/18J.
[89] Hopkins to Chancellor, September 18, 1936, T 160/840/4.
[90] Cobbold, "Interviews at Bank of France," September 17, 1936, BoE C43/343; Cobbold, Untitled memo, September 17, 1936, BoE C43/343.
[91] Hopkins to Chancellor, September 18, 1936, T 160/840/4.
[92] Phillips to Waley, September 18, 1936, T 160/840/4.

Conversations continued, and the French intimated that they wanted to announce the devaluation after markets closed on Friday, September 25.[93] On the 23rd, Mönick presented the British with draft legislation that would reduce the franc from 65.5 milligrams of gold to a range of 43 to 49 milligrams, corresponding to a mean devaluation of 30 percent – in sterling terms, roughly 98 to 112 francs per pound. The government would choose a new parity within that range at a later date, and the BdF's gold would be revalued on the 49-milligram basis, with part of the profit used to endow an exchange fund. Yet it remained unclear whether the British would be able to convert francs into gold. In part for this reason, Chamberlain was not ready to play along and urged Paris to either devalue on gold, delay a decision to allow for more negotiation, or move forward alone.[94]

But Mönick insisted that the situation was too dire for any of those options. He presented a letter from Blum to Chamberlain pleading for British support and warning that devaluation, which required legislation, would not survive the National Assembly "if the Chambers do not have a very clear impression of cooperation between the three great democratic nations."[95] To allay fears about gold, Mönick then delivered a second note, explicitly approved by Auriol, proposing that the "two Exchange Funds will concert" to maintain the new exchange rate and "will be able daily to convert into gold . . . the other currency which they hold."[96] That is, the French fund would provide gold in exchange for francs so long as the British fund did so for pounds. Talk of reciprocity had been going on in the background for several days. While Mönick's document was preliminary and the British had not yet agreed to convert sterling into gold, they interpreted the note as signifying French willingness to convert francs into gold (see Chapter 6 for discussion of the subsequent gold reciprocity arrangements). With this assurance, Chamberlain informed Blum on September 24 that, despite his many misgivings, he would go along.[97]

---

[93] Cobbold, "Meetings at Bank of France," September 22, 1936, BoE C43/343.
[94] Waley, "The French Franc," September 23, 1936, T 160/840/5. Mönick was to inform Auriol of Chamberlain's warning to delay, but subsequent events described in the following paragraph made the message moot and the British told Mönick not to deliver it.
[95] Quoted in Mouré (1991, 261).
[96] "Translation of Paper Received from Monsieur Mönick," September 23, 1936, T 160/840/5.
[97] Foreign Office telegram to Clerk, September 24, 1936, T 160/840/5.

As London explained to Washington, Blum's "pressing personal appeal" was such that Chamberlain "felt he could not refuse."[98]

Now only one problem remained. Morgenthau wanted an understanding with Britain on the sterling-dollar rate before granting his approval to the whole scheme: nothing binding as in earlier discussions but more concrete than currently existed. After speaking with Roosevelt, he told a representative of the British embassy on September 24 that "if we do go ahead with this arrangement ... we take it for granted that we are talking about a $5.00 pound" and that both countries would try to hold the rate within ten cents on either side.[99] This attempt to get the British to agree to a rate was never going to work, and the Americans likely knew this.[100] But they felt they had to try. Unsurprisingly, Chamberlain responded the following day that he had no authority to "fix the pound within gold points." "It may be," he continued, "that the natural level of the pound will in the new circumstances be 5 dollars, as Mr. Morgenthau appears to assume, but the Chancellor would have expected it to be decidedly lower."[101] Morgenthau and Roosevelt, understanding that it was not worth scuttling all the work that had been done, accepted the British position. The president drafted a reply, stating that "it is a matter of opinion" what the "natural level of the pound would be," and so long as the British understood the American position, "this is not an obstacle" to the release of statements "to carry out their broad, useful and, indeed, essential objective."[102] The countries could proceed.

As evening descended in Paris on September 25, the moment was at hand. The governments were still exchanging cables to make sure that the statements were appropriately synchronized. Because each government would issue its own, each adapted the text accordingly. The US declaration spoke of the United States Government, the British of His Majesty's Government, and the French of the French Government. The British and American statements were essentially identical save for this difference, while the French statement included additional language on its impending devaluation. With midnight approaching, the delay in finalization resulted in a bit of farce, the president of France sending word to the Americans

---

[98] Treasury telegram to Mallet, September 24, 1936, T 160/840/5.

[99] Morgenthau conversation with Mallet, September 24, 1936, MD 33/252.

[100] Morgenthau seemed nervous and unsure about the wisdom of pushing the matter with the British. Treasury meeting, September 25, 1936, MD 34/6–9.

[101] Vansittart telegram to Mallet, September 25, 1936, T 177/31.

[102] Treasury meeting, September 25, 1936, MD 34/43.

that he would very much like to go to bed so could they please hurry things up.[103] Finally, in the early hours of Saturday, September 26, each party agreed to the statements. At 1:10 a.m., Auriol announced the plans for devaluation – a new gold range for the franc and the establishment of a stabilization fund – and issued the French declaration. Publication of the British and American documents followed.[104]

The final statements were five paragraphs long. The first was a preamble, noting the governments' "common desire to foster those conditions which safeguard peace and will best contribute to the restoration of order in international economic relations and to pursue a policy which will tend to promote prosperity in the world and to improve the standard of living of peoples." The second paragraph declared that the countries would "continue" to pursue the "greatest possible equilibrium in the system of international exchanges," while caveating that they must "take into account the requirements of internal prosperity" when determining "policy towards international monetary relations." The use of the word "continue" conveniently papered over the destabilizing actions London and Washington had taken in previous years.

In the third paragraph, France stated that it would seek a "readjustment" of the franc, which the British and Americans "welcomed." The three would "use the appropriate available resources so as to avoid as far as possible any disturbance of the basis of international exchanges resulting from the proposed readjustment. They will arrange for such consultation for this purpose as may be necessary." The fourth paragraph connected economic growth to liberal policies: The parties "attach the greatest importance to action being taken without delay to relax progressively the present system of quotas and exchange controls with a view to their abolition." The final paragraph "invit[ed] the cooperation of the other nations to realize the policy laid down in the present declaration" but ended with Morgenthau's warning that the governments "trust that no country will attempt to obtain an unreasonable competitive exchange advantage and thereby hamper the effort to restore more stable economic relations."

There was no fixing of exchange rates, no commitment to remove trade barriers, no definition of "unreasonable competitive exchange advantage." There was no penalty for noncompliance, no legislative assent, no technical arrangements. As Clarke (1977, 39–40) writes, the Tripartite Agreement

---

[103] Treasury meeting, September 25, 1936, MD 34/104.
[104] "Europe's Currency Crisis," *The Economist*, October 3, 1936.

"successfully obscured the fundamental differences among the three countries." But there were now three statements, laboriously negotiated over, that offered a vision of the future far different from that of the recent past. The question as to if, and how, the countries would actually cooperate under the Tripartite Agreement would be answered only with time and experience.

6

A New Order, 1936–1939

Devaluation of the franc sealed the gold bloc's fate. After the French announcement in the early hours of September 26, 1936, Switzerland and the Netherlands put on brave faces, vowing to maintain their parities, but resolve gave way to reality in less than a day. That afternoon, Switzerland devalued, and the Netherlands shortly thereafter imposed a gold embargo. Smaller countries pegging to gold currencies, such as Latvia and Greece, devalued and realigned to sterling.[1] It was a frantic couple of days. But the gold bloc's collapse in itself was not all that shocking: It had long been a matter of when, not if. As *The Economist* remarked, "The expected has happened."[2]

What came as a surprise, however, was the manner in which France – by far the most important member of the gold bloc – devalued. France did not act in spite of Anglo-American objections: It did so with their blessing and as part of an international agreement. Monetary peace now seemed at hand. "Instead of new threats of competitive depreciation," *The New York Times* declared, "we have assurance of cooperative action to keep currencies at stable levels. . . . The three great democracies have shown a clarity of purpose and an incisiveness of action which belies the talk of an infirmity of democratic will."[3] The *Financial Times* praised the new "Triple Alliance."[4] *The Economist* was optimistic as well, though the newspaper emphasized that it would "exercise all the talents and employ all the

---

[1] Of the remaining two countries that had signed the declaration at the World Economic Conference, Italy and Poland had already turned to exchange controls, the former in 1934 and the latter in April 1936. Italy also devalued in October 1936 (Mitchener and Wandschneider 2015).

[2] "The Gold Bloc Falls," *The Economist*, October 3, 1936; "Effects of Devaluation," *The Economist*, October 3, 1936.

[3] "Democracies in Line," *The New York Times*, September 27, 1936.

[4] "France's Lead to Gold Bloc," *Financial Times*, September 28, 1936.

experience of the authorities of the three covenanting nations to preserve a genuine stability of the exchanges, a moving equilibrium between disparate national economies."[5]

Indeed, achieving this "genuine stability," as opposed to what many considered the artificial stability of the gold standard and the chaos of no-holds-barred floating, would not be simple. The exchange funds were to be the instruments for reaching this admittedly vague goal, working in coordination after years of isolation. The problem was that exchange managers felt unable to intervene given their currencies' mutual inconvertibility into gold. Officials had discussed this problem in the negotiations leading up to the accord, but nothing had been finalized by the time France devalued. It took two additional weeks for governments and central banks to hammer out arrangements.

The result: reciprocal gold facilities. Every day, Tripartite members set prices for gold in terms of their currencies. Britain, for instance, might fix one ounce of gold at £7. If the United States purchased £700,000 sterling in the market that day, it could then convert it into 100,000 ounces of gold. This gold option on the £700,000 sterling expired at day's end; the next morning Britain reset the gold price and the process restarted. In this way, the Americans could intervene in the sterling market without fear of valuation loss – they knew exactly how much gold they would get in return for any sterling purchased – and the British were not obliged to adopt a gold value for sterling for longer than a day. Reciprocity meant that London could intervene in the dollar market and convert the proceeds into gold, a welcome opportunity after three years of being unable to do so. The French likewise had such rights and obligations, and in November, Belgium, the Netherlands, and Switzerland set up similar facilities when they joined the Tripartite Agreement. Though not classical convertibility, under which the monetary authority provided gold in exchange for its currency no matter how or when it was obtained or by whom, this circumscribed twenty-four-hour convertibility cleverly balanced the desire for gold with the insistence on flexibility.

The new system of daily gold clearing had three principal benefits that served the parties well during the tumultuous years preceding the outbreak of the Second World War. First, the commitment to offer gold functioned as a token of good faith, a material expression by each party – to one another and the public – of its aim to collaborate. Gold convertibility was in this sense the price of membership in what became known as the

---

[5] "The Gold Bloc Falls," *The Economist*, October 3, 1936.

"currency club." Second, the system stitched together the members' differing monetary systems, preventing a further splintering of the world economy in the aftermath of France's devaluation. It did not matter that Britain had no official price of gold, that America had one that was subject to presidential alteration, or that France had a range of gold values within which it held the franc: All agreed to daily clearing. Finally, the very nature of the twenty-four-hour gold standard, requiring daily prices and offsetting gold transactions, meant that authorities were in touch constantly. Far from hiding their intervention amounts, they now shared them, putting an end to the suspicion that had long dogged exchange operations.

This chapter studies all of these developments, beginning with a description of public reactions to the Tripartite Agreement. It proceeds to the negotiations on convertibility and the accession of the three new members in November 1936. The chapter then focuses on the gold-clearing system, providing the first in-depth analysis. Most of the examination centers on Britain's experience, both qualitatively and quantitatively. The system squared the circle of how to enable countries to intervene in currencies that were not universally convertible into gold and played a crucial role in keeping members on the same page during a time of immense political and economic strain. It established a technical foundation for broader collaboration and, as later chapters document, was integral to the Tripartite Agreement's success in preventing policymakers from relapsing into the antagonisms of earlier years.

FIRST DAYS

Five paragraphs about future cooperation did little to assuage the humiliation many in France felt upon learning that the gold standard was defunct. Much of the immediate reaction ranged from disappointment to outright anger. One deputy castigated the government: "You have made of our franc an abstract and erratic currency, running after two wandering moneys."[6] Some observers were more hopeful. *L'Agence économique et financière*, for instance, quickly intuited international implications: "Great Britain and the United States have shown themselves ready to take their place beside us as friends—to gain an idea of the importance of this one has only to read the German Press," whose concern at the democracies working together manifested in condemnations of the Agreement.[7] And Premier Léon Blum made as much use of the Agreement as he could in

---

[6] Quoted in Mouré (1991, 267).
[7] "Franc Devaluation—News from Various Quarters II," September 29, 1936, BoE OV48/10.

selling devaluation to the public. But acceptance of the franc's new reality took time. It was only as the monetary regime became more familiar and as the Tripartite Agreement's role in fostering better relations with Britain and America became more evident that the public began to value the pact.

The response in the United States, on the other hand, was overwhelmingly positive. While some commentators complained that anything less than a return to the gold standard was a step backward or that the country was getting entangled with Europe once again, most celebrated the end of the monetary war.[8] *The Wall Street Journal* reported that the financial district considered the Tripartite Agreement "the most constructive development for world business and finance since the end of the World War."[9] The influential columnist Walter Lippmann, in a piece entitled "A Corner has been Turned," wrote that "the gentlemen's agreement reached on Friday must be accounted a great victory" and that it "is a sure foundation on which the nations can advance."[10] Even James Warburg, a former Roosevelt economic advisor-turned-outspoken critic, was so buoyed by the Agreement that he came back to the fold and publicly endorsed the president in his upcoming reelection bid.[11]

In Britain, Chamberlain deemed the Agreement to have received an "excellent reception."[12] Newspapers applauded the historic move, the *Financial Times* emphasizing the significance of the change in the US posture from the dreary days of the World Economic Conference.[13] *The Times* of London declared, "Nothing is of more importance to the economic welfare of the world at the moment than that the Three-Power Agreement to stabilize their currencies should succeed," pointing out that this stability would be one deriving from "skilful management" and would not have the "precision" of a return to the gold standard.[14] The press also celebrated the clause in the Agreement's fourth paragraph on the need to reduce trade restrictions and avoid exchange control.[15]

---

[8] "World Wonders When and If Gentlemen Break Agreements" and "Roosevelt Assailed for His Political Use of Crisis over France," *Chicago Daily Tribune*, September 27, 1936.

[9] "Wall Street Weighs Devaluation Effects on U.S. Markets," *The Wall Street Journal*, September 28, 1936.

[10] "Today and Tomorrow: A Corner has been Turned," *New York Herald Tribune*, September 29, 1936.

[11] "J. P. Warburg Goes Back to Roosevelt," *The New York Times*, October 18, 1936. Warburg also cited the Reciprocal Trade Act of 1934 as another motivation.

[12] Quoted in Drummond (1981, 219).

[13] "Devaluation by the Gold Bloc," *Financial Times*, September 28, 1936.

[14] "City Notes," *The Times* (London), September 28, 1936.

[15] "The Gold Bloc Falls," *The Economist*, October 3, 1936.

The rest of the world took note as well. Belgium expressed support at once, though it did not become a member until November 1936.[16] Representatives at the Bank for International Settlements (BIS), on the other hand, were less pleased, annoyed at having been left in the dark. Toniolo (2005, 181) writes that the "reception given to the agreement in Basel was understandably cool," with the president of the BIS stating curtly at the board meeting that the "facts must be accepted and discussion seemed idle." After all, the BIS would have little influence in a world where governments, not central banks, ran monetary relations, a transformation the Tripartite Agreement cemented.

Hjalmar Schacht, president of the Reichsbank, was among those at the monthly board meeting in Basel voicing disapproval. He explained that Germany had no intention of devaluing or joining the pact and would instead maintain its overvalued currency in conjunction with exchange controls.[17] Indeed, the British ambassador in Berlin reported home in a series of cables that the Agreement "came as a severe blow" to the Nazis. They interpreted the move as "an attempt to put political pressure" on the country, and the "fact that three democratic Governments have been able to spring a surprise on the world came as a most unpleasant surprise to them."[18]

Concerned that the Germans would attempt to sabotage the pact, Morgenthau was on the lookout for interference from Berlin. Moscow, however, seemed to attack first. On Saturday, September 26, with the Agreement only hours old, word reached the US Treasury that the Russian State Bank was selling £1 million against dollars in New York. Morgenthau was livid, seeing in the transaction a devious means to depress sterling, destabilize exchange rates, and "break down" the accord.[19] He used the Exchange Stabilization Fund (ESF) to support sterling and denounced the Soviet sale at a hastily arranged press conference.

In fact, the Russian transaction had nothing to do with the Tripartite Agreement. It was a standard operation, not even that large, to obtain

---

[16] "Text of Belgian Note to Hull," *The New York Times*, September 27, 1936.

[17] Schacht's statements around this time were muddled as he tried to balance economic instincts pushing toward devaluation with political dictates pulling in the opposite direction. He wanted to keep the line of communication open with the democracies. He had recently met with Blum in August and corresponded with Leith-Ross after the Agreement's announcement. But there was never any chance of Germany devaluing and removing exchange controls. See files in T 188/144.

[18] Phipps telegram, September 30, 1936 and October 1, 1936, T 188/144.

[19] Untitled note, September 26, 1936, MD 34/292.

dollars to pay off a debt maturing in Sweden. Ill-timed, perhaps, but nothing more than that. The blowback to Morgenthau's performance was swift. The Soviets condemned the accusation as an "absurd invention."[20] The *New York Herald Tribune*, no friend of the administration's, savored the moment, noting that the secretary's "capacity for making himself ridiculous is, of course, well known."[21] Chamberlain piled on, writing to his sister that Morgenthau had "made an ass of himself."[22] Morgenthau, likely exhausted from the week's negotiations, had acted rashly. He ignored advice from many aides to stand down. But in the process of embarrassing himself, he also demonstrated just how devoted he was to the Agreement, which, he proclaimed, would be "the turning point for general peace in the world."[23] He was determined to make it work, to prove that the big democratic nations could cooperate. He was all in.

The British government, by contrast, was more skeptical, pleased with smoothing the path for the French devaluation but unsure where developments would lead. Chamberlain sent a kind message to Morgenthau on September 28, expressing satisfaction with the Agreement and hoping it would lead to "a better understanding and more friendly relations between the nations of the world."[24] The two countries set up regular meetings between treasuries and embassies in October, helping to formalize the call for greater consultation.[25] And the British believed that there was space for additional cooperation, including gold convertibility. Even so, they did not want anybody to think that the fundamentals of their cheap money policy had changed or to get caught up in fantasies of international coordination

---

[20] Steil (2013, 37) and Blum (1959, 175–76) find the Soviet move suspicious. However, as early as June 16, the Soviet press had publicized that the government would pay off a $6 million loan to Sweden. "Soviet Dollar Deal Decided 3 Months Ago," *The Daily Telegraph*, September 29, 1936; "Soviet Explains Dollar Deal," *The Daily Telegraph*, September 29, 1936; Bluett, "Soviet Payment to the Swedish General Electric Company," October 3, 1936, T 160/840/7; Henderson telegram to Hull, September 28, 1936, MD 35/76.

[21] "A Cheap Political Trick," *New York Herald Tribune*, September 29, 1936. The newspaper suggested that the announcement was a stunt to burnish the administration's anti-communist credentials ahead of the election. While Morgenthau actually considered the Russian transaction malicious, politics were not entirely absent from his calculations. As he told Roosevelt when explaining his actions, "That answers Hearst," in reference to attacks by the Hearst press claiming the administration was soft on the Soviets. Dictation, September 26, 1936, MD 34/294.

[22] Neville to Ida Chamberlain, September 28, 1936, in Chamberlain (2005, 209).

[23] "Text of Secretary's Remarks for Paramount and Fox Movietone Newsreels," September 29, 1936, MD 36/23.

[24] Telegram to Mallet, September 28, 1936, T 160/840/6.

[25] Bingham to Chamberlain, October 16, 1936, BoE C43/327.

that were divorced from reality. There were no press conferences à la Morgenthau. Chamberlain's Mansion House address in early October celebrated the Agreement as "this most essential step forward . . . creat[ing] fresh hopes of further advance in international cooperation" but stayed away from grand pronouncements.[26]

This strategy reflected the inclinations of the civil service. Treasury officials, wary of future disappointment, did not want expectations to run out of control. Sir Frederick Leith-Ross complained to Sigi Waley that everyone "seems to think that we are all in sight of the millennium," and Waley found it amusing that the Tripartite Agreement was "welcomed as securing all the benefits of stabilisation and co-operation and all the benefits of independence simultaneously."[27] Upon hearing that Czechoslovakia was interested in joining the pact, Leith-Ross despaired: "We can scarcely explain to them that the high-sounding terms of the Declaration were simply put in to help the French Government with their internal political troubles and mean nothing."[28] These dismissive comments should not be overemphasized. Whitehall was not disappointed with the Agreement or angry at having participated; it simply did not yet expect much benefit beyond having prevented France's devaluation from setting off a further round of competitive depreciations. It also worried that if countries like Czechoslovakia joined, they would bring little to the table and end up using membership as a pretext for requesting funds. In short, the risk-averse British thought it best to proceed slowly.

There were two main avenues on which Tripartite members could move forward: reducing trade restrictions and cooperating on monetary policy. Despite several attempts, there was little success on trade liberalization. France unilaterally reduced its tariffs and quotas after devaluation to get the process started. Some in Whitehall, encouraged by this gesture, were open to reducing trade barriers, but the policy decided upon was that the British had "already made our contribution to general recovery in undertaking to refrain from monetary or commercial retaliation" to France's devaluation; the onus remained with France to make a greater effort.[29] The moment soon fizzled with no multilateral agreement. Another initiative in 1938 also failed.[30] To be sure, there were some bilateral achievements during these years, such as the Anglo-American trade agreement in 1938.

[26] "The Return of Prosperity," *The Times* (London), October 7, 1936.
[27] Waley to Rowe-Dutton, October 9, 1936, T 160/685.
[28] Leith-Ross, Untitled memo, September 29, 1936, T 177/31.
[29] Chancellor telegram, October 6, 1936, T 177/33.   [30] See Chapter 8.

But, on the whole, dreams of a united effort to unshackle trade were disappointed. Fortunately, there would be much more success in the monetary realm, which was, after all, the Agreement's primary focus.

"A NEW TYPE OF GOLD STANDARD"

The Tripartite Agreement called for cooperation, particularly between exchange funds. As *The Times* of London remarked, such inter-fund cooperation would be an "entirely new experiment."[31] For the experiment to have any chance of success, policymakers first needed to figure out how to facilitate intervention. The lack of convertibility made sustained intervention too risky; currencies needed to be convertible if funds were to operate on a regular basis. The question was, which currencies and under what rules? America's policy of converting dollars into gold for central banks on the gold standard remained intact, but it became effectively meaningless with the collapse of the gold bloc, since the only country that still qualified was Belgium, which had returned to a fixed gold price. With France's devaluation, then, none of the members could get gold from each other.

The solution, reached in three nearly identical sets of arrangements, was reciprocal convertibility. Britain and France came to an agreement quickly, as there had already been a fair amount of discussion on the subject in the days preceding France's devaluation.[32] On Sunday, September 27, Cameron Cobbold of the Bank of England (BoE) met with counterparts at the Banque de France (BdF) in Paris to hammer out details. He made it clear that the British "could only work on the basis of day-to-day co-operation." His counterpart, deputy governor Pierre Fournier, was of like mind and wrote down, in Sayers' (1976, 480) words, "a phrase that passed into the mystique of international economic relations": "ni accord, ni entente, uniquement co-opération journalière" (neither accord nor under-standing, simply day-to-day cooperation). That is, things should remain informal and operate on professional trust rather than codified rules.

This creed animated Cobbold and Fournier's arrangement on gold reciprocity. Under their plan, every morning, each central bank, acting on behalf of its exchange fund, would quote the other the price of gold in terms of its currency for the day. Any sterling purchased by the BdF could be turned into gold at the British price; any francs purchased by the BoE

---

[31] "City Notes," *The Times* (London), September 28, 1936.
[32] Cobbold, Untitled memo, September 17, 1936, BoE C43/343.

could be turned into gold at the French price. Importantly, convertibility was good only for that day: Cobbold's notes recorded that "any right to obtain gold for the currency remaining unconverted will expire" at day's end.[33] The terms agreeable to both sides, operations under the arrangement began on October 2 when the exchange market for francs reopened and Paris started holding the franc at 105 per pound, the midpoint of the range implied by the devaluation limits.[34]

All the while, France had been asking America about setting up facilities so that it could once again convert dollars into gold, since it no longer qualified under the gold standard clause.[35] Morgenthau recognized the need for altering the rules and had already set the wheels in motion.[36] Most officials in Washington took for granted that any US gesture would need to be reciprocated, but not everyone agreed. H. Merle Cochran, the financial attaché in Paris, suggested to the secretary that the United States unilaterally permit convertibility to all monetary authorities, without requiring reciprocity or limiting its terms to daily operations: America had more than enough gold, and such a policy would help "to really make an international currency of the dollar."[37] Cochran, however, was ahead of his time. Universal convertibility of the dollar for official holders would eventually become the foundation of the Bretton Woods era, but, for the moment, Morgenthau insisted on reciprocity and flexibility.

On October 5, Morgenthau was ready to move forward with France and brought in Britain, as he did not want to make a "side agreement" that left one party out.[38] Negotiations proceeded between Washington and Paris and Washington and London, with all parties kept up-to-date on the progress of the talks but no joint meetings taking place. Though the aim was to make the multilateral system coherent, so that every member could obtain gold from any member, these agreements were technically bilateral. Cochran served as the conduit between Morgenthau and French Minister of Finance Vincent Auriol. The British embassy in Washington relayed

---

[33] Cobbold, "Note of Conversations at Bank of France," September 28, 1936, BoE OV48/10.

[34] For a summary of the French exchange fund and applicable laws, see "Historique du Fonds de Stabilisation des Changes," undated, BdF 1201201101/1.

[35] Cochran telegram to Morgenthau, September 23, 1936, MD 33/52J-K.

[36] Before the Tripartite Agreement's announcement, Morgenthau had his staff draft paperwork authorizing reciprocity for France and Britain. He was surprised that the British did not press the issue immediately. "Confidential Draft of Possible Statement by the Secretary of the Treasury," September 23, 1936, MD 33/100; Treasury meeting, September 25, 1936, MD 34/49.

[37] Cochran telegram, October 6, 1936, MD 38/3.

[38] Treasury meeting, October 5, 1936, MD 37/238.

messages between Morgenthau and Chamberlain. Upon hearing the details of Morgenthau's offer of reciprocity, London, far from dragging its feet as it had in the earlier negotiations, was enthusiastic. "We can but welcome the American offer to give us gold for dollars," the BoE's Harry Siepmann minuted, "and we cannot fail to reciprocate."[39] There was little trouble working out the technicalities, which followed the Anglo-French understanding on daily prices and convertibility. The dollar price, as with the sterling and franc prices, was liable to change on a day's notice, but the expectation was that it would not. Thirty-five dollars per ounce would become, the US Treasury believed, the "pivot" of the system.[40]

The only thing left was the announcement. Morgenthau wanted to advertise the new agreements. London was hesitant, at first wary of publicizing technical arrangements, but realized there was no harm in doing so. It worked with Paris to craft nearly identical messages from their end, and the governments released the statements on October 12 to be published the following day.[41] The US proclamation was a formal alteration of its regulations, whereby the earlier rules permitting the sale of gold once the exchange rate had reached gold export point were supplemented to include the sale of gold to exchange funds "of those countries whose funds likewise are offering to sell gold to the United States." Britain and France were the only two countries meeting this qualification, and a separate statement named them in compliance. The British press release contained no regulatory changes but explained that the "day-to-day working arrangement [with America] should greatly facilitate the technical operations of exchange control" (somewhat confusingly, the British at times referred to exchange management as "exchange control;" in this context, the term signified intervention, not regulation.) "Similar arrangements have been made with the Bank of France so as to provide for effective co-operation between the three centres." The French statement added that the "chief problem" that had barred "effectual co-operation" – the inconvertibility of currencies stemming "from the very nature of the monetary régimes" – "has been happily solved."[42]

Morgenthau, as usual, held a press conference. "The level of foreign exchange, as between the United States, Great Britain and France," he

---

[39] Siepmann, Untitled memo, October 6, 1936, BoE C43/327.
[40] Treasury meeting, October 5, 1936, MD 37/212.
[41] Hopkins to Woods, October 7, 1936, T 160/585; Waley to Leith-Ross and Hopkins, October 10, 1936, T 160/585.
[42] Bank for International Settlements (1937).

stated, "may be though[t] of as a triangular plane. Each corner rests on the foundation of a stabilization fund.... No country wishes, through these operations, to accumulate too much paper currency of the other countries, and, therefore, we propose to permit each country to convert the other countries' paper money into gold, the price being fixed each day." The arrangement was nothing less than "a new type of gold standard."[43] The press cheered this demonstration of cooperation, with *The Economist* hopeful that "the new arrangement might well develop into that satisfactory working compromise between rigidity and chaos for which the need has been felt ever since it became obvious that the old gold standard could never be restored."[44]

It is worth pausing to consider why, after years of refusing to tie the pound to gold in any manner, the British were suddenly so willing to sell gold. The reason, the Treasury's Waley explained, was that there was "no harm & great advantage in a reciprocal arrangement."[45] There was "no harm" because the price of gold was good for twenty-four hours only: Britain retained full freedom of maneuver day-to-day. In addition, Britain was no longer gold-poor. In fact, it was gold-rich and perhaps even gold congested. Gold in the Exchange Equalisation Account (EEA) grew from £29 million at the end of 1932 to £150 million in 1935 and £237 million in the days after the Tripartite Agreement; gold in the Issue Department rose from £120 million to £249 million during that time.[46] Losing moderate amounts of gold was no longer worrisome. Moreover, there was "great advantage" because reciprocity was the only way to get convertibility rights for dollars and francs, which London considered the *sine qua non* for effective exchange management. There was thus no debate in Whitehall or Threadneedle Street about whether or not to proceed: all were in favor.

Right after the reciprocity announcements, the central banks of Belgium and Switzerland contacted the Federal Reserve Bank of New York (FRBNY) to discuss gold policy. The Belgians, still on a modified gold standard, wanted to know if they continued to have access to US gold under the 1934 regulations; Switzerland hoped to gain access under the same terms as Britain and France. Morgenthau informed London and Paris of these messages, and the three governments thought it useful to

---

[43] Press conference, October 12, 1936, MD 39/28–40.
[44] "Financial Notes," *The Economist*, October 17, 1936.
[45] Waley, Untitled memo, undated, T 160/840/5.
[46] EEA gold valued at cost; Issue Department gold valued at the statutory parity.

bring Belgium and Switzerland into the group. To be sure, the original members had no intention of conferring equal status to the new adherents.[47] The vast differences in economic power made equality impossible: The Big Three would chart the course. Nevertheless, they agreed that the smaller countries would benefit from inclusion in the club and the club would benefit from expansion, a further demonstration that the democracies had turned the page on the past.[48]

Morgenthau instructed Cochran to visit Belgium and Switzerland to work out the details; Britain and France engaged in bilateral discussions with these countries as well. There were some stumbling blocks. Morgenthau now wanted all gold transactions to go through exchange funds and planned to cancel the 1934 regulations that permitted the export of gold by arbitrageurs once the dollar reached gold export point. Belgium did not have an exchange fund and wanted its central bank to enter into the arrangement.[49] Morgenthau insisted that governments be the principals and central banks the agents. Much back-and-forth ensued. Sir Frederick Phillips thought Morgenthau's "dislike for Central Banks is becoming almost a mania" and could not understand the emphasis on what seemed so minor a point.[50] A muddled solution whereby the Belgian government provided a secret guarantee to the US Treasury for the central bank's transactions patched things over.[51]

The Dutch soon joined the negotiations, and on November 24, 1936, the world awoke to yet another series of coordinated statements. Switzerland and the Netherlands "adher[ed] to the general principles" of the Tripartite Agreement, Belgium having already done so back in September.

---

[47] As Morgenthau told the British, he did not think that the new countries would be "members of this tri-partite agreement. I want to call them junior partners, but Lochhead does not like this." To which the British representative replied, "Satellites." "Yes, satellites," Morgenthau responded, "they revolve around us." In the end, there was no formal distinction in membership, but the original three led the group. Morgenthau conversation with Bewley and Mallet, October 21, 1936, MD 41/58.

[48] Siepmann considered the "extension of the membership ... technically almost meaningless" since, from Britain's perspective, the dollar and the franc were by far the most important currencies. Nevertheless, the expansion "was helpful because it confirmed this impression of a new leaf turned over, with more to follow." Siepmann, "The Tripartite Agreement," September 3, 1937, BoE G1/304.

[49] Belgium had created an exchange fund after leaving the gold standard in 1935 but got rid of it upon returning to gold in 1936. "Devaluation of the Belga," *Financial Times*, April 2, 1936.

[50] Phillips to Hopkins, October 27, 1936, BoE C43/327.

[51] de Man to Morgenthau, November 9, 1936, MD 44/195. For a summary of all of these developments, see Cochran to Morgenthau, December 28, 1936, MD 43/part II.

Washington amended its gold regulations, striking the language on the gold export point and expanding the reciprocity clause so that Belgium satisfied the criteria. Britain and France welcomed the new members and celebrated the extension of technical facilities.[52] In the days after the club's expansion, *The Economist* concluded that "the world is now passing under a form of quasi-gold standard, the key to which lies in semi-rigid gold parities maintained by official international transfers of gold."[53] Six countries did not constitute the world, but the new system certainly defined the democratic world's approach, one that revolved around gold.

GIVE GOLD, GET GOLD

In late October 1936, Harry Siepmann tried to make sense of all that had happened in the past month. He believed it essential, he wrote to the FRBNY's Allan Sproul, that "we should convince the world that a decisive corner has been turned." No doubt, doing so involved "a certain amount of bally-hoo." But he thought the new system, where exchange funds now "agree[d] to clear with one another in gold and, with that reassurance behind them, to supply the exchange markets with any currency," might just work. Perhaps, he hoped, its success could lead to "monetary problems as a whole ... sinking into the background."[54] After five years of currency turmoil dominating the headlines, calm would be a triumph in itself.

Exchange markets did settle down. The volatility of the pound's exchange rate against all of the club currencies – save for the franc – more than halved in the years after the Tripartite Agreement as shown in Table 6.1 (see also Figure I.1). But unfortunately for Siepmann, monetary issues did not recede from the front pages. In the years after the Agreement, financial turbulence did not suddenly vanish, nor did the adherents agree on all things at all times. As later chapters document, old problems – foremost the weakness of the franc – recurred, and new problems – the apparent oversupply of gold and the descent into war – emerged. But the tone and substance of policymakers' responses changed. The default was no longer how to maximize leverage against other countries; it was how to minimize disturbances to the system. The Tripartite Agreement provided a foundation upon which countries could work together to mitigate these problems.

---

[52] Bank for International Settlements (1937).
[53] "Financial Notes," *The Economist*, November 28, 1936.
[54] Siepmann to Sproul, October 27, 1936, BoE C43/343.

Table 6.1 *Exchange rate volatility before and after the Tripartite Agreement (average weekly change, percent)*

	Before (percent)	After (percent)
Dollar	2.2	0.5
Franc	1.3	1.9
Swiss franc	1.4	0.4
Belga	1.9	0.5
Guilder	1.3	0.5
Group	1.6	0.7

Note: The "Before" period refers to January 1932 to August 1936; the "After" period refers to October 1936 to June 1939.
Source: Eichengreen (1992, table 12.6)

And the system of gold clearing – the prose complementing the poetry of September 26 – provided the technical means for doing so. Yet, despite its centrality, there has been no comprehensive study of the mechanics of gold clearing.[55] How were prices determined? Did members make use of the facilities? What types of intervention did they undertake? Did they convert their holdings every day? How often did gold move between central banks? How much flexibility was there? Reviewing operations in general and digging into Britain's experience in particular sheds light on these questions.

In setting up a system of gold clearing, the first issue to solve was the price for gold. The answer was simple for Belgium and the United States as they both had gold parities. The other members had to be more creative; indeed, given the bilateral nature of the agreements, they needed methodologies that made sense for each partner. For example, Britain and France both based their prices for each other on their exchange rates with the dollar. With the US gold price $35 per ounce, if the sterling-dollar rate was $5, the BoE would purchase gold from or sell gold to the BdF in London at £7 per ounce (minus shipping costs to Paris). If there was substantial movement in exchange rates during the day, the two central banks would get in touch again – communication was simplified by a new direct line from the BoE to BdF – and alter the prices for transactions moving forward, maintaining the previous price for transactions already consummated.[56]

[55] See Oye (1985) for a discussion of the facilities from a political science perspective.
[56] Siepmann to Phillips, September 30, 1936, BoE C43/343; Cobbold, "Note of Conversations at Bank of France," September 28, 1936, BoE OV48/10; "Terms of day-

The Anglo-American arrangement operated differently. The US Treasury had a single policy on gold transactions with all club members: It sold gold in New York at $35 plus 0.25 percent handling charges ($35.09) and bought gold in New York at $35 minus 0.25 percent ($34.91). Barring announcement of a change, these prices were to remain in force indefinitely. As for the sterling price, the small overlap in market hours between New York and London and the relatively high cost of communication between the two meant that, unlike in the Anglo-French arrangement, one price per day would have to do. Rather than basing this price directly on the sterling-dollar rate, the British used the price at the gold fixing, a daily ritual in London that provided a benchmark price for gold. Doing so made sense given that the fixing provided exactly what was needed: a sterling price for gold. It also served to reinforce London's importance in international finance.[57]

Notwithstanding these nuances – and those in the dealings with other club members – the essence of the arrangements was simple: Each country would provide gold in exchange for its currency (eliminating the risk of intervention purchases) and provide its currency in exchange for gold (facilitating intervention sales) at prices quoted each day.[58] The prices at which these transactions occurred, save for those that were official parities, were not shared with the public.

Figure 6.1 illustrates the mechanism of gold clearing, depicting the relationship between intervention and conversion for the BoE (on behalf of the EEA) and FRBNY (on behalf of the ESF). As Figure 6.1a shows, the FRBNY gold facility allowed the BoE to convert any purchases of dollars from the market into gold. On the other hand, BoE sales of dollars to the market were financed through sales of gold to the FRBNY, as depicted in Figure 6.1b.

---

to-day working arrangements with Central Banks," November 2, 1936, BoE C43/343; Smeeton, "Tripartite Currency Agreement," November 21, 1973, BoE C43/463. The more frequently the price changed, the less the gold facilities acted as a stabilizing force and the more they mimicked market forces.

[57] The BoE did not impose a spread at first, but in the spring of 1937, it instituted a spread of 2 pence on either side of the fixing price, equating to a total spread of around 0.25 percent when gold was £7 per ounce (half the US spread). Bolton, "U.S. Exchange Fund Operations," March 11, 1937, BoE C43/327; Siepmann, Untitled memo, March 11, 1937, BoE C43/327; Knoke conversation with Bolton, March 16, 1937, FRBNY C261; "Daily Gold Price Given to the Federal Reserve Bank of New York," December 29, 1938, BoE C43/314.

[58] For a description of the various arrangements, see "Terms of day-to-day working arrangements between Central Banks," October 28, 1936, BoE C43/343.

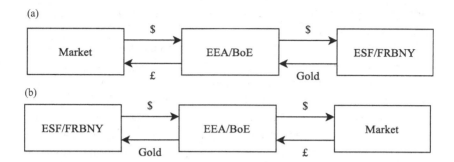

Figure 6.1 Reciprocal gold facilities.
(a) BoE converting dollars purchased in the market into gold at FRBNY.
(b) BoE obtaining dollars from FRBNY to sell in the market.

Importantly, the selling price for gold was valid only for exchange transactions undertaken that day: Foreign exchange balances amassed in the past did not automatically have the right of conversion at that, or any, price. Policymakers likely agreed to this convention to minimize the accumulation of large gold claims on one another, which, as the early years of the decade had revealed, could become a source of instability. Since members did not want to hold foreign exchange anyway, they almost always converted within the day so that the restriction was usually not binding. To streamline the process, central banks created new accounts that segregated intervention transactions on behalf of exchange funds from other transactions that would not be eligible for conversion.[59]

Most of this intervention was in the spot market, as exchange managers tended to view forward operations with suspicion. The BoE's "traditional view," Sayers (1976, 2:420) explains, "was that forward markets were dominated by speculators and were therefore anathema." Prior to the Tripartite Agreement, the EEA had ventured into forward markets on occasion, such as the forward sales of francs to avoid the two-day usance risk described in Chapter 5. But the aim was to protect the EEA and not to influence forward rates. During the Tripartite years, the preference for spot intervention continued, notwithstanding some notable exceptions, such as

[59] For instance, the BoE created two new accounts for the FRBNY: a sterling account No. 3 and a gold account B. The FRBNY created two new accounts for the BoE: a dollar account G and a gold account No. 3. These accounts were to be used "exclusively for the purpose of clearing any exchange control operations." Knoke telegram to Bolton, October 10, 1936, FRBNY C261; Peppiatt telegram to Knoke, October 14, 1936, FRBNY C261.

Britain's large sales of forward dollars during the Munich crisis in 1938 (discussed in Chapter 9).

Each day, then, the countries set prices for gold at which they were willing to deal and then intervened in exchange markets. At the end of the day, the question of convertibility came up. Unsurprisingly – since they had all negotiated for this right – they almost always exercised their option to obtain gold.[60] While extant data do not permit tracing precisely what percent of exchange intervention was converted into gold each day, they reveal that exchange holdings constituted a very small fraction of reserves, consistent with gold clearing.[61] As Figure 3.4 shows, the EEA was for all intents and purposes a gold fund. By 1937, foreign exchange accounted for less than 1 percent of the EEA's reserve assets by value. The FRBNY's Arthur Bloomfield, in a 1943 report, summarized the practice on conversion: "Currencies acquired by each fund in the course of its daily operations were invariably liquidated within the specified twenty-four-hour period by conversion into gold, unless, of course, pressure on the foreign exchange rates reversed itself within this period, in which case the various funds would simply take the opportunity of instead selling these balances in exchange for their respective domestic currencies."[62] Foreign exchange balances were thus low, so when managers wanted to sell foreign exchange to the market in order to strengthen their currencies, they usually obtained it by selling gold to the respective central bank.

Gold transactions between club members, reflecting the conversion of exchange intervention, skyrocketed after the implementation of the new system – both in magnitude and frequency. Using data from the EEA's gold ledgers, Table 6.2 depicts the average transaction size and the percentage of market days during which there was a transaction between

[60] There were exceptions. For example, the large spread in US gold prices sometimes led exchange managers to hold onto dollars if they expected to sell them shortly. Indeed, the US spread was a sore point throughout these years as it complicated dealings in what was becoming the world's most important currency. One result was the aforementioned hesitancy, at times, to convert. The other was that exchange funds often cleared their dollar transactions through London rather than New York. "A tariff wall is put round American gold," Siepmann explained, "and a strong inducement is given to all controls to clear their position, when they are long of dollars, anywhere but in the clearing provided for under the new arrangements." Siepmann, "T. K. B.'s letter of the 12th October," October 24, 1936, BoE C43/327; Knoke conversation with Cariguel, December 31, 1936, FRBNY C261.

[61] The Swiss in 1937 temporarily bucked this pattern, as explained in Chapter 7.

[62] Bloomfield, "The Tripartite Agreement of 1936 as an Alternative to the Keynes and White Plans," May 8, 1943, FRBNY FF4608.

Table 6.2 *BoE gold transactions with Tripartite central banks*

	Period 1	Period 2	Period 3
	Before Tripartite	After Tripartite	After Tripartite
	1/1/36– 9/25/36	1/1/37– 9/25/37	11/24/36– 12/31/38
United States			
Transaction frequency (percent of market days)	3%	26%	29%
Average transaction size (thousand £)	227	760	1,180
France			
Transaction frequency (percent of market days)	37%	70%	67%
Average transaction size (thousand £)	1,675	1,203	1,478
Switzerland			
Transaction frequency (percent of market days)	6%	13%	20%
Average transaction size (thousand £)	134	464	365
Belgium			
Transaction frequency (percent of market days)	0%	13%	30%
Average transaction size (thousand £)	N/A	149	263
The Netherlands			
Transaction frequency (percent of market days)	11%	40%	43%
Average transaction size (thousand £)	168	315	448

Note: Transaction frequency refers to the percent of market days when the BoE transacted in gold with the listed central bank.
Source: BoE 2A197/2 and C139/1 and author's calculations

Britain and other countries before and after the Tripartite Agreement. The pre-Tripartite era, Period 1, is from January 1, 1936 to September 25, 1936. There are two post-Tripartite periods. Period 2, from January 1, 1937 to September 25, 1937, looks at the corresponding months the following year. Period 3, from November 24, 1936 to December 31, 1938, considers a longer time frame and begins once all reciprocal facilities were in effect. Britain and America had almost no dealings before the Agreement, with transactions occurring on only 3 percent of market days; after the Agreement, the frequency was an order of magnitude higher at almost 30 percent. The average size of these transactions was

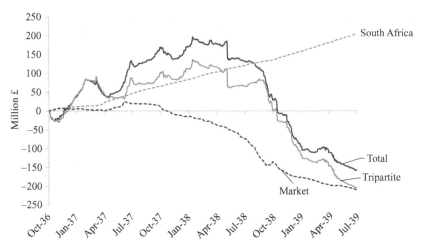

Figure 6.2 EEA cumulative gold gains, 1936–1939 (million £, at cost).
Note: Chart depicts cumulative gold gains, defined as net gold purchased from source since October 1, 1936.
Source: BoE 2A197/2 and C139/1 and author's calculations

also much higher. The frequency of dealings with other members increased substantially as well, nearly doubling for France and almost quadrupling for the Netherlands.[63]

For Britain, these club transactions accounted for the bulk of the changes in the EEA's reserves, as shown in Figure 6.2. The EEA bought gold from South Africa but sold most of it to the market, leaving Tripartite gold flows as the most important on a net basis. And as Figure 6.3 illustrates, France and America were the two most important club counterparties, with London gaining the most gold from Paris and losing the most gold to New York. Gains of French gold began in November 1936, and they continued, albeit with the occasional reversal, through November 1938. Losses of gold to the United States also began soon after the Tripartite Agreement, but they did not become serious until the summer of 1938 and the Munich crisis. In addition, the British sold a large amount of gold to the Netherlands, while gold flows with Belgium and Switzerland were relatively muted.

Gold dealings with France were the most significant but it is important to note that the British usually did not instigate them. The French largely

---

[63] This increase is not necessarily wholly attributable to the Tripartite Agreement; had the countries not come to an understanding in 1936, dealings could perhaps have risen as the international monetary situation evolved.

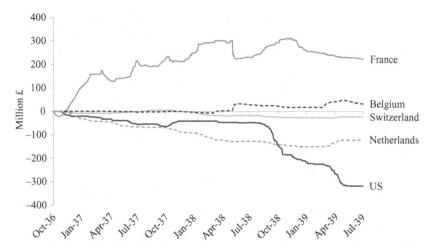

Figure 6.3 EEA cumulative gold gains with Tripartite members, 1936–1939 (million £, at cost).
Note: Chart depicts cumulative gold gains, defined as net gold purchased from source since October 1, 1936.
Source: BoE 2A197/2 and C139/1 and author's calculations

took control of the sterling-franc rate, holding it at various sterling pegs throughout these years. With the franc often weak, Paris sold sterling to support the franc; London provided that sterling in exchange for gold. This practice was in contrast to the pre-Tripartite years, when London operated in the franc market and then cleared in gold in Paris. In fact, whereas 80 percent of transactions between the two central banks prior to the Tripartite Agreement had been on a franc basis – reflecting British initiative in the market – 90 percent of transactions after the Agreement were on a sterling basis – reflecting French initiative.[64] That the British only rarely transacted in francs after the Agreement did not mean they were not cooperating. Their willingness to sell sterling in exchange for gold demonstrated their commitment to the pact, especially when gold inflows became excessive during the Gold Scare (as discussed in Chapter 7). Moreover, London now intervened heavily in the dollar market, a stark change from earlier years when it had effectively refused to operate in the currency.

[64] In the weeks leading up to the Tripartite Agreement, London insisted that "we could not agree to allowing the French authorities a larger say in the sterling/franc rate than we had ourselves," but in the end it acquiesced to Paris pegging to sterling. Cobbold, "Note of Conversations at Bank of France," September 28, 1936, BoE OV48/10.

The purpose of intervention under the Tripartite Agreement was, according to the BoE, "not a rate but wide and orderly markets," so that there was "day to day stability" and the possibility of "long range fluctuation."[65] That is, minimize short-term volatility but allow for some movement in rates over the longer term in response to persistent market forces. These objectives were not fully held by all members. France, in particular, tended to favor fixed rates. But most policymakers understood that exchange rates might have to change significantly when domestic trade-offs became untenable. This recognition foreshadowed the adjustments for "fundamental disequilibria" in the Bretton Woods era.[66]

Studying intervention patterns suggests that exchange managers did, indeed, aim to reduce fluctuations during the Tripartite years. As the analysis in Appendix A shows, Britain's daily purchases and sales of foreign exchange pushed against market forces: When the exchange rate was weakening, London sold reserves; when it was strengthening, London purchased reserves. The baseline regression suggests that a 1 percent depreciation of the pound against the dollar resulted in the EEA selling roughly £1.5 million of dollars into the market. The United States similarly acted in a manner consistent with leaning against the wind, though in a less intense fashion: A 1 percent depreciation of the dollar against the pound resulted in the ESF selling roughly £150,000. The United States was less aggressive because it continued to buy and sell gold at a fixed price and thus did not employ the ESF as regularly as Britain used the EEA. Comparable analysis of French intervention is more difficult given the strict peg they attempted to hold for long stretches, but the sheer loss of reserves is proof enough that Paris was not pushing the franc down. The countries were now working toward more stable rates. Whatever competitive intent existed in the first half of the decade was not apparent in the second half.

All of these gold transactions did not lead to flotillas of steamers traversing the waters, transferring gold between members every day. Central banks took advantage of earmarking to facilitate the process. As a general rule, country A's intervention in currency B resulted in gold movements in country B. When the British purchased dollars in the market and converted them into gold, the United States added gold to the BoE's account at the FRBNY; when the British needed dollars to sell in the market, the United States took gold from the BoE's account at the FRBNY. As always, there were exceptions. For instance, the BoE continued

---

[65] "The Agreements," December 15, 1936, BoE C43/327.
[66] Cesarano (2003) explores the historical meaning of "fundamental disequilibrium."

to receive orders from the FRBNY allowing the former to sell gold to the latter in London in return for dollars, so that the British had the privileged ability to obtain dollars against gold either in New York or London (up to a limit).[67] But the "simple principle," as Siepmann put it, was that action in a currency should generally move gold in the issuing country.[68]

While earmarking facilitated the system's operations, holdings of gold abroad could be undesirable. Gold was a physical asset, and its value depended on its location. Sometimes officials became queasy at having too much gold in other countries. The main fear was that war would break out in Europe and trap earmarked holdings, making it impossible to ship them home or even use them overseas. Morgenthau expressed this concern as early as December 1936, fretting to his staff, "I don't like all the gold we got in England. . . . It makes me nervous. They might have an air raid over there any time and I think I'm subject to criticism."[69] For this reason, the United States repatriated some of its overseas gold from time to time. British policymakers had similar reservations about accumulating too much gold in Paris and imposed limits on how much was safe to hold there. As war seemed ever likelier, London began a concerted effort to transfer much of its gold out of the continent to safer spots in the Empire.[70] These shipments did not alter the system's essence, but they did reduce its elasticity. When Washington wanted to lower its gold holdings in London, for instance, it could become less willing to purchase sterling in the market until it had shipped some gold back home. The more the parties required gold to move locations, the more friction.

Because gold clearing was done daily, support of another country's currency did not extend beyond the day. There was no buying and holding. Any support offered to a member's currency resulted in a decrease in that member's gold holdings at the end of the day. In Bloomfield's words, there was no "genuine mutual support of currencies."[71] Policymakers were not

---

[67] London was, however, hesitant to rely too much on this facility. As Siepmann cautioned, "it must never be regarded as our chief resource for the defence of sterling because it is only a facility granted to us at will by the F[ederal].R[eserve].B[ank]., whereas we have the right to create dollars, without asking permission, by delivering gold in New York." Siepmann, "Limits to the Defence of Sterling on the Dollar," March 21, 1938, BoE C43/327.

[68] Siepmann, Untitled memo, October 7, 1936, BoE C43/327.

[69] Treasury meeting, December 7, 1936, MD 47/247.

[70] "Gold Held Abroad," February 27, 1939, BoE C43/26.

[71] Bloomfield, "The Tripartite Agreement of 1936 as an Alternative to the Keynes and White Plans," May 8, 1943, FRBNY FF4608.

oblivious to this shortcoming: At times they considered holding currencies for longer periods to aid a member in need. But the memories of losses on exchange holdings from the decade's early years in conjunction with perceived political limits meant that they never took the leap.

Perhaps the best summary of the principles underlying these arrangements comes from a BoE note given to the National Bank of Belgium during negotiations in October 1936. The memo succinctly explained the purpose and operations of the prospective reciprocal facilities:

1. Bilateral.
2. Tacit.
3. Day-to-day.
4. To be applied in practice as may be agreed, according to circumstances.
5. Positions resulting from exchange intervention to be cleared in terms of gold delivery two days ahead.
6. Bank of England's operations move gold in Brussels, National Bank's operations move gold in London.
7. National Bank's statutory prices apply to any dealings in belgas for account of the EEA.
8. Belgian intervention in sterling is cleared at the Bank of England through a special account, at prices to be agreed as required, on the basis of the exchange rates.
9. Paris gold may be used to clear whenever mutually agreed.[72]

Point 1 noted that the clearing arrangement was bilateral. Points 2 through 4 stressed that everything was informal. Point 5 expressed the principle that all exchange intervention proceeds should be cleared in gold. Point 6 stated that when the British purchased belgas, they would obtain gold in Brussels; when the Belgians purchased sterling, they would obtain gold in London. The central banks could agree to modify where the gold moved, however, as suggested by point 9. Finally, points 7 and 8 reflected the fact that there were different ways to set the gold price depending on each currency's relation to gold.

To make this system operational, communication was essential, and it reached unprecedented levels, especially between Britain and the United States. Just two weeks before the French devaluation in September 1936, as catastrophe loomed, the FRBNY had called the BoE "merely to keep in touch ... inasmuch as we hadn't had a direct conversation for some time."[73] After the Tripartite Agreement, phone calls were often daily, cables at least that frequently.[74] While the BoE and BdF had already begun communicating more in the pre-Tripartite years, the fundamental disconnect between their monetary policies during that bleak time had reduced the cooperation purely to upholding the status quo. But, Sayers (1976, 2:464) writes, "when at last, in 1936, 'the three great democracies' were ready to make an open step forward, the accumulated experience of day-to-day cooperation between the central bankers of Paris and London ensured that there should be substance behind the fine words of the governments."

Daily contact went through central bank exchange managers: George Bolton of the BoE, L. Werner Knoke of the FRBNY, and Charles Cariguel of the BdF. Others with key roles in facilitating cooperation were Cobbold and Siepmann from the BoE and Sproul of the FRBNY. These officials discussed the state of the markets, interpreted political developments, relayed messages from higher-ups, and speculated about the future. The most important information shared was the extent of intervention. The reciprocal facilities and their restriction to daily convertibility meant members necessarily had to inform one another of their intervention. If the United States purchased sterling and did not tell the British about it that day, there was no guarantee that it could later convert that sterling into gold at the BoE. Thus, the system was predicated on transparency, on sharing the very information that had been withheld – to the detriment of monetary comity – in previous years.[75]

Not only did the members inform one another of their interventions, but they also jointly oversaw the markets. Rather quickly after the Tripartite Agreement's announcement – indeed, while reciprocity was still being negotiated – the parties worked out a method of market control that lasted until the war. Britain and France were responsible for intervening

---

[73] Sproul conversation with Catterns, September 10, 1936, FRBNY C261.

[74] Clarke (1977, 55–56).

[75] While members informed one another of their daily interventions, they did not share all reserve data. Usually the daily data was more than sufficient to understand general trends. But at times, members wanted more cumulative information. For instance, when sterling fell in the autumn of 1938, Washington requested more information on exactly how much gold the EEA still had and London provided the information. Bewley telegram to Treasury, November 22, 1938, T 188/232; Cochran, Untitled memorandum, December 3, 1938, MD 154/232.

when the European markets were open; once Paris and London closed for the day, New York would take over. And, in general, the country whose currency was under pressure would take the lead in determining how much to support it.[76]

All of these interactions helped make sure the countries did not work at cross-purposes, transforming the exchange funds – in the perception of the public and governments – from weapons of war to instruments of peace. The turnaround in sentiment was so complete that thereafter collaboration seemed unsurprising, indeed the natural state of things. Newspapers now wrote of the "funds" (plural) jointly attempting to quell market disturbances rather than of one fund seeking to gain an advantage at the expense of another. Siepmann discussed the benefit of contacts in 1938:

As currency relationships are reciprocal, it is evidently possible that two "controls" differing (even though only slightly) in their policies and objectives, might find themselves pulling at opposite ends of the same rope. The question is sometimes asked, how cooperation succeeds in avoiding such a situation. The answer is: by constant exchange of information and views, by mutual give and take, and by understanding and sharing one another's difficulties which are apt to be those of one "control" to-day and of another to-morrow.[77]

How much things had changed from 1935, when London had no interest in engaging Washington.

Give gold, get gold. Reciprocal and transparent. Informal and flexible. The twenty-four-hour gold standard was "based," the BoE reported in May 1937, "ultimately, upon the use of gold as the one recognised means of clearing the residual indebtedness between nations."[78] More than eight decades later, the reliance on gold appears quaint if not absurd. The question seems inescapable: Why leave the gold standard only to keep the metal on such a high pedestal? But the question misses the point. Gold remained the preeminent reserve asset *because* countries left the gold standard. Many of the club members had been burned holding foreign

---

[76] Morgenthau conversation with Knoke, September 28, 1936, MD 35/34–36; Bloomfield, "The Tripartite Agreement of 1936 as an Alternative to the Keynes and White Plans," May 8, 1943, FRBNY FF4608.

[77] "Mr. Siepmann's Memorandum for the Treasury," February 14, 1938, BoE C43/65.

[78] "Foreign Exchange and Gold," May 26, 1937, BoE G1/502. In this light, it is instructive to consider one of Keynes' most memorable lines. In 1923, he asserted, "the gold standard is already a barbarous relic." But as he declared a decade later, "A barbarous relic, to which a vast body of tradition and prestige attaches, may have a symbolic or conventional value if it can be fitted into the framework of a managed system of the new pattern." "Should Britain Compromise on the Gold Standard?" *Daily Mail*, February 17, 1933.

exchange in the past, and they set up a system to prevent that from happening again. Of course, no system is without risk. As discussed in Chapter 7, even the value of gold came into doubt at times. But in the choice between paper and metal, currency club members would line up again and again behind the latter.

Gold convertibility was just one aspect of the Tripartite Agreement. It provided the glue that helped hold things together when crises threatened the pact. The system was not intended to, nor could it, solve every problem. But it was a decided improvement on the chaos of the past.

7

Gold and Dollars, 1936–1937

The train had armed guards and darkened windows. A decoy train ran several hundred yards ahead. Sentries with machine guns secured the perimeter at the arrival station, and the Seventh Cavalry readied a motor escort to the army base. The precautions were extreme but necessary, for the train arriving at Fort Knox on January 13, 1937, carried precious cargo – indeed, national treasure. Nearly one hundred million dollars of gold was onboard, the first shipment of reserves to the newly constructed bullion depository. The US government built the massive, bomb-proof vault in Kentucky to safeguard the nation's holdings, which were concentrated on the coasts and thus exposed in the event of foreign invasion. Week after week from January to June 1937, trains (and their decoys) made their way from Philadelphia and New York to Fort Knox, transporting the metal for storage in the fortress.[1]

While gold was, of course, immensely valuable, there was a bit of irony to all of this security. Around the time the first shipment reached Fort Knox, the world was starting to wonder if there might be too much gold floating around the monetary system. It was an odd thought, given that a shortage had been the great fear during the past decade. But talk of a "glut of gold" – a function of record supply and meager demand – soon became ubiquitous. Rumors spread that the United States would slash its statutory price to bring the two in line. By spring, the world was obsessed with the matter. As bar after bar of America's gold reserves journeyed across the country, guarded to the hilt, investors around the globe were trying to ditch the metal as quickly as they could. Markets on both sides of the

---

[1] "First Lot of Gold Safe at Fort Knox," *The New York Times*, January 14, 1937; "$120,000,000 in Gold Arrives at Fort Knox," *New York Herald Tribune*, January 21, 1937; "Transfer of Billions to Fort Knox Finished," *The New York Times*, June 23, 1937.

Atlantic seized from April to June until Britain and America made clear their intention to support the current price.

This "Gold Scare" was just one of the challenges confronting the Tripartite nations during the last years of peace. A massive recession in the United States, for instance, threatened to derail global recovery from depression. In Europe, Hitler's provocations made war ever likelier, setting off new rounds of capital flight, even as many clung to the hope that yet another deal could ensure "peace for our time."[2] And with zero hour approaching, the demands of total war forced policymakers in London and elsewhere to rethink the fundamentals of economic policy.

At one time or another, gold, dollars, francs, and pounds, the building blocks of the Tripartite system, came under stress as a result of these developments. One crisis – the frenzy over the price of gold in the spring of 1937 – tested core assumptions about the metal's monetary role. Another – the dollar's weakness during the 1937 recession – revealed differences in opinion on the duty to intervene. Some problems largely reflected internal issues, such as the franc's interminable struggle to stay afloat; others mostly external factors, as with sterling's plunge during the Munich crisis in the autumn of 1938. Disagreement on how best to handle these problems could be intense, but through it all, the currency club remained intact. In fact, the Tripartite Agreement – with its emphasis on consultation and joint responsibility – provided the lens through which policymakers considered and responded to these problems. Even Britain, which had been skeptical of the Agreement at its launch, grew to rely on it, both as a framework for its own policy and as a means to understand and influence others'. By the middle of 1937, Harry Siepmann of the Bank of England (BoE) deemed the Agreement "[o]ur greatest asset."[3]

This chapter picks up the narrative of Britain's international monetary relations during the Tripartite years, exploring the first fifteen months, from the end of September 1936 to the end of 1937. Though much happened during this time, the focus is on two events that preoccupied monetary authorities: the Gold Scare in the spring of 1937 and the Dollar Scare that autumn. (The franc's evolution during this period and beyond, of profound concern to London and Washington, is the subject of Chapter 8.) The Gold Scare, the more significant of the two episodes, revolved around fears that Britain and the United States, having stuffed their coffers with gold, would tire of purchasing the metal and allow its

---

[2] See Parker (2002) for a study of Chamberlain and appeasement.
[3] Siepmann, "The Price of Gold," May 7, 1937, BoE C43/141.

price to fall. The rumors wreaked havoc in markets, not just for gold but for foreign exchange and more. Ultimately, the countries resolved to maintain gold's price and anxiety subsided. Not content with the status quo, market sentiment soon underwent a dramatic turnabout, with investors fearing that the United States would increase the price of gold (depreciate the dollar) in response to the worsening recession in what, rather derivatively, became known as the Dollar Scare. Here too there was no alteration and the alarm petered out.

Since there was no change in the price of gold in either case, neither crisis has received much attention in the literature. Studying them closely, however, reveals a great deal about the management of sterling, the architecture of the international monetary system, and the operation of the Tripartite Agreement. The twenty-four-hour gold standard was predicated on gold being a safe asset; if it suddenly became risky, the entire structure could crumble. London and Washington did worry about absorbing too much gold during the early months of 1937 – they were "suffering from gold indigestion" in Sir Frederick Phillips' phrasing – and they even considered reducing its price.[4] But both sides, agreeing that they needed to be on the same page, concluded that no asset would suffice as a substitute for gold in clearing international transactions and its value therefore needed to be maintained. The Dollar Scare, for its part, brought to light differences of opinion between Britain and America on which party should intervene when. They were now discussing these disagreements, however, rather than allowing them to fester, signifying just how much had changed. Throughout, the Tripartite Agreement was front and center, guiding policymakers as they sought steadiness during this dizzying time.

TOO MUCH OF A GOOD THING

In the first weeks after the Tripartite Agreement's announcement, all eyes were on the exchange markets. When trading in francs reopened on October 2, 1936, Paris began intervening to hold the currency at 105 to the pound, right in the middle of the effective range implied by the gold bounds in the new monetary law. As for sterling, it immediately fell from $5.04 to $4.94 and soon neared the old parity of $4.86, as shown in Figure 7.1. But this drop was largely expected as French capital returned home from across the Channel. Far from threatening the pact, sterling's fall

---

[4] Phillips, "The Present and Future of Gold," May 1, 1937, T 177/39.

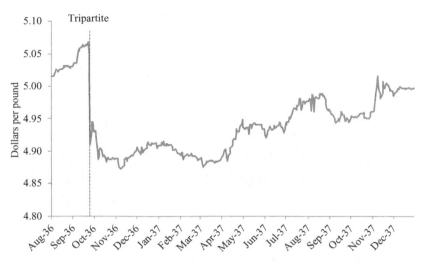

Figure 7.1 Sterling-dollar exchange rate, 1936–1937.
Source: Global Financial Data

and London's response reinforced it. The Exchange Equalisation Account (EEA) sold over £20 million of gold to the new French fund and additional gold to the Exchange Stabilization Fund (ESF) in the Agreement's first month. The French were thus able to begin rebuilding their depleted reserves, and Washington interpreted the transactions as proof of London's commitment to cooperate. "England has spent far more money in the past two weeks keeping the price of sterling up than we have spent," Secretary of the Treasury Henry Morgenthau told a group of officials in October. "She has absolutely kept good faith, and no one could ask for a better partner than we have had during the last couple weeks."[5]

As the year ended, however, focus shifted from exchange rates to gold and the possibility of a surfeit. The concern was not completely new: Back in 1935, Phillips had predicted that "one day the [gold] boom must break and the value of gold decline."[6] After all, the sterling price of gold was some 70 percent higher in 1935 than it had been just four years earlier. By the end of 1936, Phillips' theory started to catch on more widely. That year alone, Britain's gold reserves rose more than 40 percent in value, as shown in Figure 7.2. US reserves, much larger to begin with, rose a still substantial 11 percent. Authorities in both countries started to wonder how much

---

[5] Meeting with government economists, October 12, 1936, MD 39/53.
[6] Phillips, Untitled memo, January 26, 1935, BoE G1/487.

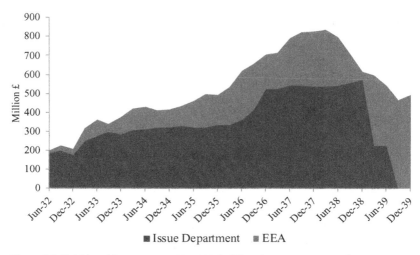

Figure 7.2 British gold reserves, 1932–1939 (million £, at current prices).
Source: Bank of England (1968)

more gold they could handle at its current price. This unease about increasing reserves may seem odd given that, in earlier years, monetary officials around the world had done all they could to husband their gold. And with hindsight, it seems doubly bizarre given the shortage of reserves that would soon plague Britain in the run-up to war. Yet a range of forces materialized that gave rise to legitimate, if exaggerated, concerns that an excess supply of gold was distorting the global economy and threatening control of monetary policy.

There were two components to the superabundance theory: too much supply and too little demand. In part, they reflected improved prospects for the world economy. The early years of the Depression had witnessed a rush into gold, as individuals sought safety in the one asset that seemed incapable of losing value. This hoarding – the bane of monetary authorities – had been attractive when the investment outlook was lackluster and devaluation appeared perpetually around the corner. But the smoother-than-expected devaluations in September 1936 boosted confidence, fundamentally altering the calculus about where to best place capital. Holding gold was no longer so appealing. Whereas Europeans had hoarded roughly £360 million in gold between January 1931 and October 1936, they sold £200 million from October 1936 to June 1937.[7]

---

[7] "The Gold Scare of 1937," December 31, 1953, BISA 9.1 002 CB 249. The text quotes figures in dollars as $1.8 billion hoarded and $1 billion sold, respectively.

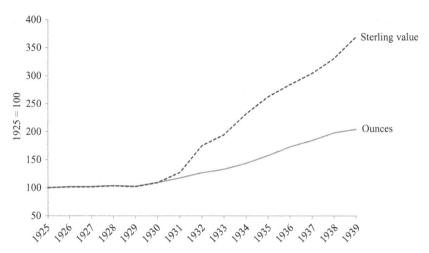

Figure 7.3 World gold production by weight and value, 1925–1939 (1925 = 100).
Source: US Gold Commission (1982, table SC-2) and *Financial Times*

This decrease in private holdings was only part of the increase in the available gold supply. Gold production, stagnant throughout the 1920s, surged with the devaluations of the 1930s, setting new records each year. When Britain suspended gold convertibility in 1931, the sterling price of gold leapt over 40 percent within months. The profitability of mining jumped as a result. Just over two years later, Roosevelt's devaluation of the dollar imposed a 70 percent increase in the dollar price of gold, further incentivizing production. By 1936, annual world gold production in ounces was nearly 50 percent greater than it had been in 1931; in sterling terms, production was over 120 percent greater, at more than £230 million. Figure 7.3 shows gold production by weight and by sterling value, demonstrating the steep increase relative to the 1920s.

With private demand weak and new production increasing, official buyers needed to fill the gap if the price was not to fall.[8] In 1936, reported gold reserves totaled £4.5 billion. The three largest holders were America with £2.3 billion, France with £611 million, and Britain with £523 million.[9] These three countries would need to take up the majority of gold on offer. The junior members of the club held sizeable reserves relative to their

---

[8] Demand from industry and the arts was paltry, averaging less than 7 percent of total supply (Bank for International Settlements 1938, 45).

[9] Ibid., 49. Estimated from dollar figures using the $4.90 sterling-dollar rate at the end of 1936. These figures do not include exchange fund holdings, which were not reported.

economies but not at a scale to make a serious dent. Moreover, countries that previously would have helped soak up gold, such as Germany, now had no interest in purchasing the metal, content as they were with exchange controls and determined not to lend support to a commodity of which they held almost none and the democracies held in bulk.[10] Further concentrating the "burden" – a term frequently employed at the time – on Britain and America was that France was not in a position to draw in much gold. In the weeks after devaluation, it had gained a good amount, but by the end of October, renewed concern about the franc's prospects resulted in an outflow, including £100 million to Britain in just over two months.[11]

The upshot was that America and Britain could expect to purchase substantial amounts of gold for the foreseeable future. Importantly, each dealt in gold differently. The United States purchased at $35 per ounce in New York from anybody at any time. With America running a trade surplus and serving as a safe haven during war scares, gold tended to flow toward it. Britain, on the other hand, had no fixed price or standing facility for accepting gold, but it housed the world's gold market in London, from which much of the globe's gold made its way, via private arbitrage, to the United States. The sterling price of gold and the all-important sterling-dollar rate were, of course, inextricably connected given the fixed dollar price of gold. The BoE therefore intervened in the gold market to influence the price of gold and complement its efforts in exchange markets. Gold from South Africa was also consigned to the BoE and either taken up by the EEA or sold in the market to meet demand. And the gold reserves of both Britain and America changed in response to operations of the reciprocal facilities, which for Britain accounted for the greater part of the fluctuations in the EEA's holdings.

---

[10] Germany, for example, had under £10 million of gold. While Germany had little interest in purchasing gold, it made sure to raid the gold reserves of countries it invaded, including Czechoslovakia. The BoE's role in facilitating the transfer of Prague's gold to the Reichsbank's account at the BIS came under much scrutiny at the time and after (Blaazer 2005).

[11] Not all of this gold directly reflected exchange operations: The French shipped £40 million in gold for repayment of the government's credit from London banks. In 1933, 1936, and 1937, Chamberlain and Norman allowed private credits to the French government and railways (approval for private loans being necessary due to restrictions on foreign lending). The BoE helped handle the conversion of foreign exchange, accepting the French gold and paying out sterling to the bank syndicate. Sayers (1976, 2:466) and files in BoE C43/420.

Buying gold was not without complication, however. The British did so through the EEA, which had a limited size, meaning that purchasing more gold today meant fewer resources to purchase gold tomorrow. At the beginning of November 1936, the account had roughly £75 million in free sterling; by the start of December, only £50 million. With the trend likely to continue or even intensify, the EEA risked running dry early in the new year. To boost the fund's firepower, Whitehall could seek parliamentary authorization for a further increase in capital, but it was hesitant: Requesting additional funds could open up the EEA to scrutiny and fuel greater demands for transparency. Instead, officials transferred £65 million of gold from the EEA to the Issue Department at the BoE on December 15.[12] In return for the gold, the EEA obtained sterling assets, which it then used to purchase gold as needed. This expedient could not be repeated indefinitely, however: Should large inflows of gold continue, either Parliament would have to increase the EEA's size or the EEA would have to restrict how much gold it purchased.[13]

The United States, on the other hand, had no limit to how much gold it could buy. But unlike Britain, it did not routinely sterilize gold flows and instead monetized them. As a result, the onslaught of gold coming ashore and the corresponding increase in the banking system's excess reserves raised alarms of an impending inflationary boom. Roosevelt ordered a review of how to limit what he derided as "hot money" flows. Newspapers were rife with stories documenting the latent threat that excess reserves posed.[14] Already in August 1936 the Federal Reserve had increased reserve requirements, but the hike did little to quiet fears. Morgenthau, feeling trapped between "four gold walls with no door," believed that sterilization would free him, and in mid-December he announced that all gold flows would henceforth be sterilized – purchases of gold would now be financed by debt rather than money creation.[15] Many saw the move as a reasonable

---

[12] The transfer of gold to the BoE's Issue Department would have resulted in a one-for-one increase in the note issue, but officials simultaneously reduced the Fiduciary Issue by £60 million, so that the actual increase was only £5 million. Fisher, "Note on Fiduciary Issue and Bank Return," June 12, 1937, T 160/660.

[13] Transferring gold to the BoE resulted in the immobilization of some of the EEA's sterling assets. The EEA, by law, was responsible for carrying any difference between the cost of gold it sold to the BoE and the BoE's valuation of the gold at the statutory parity. The £65 million of gold entering the BoE's books had cost the EEA £108 million, meaning the EEA's potential sterling resources fell by £43 million.

[14] "Roosevelt Studies Threat to Markets in Inflow of 7 Billion Foreign Funds," *New York Herald Tribune*, November 14, 1936; "Morgenthau Maps Treasury Moves," *The New York Times*, November 20, 1936.

[15] Treasury meeting, November 24, 1936, MD 46/208.

response. *The Economist* was "glad that the United States is following the British precedent" on sterilization, joyful that the New World could still learn from the Old.[16]

But sterilization was not celebrated by all. The budgetary cost, while minor given low interest rates, fueled opposition from those carrying the banner of fiscal orthodoxy. Then there was the physical dimension. The US Treasury started transferring the nation's gold to Fort Knox in 1937. The notion of borrowing money to buy gold to bury in Kentucky struck many as nonsensical. "[W]e now sterilize all this excess gold, which we go right on buying at the same old swollen price," Senator Arthur Vandenberg decried. "We sterilize it, which is to say that we bond ourselves to buy it before we bury it."[17] Of course, sterilization and burial did not mean the gold was in any monetary sense lifeless: It still mattered. Continuing to purchase gold prevented an appreciation of the dollar; in addition, if and when gold flowed out, there would be no need to tighten domestic credit.[18] But these benefits did not convince the Vandenbergs of the world.

Besides complicating monetary management, the high price for gold seemed to be distorting the economy. It surely benefitted gold producers, many of the most important ones being in the British Empire. But investment in gold mining was heating up a global economy that was approaching a boom. This prospect fed concerns that inflationary exuberance could lead to bust. Wholesale prices rose 16 percent in Britain during the second half of 1936 and 6 percent in America, as shown in Figure 7.4. While prices were still below their 1929 levels, fears of runaway inflation remained strong. The press wrote often of the specter of an "inflationary boom" as the new year commenced, and Roosevelt warned in a fireside chat in March 1937 that "recovery is speeding up to a point where the dangers of 1929 are again becoming possible."[19]

Britain and America were therefore expending record amounts to buy a monetary metal that did not directly enter the money supply; even so, inflation seemed on the verge of running amok. London could not continue to buy gold without an eventual increase in the EEA's capital;

[16] "American Exchange Control," *The Economist*, December 26, 1936; "The Treasury's Gold Policy," *The New York Times*, December 23, 1936.

[17] 75 Cong. Rec. S3934 (April 29, 1937).

[18] Morgenthau was most enthusiastic about sterilization precisely because it would prevent a tightening of domestic conditions should gold flow out. Morgenthau conversation with Roosevelt, December 17, 1936, MD 48/262.

[19] "The Control of Inflation," *The New York Times*, March 21, 1937; Roosevelt, Fireside Chat, March 9, 1937, RMSF 1041A.

Figure 7.4 Wholesale prices in Britain and the United States, 1929–1939 (January 1929 = 100).
Source: Global Financial Data

Washington could continue only so long as political realities allowed it to. Perhaps, some policymakers began to think, the solution was to reduce the price of gold rather than try to find ways to keep buying at the current price. There was no reason why $35 – and the corresponding London price of roughly £7 when the exchange rate was around $5 – should necessarily be correct; if anything, the nonstop flow of gold to the United States and Britain suggested it was not. A lower price would reduce the incentive to mine gold, lessen the accumulation by monetary authorities, and dampen inflationary pressures. To the extent that the dollar and pound appreciated against other currencies, it could also redress payments imbalances.

There were drawbacks, however. Lowering the price would diminish the value of existing holdings; harm gold producers; potentially spark a recession; and, most significantly for the functioning of the monetary system, raise questions about the role of gold. The Tripartite system revolved around gold precisely because it seemed sure to maintain its value against the domestic currency, unlike foreign exchange. If gold's value could drop, then it might no longer fulfill its function as the safe asset around which countries orchestrated their interventions, throwing the club into confusion. And if London and Washington did not act in concert on the matter, all the progress since the summer of 1936 could vanish.

The BoE started thinking through these issues in late 1936 and early 1937. Siepmann pondered in a note to Governor Montagu Norman in February 1937 whether Britain and America should "put down the price of gold by say 5 per cent."[20] The following month, Henry Clay worried that "[i]f nothing is done, the accumulations of gold will reach a point at which they break down the willingness or capacity of Governments to carry gold which they do not use for monetary purposes. Gold will then rapidly lose its value, and large areas of the Empire will be ruined." He believed a moderate reduction in the price now was necessary to forestall a "calamitous fall" later.[21]

Across the Atlantic, the US Treasury studied the problem and the potential for a reduction in the price.[22] The two sides also discussed the topic with each other in several meetings in March, with Clay pointing out to the US financial attaché that "under the tripartite monetary arrangement no action could be taken individually."[23] For the moment, most policymakers did not find the matter urgent; the problem seemed to require sober examination but did not call for any rapid response. At the beginning of April, however, the sudden eruption of the Gold Scare smashed any sense of complacency.

"THAT GOLD WORRY"

On April 6, George Bolton, foreign exchange manager at the BoE, reported that certain US banks had advised their London offices not to engage in gold arbitrage to New York. The reason appeared to be that the "Head Offices fear a possibility of a reduction in the United States Treasury buying price for gold" – any gold in transit would suffer a loss in such an event.[24] What exactly triggered these orders is unclear. Perhaps large Russian sales of gold in March spooked traders into thinking that much more would come on the market and exceed the buying capacity of Britain

---

[20] Siepmann to Norman, February 3, 1937, BoE C43/25.
[21] Clay, Untitled memo, March 18, 1937, BoE G1/488; Clay, "Gold," March 15, 1937, BoE C43/141.
[22] Schmidt to White, "The Lowering of the United States Purchase Price of Gold as a Method of Checking Capital Flows," March 2, 1937, JVP B49F6.
[23] Conversations on gold occurred between Clay and Butterworth, Morgenthau and Bewley, and Butterworth and Waley. Butterworth telegram to Treasury, March 25, 1937, MD 61/145–47; Morgenthau conversation with Bewley, April 1, 1937, MD 61/155A-B; Bewley, Untitled memo, April 14, 1937, T 177/35; Butterworth telegram to Treasury, April 2, 1937, MD 62/203–04.
[24] Bolton, "The Dollar Price for Gold," April 6, 1937, BoE C43/92.

and America. Maybe it was a comment by Oliver Sprague, a Harvard economist who had previously worked at the BoE and US Treasury, that the price of gold was too high.[25] And though there is no direct evidence, there is always the possibility that word of the conversations on gold between Britain and America leaked.

Whatever factors set off the warnings to London, the response was immediate. The Gold Scare broke out on April 7, the day after Bolton's memo, and lasted through the end of June.[26] "[A]part from the all-important question of war and peace," Einzig (1937, 1) writes, "there was during that period no question which received so much publicity." The *Financial Times* reported on April 8 that "spasms of weakness" afflicted markets within minutes of hearing the rumors of a potential cut in the price of gold.[27] The following day, the *Financial News* declared that "not merely the value but even the status of gold has been called into question."[28] The crisis fed on itself over the following months. J. P. Morgan partner Thomas Lamont found the "matter of gold" to be "on the minds of almost every one" during a trip to Europe in May.[29] And the financial press in America discussed it endlessly.

That the US administration refuted the rumors made little difference. There were so many dimensions along which the president, by his own authority, could reduce the effective price of gold – dropping the statutory parity to as low as $34.45, increasing the 0.25 percent handing cost, imposing a tariff on gold imports, or even embargoing them – that no denial seemed categorical enough.[30] Moreover, Roosevelt's word was not worth much when it came to the dollar: His gold experiments in 1933 had harmed his monetary credibility. The rumors also broadened to suggest that the British authorities would likely allow the sterling price of gold to fall in tandem; if they did not, the dollar would appreciate and the Tripartite Agreement might crumble. Whitehall tried to tamp down

---

[25] This section builds on discussions of the Gold Scare in Einzig (1938, part II), Sayers (1976, 2:483–85), Drummond (1981, 226–35), and Sumner (2015, chapter 9).

[26] Whereas the beginning of the Gold Scare was abrupt and thus easy to date, the end was not as clear-cut. June 30 is taken as an end date for convenience here, though some authorities argue that it continued into the early days of July. See, for instance, Einzig (1938, 62).

[27] "An Unsettled Day," *Financial Times*, April 8, 1937.

[28] Quoted in "The Gold Scare of 1937," December 31, 1953, BISA 9.1 002 CB 249.

[29] Lamont to Grenfell, May 28, 1937, TWLP 103/112–19.

[30] Congressional agitation further fueled the rumors. For example, representatives introduced legislation to limit the buying price of foreign gold to $25 per ounce. "Topics in Wall Street," *The New York Times*, April 29, 1937.

speculation but to little avail. Not everyone bought into the rumors – *The Economist* found the idea of a reduction in the price sheer "absurdity," an overreaction to a transient phenomenon – but they gathered momentum nonetheless.[31]

Though the Scare centered on speculation about Washington's intentions, the drama played out largely in London's gold market. Gold arbitrage came to a standstill due to concerns that the price would fall during the five-day journey across the Atlantic.[32] When banks refused to purchase gold in London to ship to New York, a shortage of dollars resulted. The EEA and ESF intervened during these times to provide dollars, using the reciprocal facilities in the process. The refusal to arbitrage was not round-the-clock, however: It ebbed and flowed with the gossip of the day. When banks felt momentarily reassured that no change in price would occur in the near-term, the profit margin on shipping gold to New York was substantial and massive amounts of the metal crossed the sea. The Gold Scare thus did not have a persistent effect on the sterling-dollar rate, and the dollar actually depreciated slightly from $4.91 to $4.94 overall, as shown in Figure 7.1.[33]

As for gold, the decline in its price was not as drastic as one would expect given that the event was predicated on the belief that the present price was too high. Over the three months, it dropped from roughly £7. 2s. to £7. 0s. per fine ounce. But the relatively muted fall was in part a result of near-constant intervention by British authorities. The EEA purchased gold from the market frequently and at times took the majority of the metal offered on the London market to prevent the price from crashing.[34]

The stress in the gold market showed up instead in what was termed the "discount on the dollar parity." An arbitrageur earned $34.77 per ounce of gold shipped from London to New York, the 23-cent difference from the

---

[31] "Financial Notes," *The Economist*, April 10, 1937.

[32] The same concern about a revaluation of the dollar during the gold clause cases in 1935 had brought arbitrage to a halt but that event was more limited in time and had a smaller impact.

[33] However, the forward discount on the dollar – indicating expectations of a revaluation – increased during these months. An additional factor affecting the sterling-dollar rate was the coronation of George VI in May, which temporarily led to a surge in demand for sterling.

[34] See, for instance, Knoke conversation with Bolton, June 1, 1937, FRBNY C261. Net purchases of gold from the market were positive for forty-five days during the Scare as compared to nine days during the previous three months according to the EEA's gold ledgers.

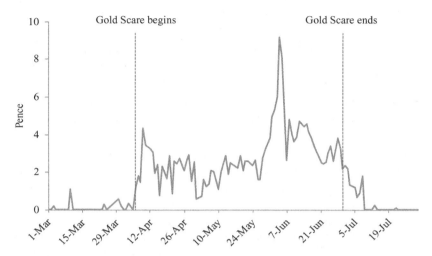

Figure 7.5 Gold discount on dollar parity, 1937 (pence per fine ounce of gold).
Source: *Financial Times* and author's calculations

$35 statutory price representing the US handling charge as well as costs of shipping. When the sterling exchange rate was e, the sterling value of the $34.77 outturn was $\frac{34.77}{e}$. Letting g represent the sterling price of gold in London, the discount was $d = \frac{34.77}{e} - g$. A positive discount implied that shipping gold from London to New York was profitable, similar to when sterling was at gold export point under the gold standard. Discounts were rare and almost never exceeded one or two pence per ounce since any discount was usually a strong incentive to arbitrage. But during the Scare, when operators refused to act, the discount surged, nearing 10 pence as shown in Figure 7.5.[35] The higher the discount, the riskier gold appeared – certainly, holders of gold thought, something must be awry if experts refused to buy the metal for what seemed like guaranteed profit – leading to greater sales and bigger discounts. The BoE worked to reduce the discount through the EEA's gold purchases but did not eliminate it, leading many in the press to criticize the managers for not buying more gold and quashing the discount.[36]

---

[35] These estimates of the discount are based on the gold fixing price and the closing exchange rate of the day and thus differ slightly from the discount at the time of fixing, which depended on the exchange rate at that moment.

[36] "Some Reflections on Dealing for Profit: A Rather Discursive Essay," October 7, 1937, BoE C43/77; Butterworth telegram to Treasury, June 5, 1937, MD 71/362–65.

Beyond the gold market, the Scare infected gold mining shares in London, since the industry would become less profitable if the price of gold fell. Trouble in this sector – one of the most widely traded on the exchange – then spread more broadly. By the end of June, gold mining stocks had plummeted 16.5 percent from the Scare's onset and industrial stocks overall had fallen 4.4 percent. In the United States, *The New York Times*' average of fifty industrial stocks fell 9 percent. Wholesale prices in both countries flatlined. While there was much else going on at this time – the Federal Reserve increased reserve requirements again in May, for example – there is no doubt that the Scare contributed to the disinflationary mindset.[37] Economies had recovered significantly after devaluations; many worried the process would reverse with revaluation.

The Scare was not constant. Fears would abate, only to be rekindled by new rumors. The *Financial Times* declared the "Gold Scare finally scotched" on April 21. "That Gold Worry" then reappeared, and after some more twists and turns, it climaxed in June, when, "[l]ike the ghost of Hamlet's father on the battlements of Elsinore, the Gold Bogy stalked throughout the world's markets."[38] Experts tugged public opinion from side to side. In a *Daily Mail* column, Gustav Cassel, preeminent Swedish economist, advocated a reduction in the price to "somewhere halfway between the old and the new" as a way to guard against inflation.[39] John Maynard Keynes, bedridden after his first heart attack, wrote a letter to *The Times* of London urging calm.[40] He was not sure that Britain had more gold than was reasonable, and even if it did, he thought there were better policies to alleviate the problem than cutting the price. Others argued that a reduction was not strictly necessary – the United States could lower tariffs to reduce its trade surplus or London and Washington could lend gold to countries in need – but considered it likely given domestic and international political realities.

British authorities responded to the Scare on two fronts. First, they had to contend with the immediate issue of market distress. As the Treasury's Phillips commented, "although the Tripartite Monetary Agreement does not bind us to offer any definite price for gold, it does bind us to take

---

[37] The Federal Reserve had already announced the changes in reserve requirements at the end of January, so the increase in May was expected. "Board's Order Raising Reserve Requirements," *The New York Times*, January 31, 1937.

[38] "A Sting in the Tail," *Financial Times*, April 21, 1937; "That Gold Worry," *Financial Times*, May 11, 1937; "The Ghost Walks," *Financial Times*, June 4, 1937.

[39] "The Price of Gold Should be Cut," *Daily Mail*, June 9, 1937.

[40] Skidelsky (1994, 634); "The Gold Problem," *The Times* (London), June 10, 1937.

reasonable steps for avoiding undue fluctuations in the Exchange."[41] London intervened in gold and exchange markets to this end. Commentators found fault with the EEA's managers for not acting more forcefully and pushing the discount down further, but there was more going on than appeared at first glance. In addition to purchasing gold in the market, the fund obtained tremendous amounts – nearly £87 million during these months – from France, which needed sterling as it battled its own currency crisis at this time. As a result of all of these purchases, the EEA's sterling resources fell from £82 million at the beginning of April to nothing at the end of June. The EEA simply did not have the firepower to buy all of the gold on offer. Nevertheless, critics were likely correct that a more activist policy in April and May, when the influx from France had not yet peaked, might have nipped the gold problem in the bud.

Second, policymakers needed to decide on their long-term policy regarding the price of gold. Should they continue to support the present price or allow it to fall, and if so, should they work with other countries? The BoE and Treasury were unanimous that any response had to involve consensus among club members, which effectively meant in coordination with the United States, with the support of the French, and at least the acquiescence of the others. The BoE believed that "[o]ur *chief resource* is the Tripartite Agreement."[42] Phillips, who found the situation "extremely pressing," wrote in May that the British should "decline to commit ourselves to any change unless it was agreed generally by all members of the Currency Club."[43]

The Americans shared this sentiment. In late March, before the Gold Scare erupted, Morgenthau told T. K. Bewley, the British financial attaché, that while the Tripartite Agreement's text did not explicitly mention the price of gold, "if any member of the Tripartite Agreement was considering dropping the price of gold that we should consult with one another."[44] After all, the price of gold directly impacted exchange rates. If the United

---

[41] Phillips, Untitled memo, June 4, 1937, T 177/39.

[42] "Gold: A Programme," May 11, 1937, BoE G1/488.

[43] Phillips, "The Present and Future of Gold," May 1, 1937, T 177/39. During the Imperial Conference in May and June, which followed the coronation of George VI and brought delegates from around the Empire to discuss a host of issues, South Africa and Australia wanted a joint statement reaffirming the present price of gold. But London would not make any pronouncement, in part because, as a Treasury note explained, "the question is essentially one between the United States and the United Kingdom (and in a minor degree France)." Memo to Hopkins, undated, T 175/94; Drummond (1981, 231–33).

[44] Morgenthau conversation with Bewley, April 1, 1937, MD 61/155A.

States reduced its buying price for gold, the dollar would appreciate unless the British allowed the sterling price of gold to fall by the proportionate amount. If the British allowed the sterling price of gold to fall and the United States maintained its buying price, sterling would appreciate. Both actions, not to mention the reactions of other members, threatened the club's commitment to exchange stability.

There was also consensus in London on the various trade-offs at play. Authorities believed that the gold inflow was too large to continue indefinitely and feared that the current price, if maintained, could become untethered from reality. They realized that other countries, notably France, were struggling with too little gold, and that the problem could have been one of distribution rather than supply – in hindsight it clearly was. But there was so little faith that the French would be able to right their ship that policymakers felt unable to orient their strategy around a French recovery.[45] Decreasing the price carried risks, however. Officials agreed that a reduction could devastate parts of the Empire and damage confidence in growth prospects. Britain also held a ton of gold – well over 3,000 tons in fact – and would take a paper loss should the price fall.[46]

The most important factor, however, was the necessity of maintaining trust in gold for international purposes. As Phillips argued, "[g]old is a monetary metal," and "[u]nless some great powers were willing to buy any amount at an approximately fixed price … gold ceases to be a monetary metal." Were that to happen, "chaotic conditions" would ensue, "[f]or the dollar, franc and sterling are only kept on a steady footing, because there is a fourth money, gold, which the United States, France and ourselves are willing to buy and sell from each other."[47] Despite the many weaknesses of gold, there was no alternative reserve asset that exchange managers were willing to consider. The Gold Scare did not lead policymakers to question gold's monetary status: It reaffirmed the necessity of the metal's international function. R. H. Brand, a director at Lazards well-connected to official circles, asserted in a three-part series for *The Times* of London that governments needed "to maintain confidence in gold as the ultimate

---

[45] As Sir Richard Hopkins wrote, "Until recently we have been trying to believe that the worst of the French crisis was over and that there would be at any rate some moderate tendency for the gold which had come out of France to go back there. It seems wiser to abandon any hopes of that kind." Hopkins, Untitled memo, May 25, 1937, T 177/39.

[46] Gold in the Issue Department had not yet been revalued, however, so a moderate reduction in the price of gold would not impact the book value of Issue Department gold (though it would impact the book value of EEA gold).

[47] Phillips, "The Present and Future of Gold," May 1, 1937, T 177/39.

standard of value and the common denominator between currencies." If gold lost its status, "the whole world would be thrown into chaos and confusion."[48]

The desire to uphold gold's role did not actually dictate whether or not to alter the price. Norman strongly favored a cut coordinated through the currency club as a preventative move to forestall a later collapse in the price. Whitehall was more circumspect, believing that maintaining the price was the best way to preserve faith. Strategies differed as a result: The BoE wanted to engage the Americans into bringing about a change, whereas the Treasury was inclined to wait things out.[49] The Treasury's hesitancy resulted as well from the upcoming Cabinet rearrangement, whereby Neville Chamberlain was to succeed Stanley Baldwin as prime minister at the end of May. All believed, however, that the proper course hinged on what the United States would do. If Washington thought reducing the price advisable, London seems to have been willing to take the plunge; if Washington thought not, London would not act alone.

The United States was of like mind. The two countries needed to be on the same page. And gold had to maintain its importance or else the Tripartite Agreement would fall apart – not to mention the hit to the value of reserves buried at Fort Knox.[50] Because Morgenthau was never one to have his hand forced, any interest he had in reducing the price of gold fell as speculation that he would do so rose. He also did not find the situation as pressing as Britain because a continuation of the status quo was possible for him without any proactive step, whereas the British were limited by the

---

[48] "Gold," *The Times* (London), June 16, 17, and 18, 1937.

[49] Norman was most fervent in pushing for action. At a meeting with Treasury officials, he "pressed the view that it was a waste of time to attempt to formulate any programme or policy for dealing with gold, until we knew what the Americans were prepared to do or not prepared to do. The only possible immediate step was for H.M. Treasury to get into touch with the U.S. Treasury." Hopkins found Norman "unduly alarmist," but in late May he thought it prudent to offer to send Phillips for discussions in Washington in response to an earlier suggestion by Morgenthau. Simon eventually did so in late June, the delay likely resulting from the required time to get up to speed on his new portfolio. "Memorandum of Discussion," May 21, 1937, BoE G1/304; Hopkins to Fisher and Chamberlain, May 24, 1937, T 177/39; Simon to Morgenthau, June 24, 1937, MD 74/58.

[50] Insight into US thinking comes from sixty pages of fictitious Congressional testimony written by the Treasury's Harry Dexter White, who used the exercise as an opportunity to wrestle with the issues at hand. As he argued, "We have too much interest in the future of gold to so threaten its use as a medium of exchange among nations." The imaginary testimony is illuminating to the historian. At the time, however, White admitted to Morgenthau that the "chief merit" of this exercise would likely "prove to be its possible use as a mild cure for insomnia." White, "Transcript of Imaginary Hearings," May 28, 1937, HDWP B2F8; White to Morgenthau, May 28, 1937, HDWP B2F8.

EEA's resources: "The shoe," Morgenthau thought, "would pinch" on London first.[51] So while Washington looked into various options for handling the problem, such as reducing the price, imposing quotas on gold production, and purchasing gold only from monetary authorities, it felt confident riding the crisis out.[52]

The two countries were committed to acting as one. Both sides were in constant contact, with the American financial attaché in London, W. Walton Butterworth, frequently meeting with Phillips, Sigi Waley, and others, not to mention messages between the two finance ministers and daily central bank contacts, all of which helped to clarify each other's positions.[53] There was no grand summit where the two parties reached a joint position – the change in Cabinet in London likely contributed to the inaction – but suffice it to say that the potential for a price reduction ended when Morgenthau informed the British at the beginning of June that he did "not feel that the solution lies through dropping the price of gold."[54] Precisely why Morgenthau made this statement when he did is not entirely clear. Certainly, inertia contributed. The troubles in the stock market were also a window into what might happen if the price actually did fall, making the idea much less attractive. But there can be no doubt that he believed that sticking with the current price of gold would best protect its monetary status and all the attendant benefits.

For the British, this decision effectively settled the matter. There was no interest in altering the price independently of the United States. By this time, Sir John Simon was chancellor, having taken over the office at the end of May as part of the Cabinet reshuffling. Simon's resume was exquisite. After obtaining a first at Oxford, he embarked on a brilliant career as a barrister and then occupied a slew of high Cabinet offices. He had a mind that few could rival. His personality and training, however, made him ill-suited for the chancellorship. A master at arguing any side, he had a tendency for indecision when governing. As a briefing for Morgenthau read, Simon "quickly acquired a reputation of never saying 'yes' or 'no.'"[55] Simon's colleague-turned-rival David Lloyd George was

---

[51] Morgenthau conversation with Butterworth, April 19, 1937, MD 65/198.

[52] White, "The Gold Problem," undated, HDWP B2F9.

[53] See, for instance, Butterworth telegram to Treasury, April 16, 1937, MD 65/114–17; Butterworth telegram to Treasury, May 4, 1937, MD 67/65–68; Butterworth telegram to Treasury, May 27, 1937, MD 70/202–07; Cochran telegram, June 21, 1937, MD 73/343–46.

[54] Morgenthau conversation with Mallet, June 7, 1937, MD 72/35.

[55] "Some Observations on Sir John Simon," undated, MD 71/34.

more scathing: "Simon has sat on the fence so long that the iron has entered into his soul."[56] His admitted ignorance of financial matters compounded this shortcoming.

Upon hearing Morgenthau's opinion on gold, Simon wrote the secretary that he "had really no opportunity to form a considered judgment on many of these difficult questions." The arguments against a reduction appeared compelling enough and seemed to be the more cautious approach, which suited him. Indeed, it appears that Simon's lack of confidence pushed him to rely on the Tripartite Agreement more than Chamberlain had, as well as to view Morgenthau more favorably.[57] To further develop ties, Simon suggested Phillips, who would be in Canada in September, visit Washington "for discussions . . . both upon the gold question and generally upon problems of mutual interest to us both."[58] Two years earlier, Morgenthau had refused an unofficial call by Sir Frederick Leith-Ross as the latter traveled to Canada, so distrustful was he of the British; now he welcomed Phillips' visit as a chance to strengthen their partnership.[59]

In the meantime, the price of gold would not maintain itself. "We must be prepared to buy gold ourselves if we expect the Americans to," a BoE memorandum stated. "This means enlarging the E.E.A."[60] Simon requested parliamentary authority on June 25 to augment the EEA's capital by £200 million to £571 million "in support of our undertakings and objectives under the Tri-partite Monetary Agreement."[61] This injection of funds was essential as the EEA had no more sterling left with which to buy gold.[62]

To ensure swift passage, Whitehall knew it needed to provide more transparency on the EEA. The decision reached by the Treasury, in consultation with the BoE, was to release aggregate information about the fund's holdings every six months, three months in arrear (in other words, at the end of each June and December, the chancellor would announce the figure for the total amount of gold held at the end of the

---

[56] Quoted in Dutton (1992, 337).

[57] For instance, almost immediately after Simon took over the chancellorship, he sent Morgenthau draft responses to parliamentary questions for his input. "Meeting re answer to Sir John Simon," June 4, 1937, MD 71/250–72.

[58] Simon to Morgenthau, June 24, 1937, MD 74/58–60.

[59] Morgenthau originally suggested holding a high-level meeting. Morgenthau conversation with Butterworth, April 19, 1937, MD 65/196; Morgenthau to Stamp, July 9, 1935, MD 8/46.

[60] "Notes and Comments," June 18, 1937, BoE G1/304.

[61] 325 Parl. Deb. (5th ser.) (1937) col. 1662.

[62] The BoE had to intervene on its own account for several days. "EEA and Banking Department," July 5, 1937, BoE C43/25.

previous March and September, respectively).[63] Simon's removal of what he termed the "veil of mystery," while leaving some members of Parliament unsatisfied, did the trick and the bill was passed.[64]

This increase was the EEA's second boost, following the enlargement in 1933. The first increase, appearing as an aggressive move to counter Roosevelt's depreciation, had further poisoned relations with the United States. This time, the action garnered widespread approval. Simon notified Morgenthau of the plan prior to informing the public, and the latter responded that he was "glad," since the addition was "well calculated to restore confidence."[65] *The Baltimore Sun* enthused that Britain's decision represented "a further step in the program of monetary cooperation which was initiated in the tripartite monetary agreement of last September."[66] A sea change had occurred. At the beginning of the decade, large exchange funds provoked suspicion and anger. Now, with the widespread understanding that funds were working together and with gold's future on the line, they were the epitome of cooperation.

By the second week of July, the *Financial Times* could write, accurately, of the "complete disappearance of the gold scare."[67] The discount on the gold parity was gone. In part, the crisis ended because of the EEA's augmentation, which spoke louder than any statement could as to Britain's willingness to buy gold as necessary. The United States also kept purchasing the metal at $35 an ounce, eventually putting the rumors to rest. In addition, signs of a boom began to recede, making the possibility of a reduction less likely. Finally, France's political and monetary crisis, which resulted in the fall of the government and devaluation of the franc, diverted attention from gold.

Though the Scare had ended in public, the matter was not yet resolved behind the scenes. The solution was to maintain the price of gold, and this hinged on monetary authorities cooperating by holding gold rather than selling it. As Threadneedle Street viewed the matter, "our obligations under the Tripartite Agreement make it obligatory upon us to accept gold freely."[68] During the height of the Scare, however, Switzerland sold large amounts of gold to the United States in exchange for dollars, dumping gold

---

[63] In addition to the amount of gold held by the EEA, the chancellor routinely stated that it had a "trifling" amount of foreign exchange. See the files in T 233/1038.

[64] 325 Parl. Deb. (5th ser.) (1937) col. 1664.

[65] Taylor conversation with Trentham, June 23, 1937, MD 74/11–17; Taylor to Trentham, June 24, 1937, MD 74/51.

[66] "British Cooperation," *The Baltimore Sun*, June 27, 1937.

[67] "More Evidence of Progress," *Financial Times*, July 8, 1937.

[68] "Reasons for Holding so much Gold," undated, BoE C43/25.

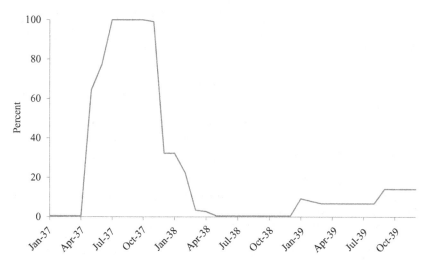

Figure 7.6 Swiss fund holdings of foreign exchange, 1936–1939 (foreign exchange as percent of total reserves).
Source: SNB 231.5

to avoid any loss should its price fall. Figure 7.6 depicts the Swiss fund's sharp move into foreign exchange, going from nearly all gold in April to almost all foreign exchange in July.

Club members found the Swiss maneuvers distinctly unhelpful. The president of the Netherlands Bank was, according to the BoE, "very annoyed with the Swiss, whose gold sales he thinks contrary to the spirit of Tripartite Agreement."[69] The British and French also found Switzerland's policy troublesome.[70] Of course, conversion of gold into dollars would have been celebrated in America during the early years of the decade when it was struggling to maintain the gold standard. But during the Gold Scare, the monetary world had become warped, and Washington now believed stability required everyone to hold onto their gold.[71]

---

[69] "Note of conversation with De Jong," June 14, 1937, BoE OV48/11.

[70] In September 1937, Siepmann wrote, "the Swiss are the least amenable members of the 'currency club.'" This characterization occurred in the midst of a French financial crisis that resulted in further depreciation of the franc, as described in Chapter 8. It is instructive that he singled out the Swiss and not the French. Siepmann, "Tripartite Agreement," September 3, 1937, BoE G1/304.

[71] Einzig (1938, 239–40) is unsparing in his criticism of the Swiss, calling their actions "very selfish" and comparing them to "rats leaving a sinking ship" – only less justified because the ship did not in the end sink.

After some back-and-forth, Morgenthau decided in July to draft a letter to the Swiss. In the note, quoted at length below, he set forth his conception of the responsibilities of club membership:

At the present time, we who have joined in the tripartite accord are engaged together in an attempt to bring a greater measure of stability and of genuine equilibrium into the market for foreign exchanges. This market has, as you know, in recent years been characterized by exceptionally large movements of capital, many of which do not represent normal financial or commercial transactions. Under these circumstances, some of us are likely to be called upon, at least temporarily, to hold exceptionally large quantities of gold. I do feel, however, that the central banks and treasuries of these countries which have declared their adherence to the tripartite accord should refrain from increasing these movements by unilateral decisions to transfer their gold reserves into foreign currencies.

In our opinion, the normal function of international gold movements is to liquidate international balances of payments arising from the natural flow of international commercial and financial transactions. Governments and central banks should, we believe, in their own operations conform as closely as possible to this general principle. We believe that this principle makes it incumbent upon the adherents of the tripartite declaration to hold their reserves in the form of gold either at home or earmarked abroad, and where a central bank deems it desirable to maintain foreign balances, such balances should in the main be kept with the Central Bank of the selected country and should, furthermore, be maintained essentially as working balances. We further feel, and especially in the case of those countries that have adhered to the tripartite declaration, that central banks or governments should make investments in other countries only after consultation with, and perhaps only at the invitation of, the government concerned.

We suggest that an acceptance of the above principles would be a constructive development of the spirit of monetary cooperation envisaged in the tripartite declaration, and would contribute toward enduring stability in the international monetary field. We hope that the other adherents to the tripartite declaration share this interpretation of its implications.[72]

Reserves, then, were to be exclusively in the form of gold save for working balances in foreign currencies. The gold facilities were meant to enable intervention to stabilize rates, not to provide a means for altering reserve composition. And each member of the currency club had to do its share, holding enough gold so that the metal retained its monetary properties.

Before presenting the letter to the Swiss, Morgenthau sought input from Paris and London. Siepmann felt that "the general principles and apparent intentions underlying Mr. Morgenthau's draft are in fact entirely

---

[72] Morgenthau telegram to Butterworth, July 14, 1937, MD 78/329–31. Clay (1957, 431) appears to be the only work that refers to this episode, though he maintains discretion by referring to the Swiss National Bank as a "European Central Bank."

acceptable." But he believed it ill-advised to "formulate a code for Controls."[73] More important, the British worried that the Swiss could interpret the letter as suggesting that Washington itself was wary of purchasing gold. Replying to Morgenthau on July 19, Simon gently asked, "May it not also be wiser at the present moment when confidence in gold is recovering to avoid putting into the minds of the junior members of the Currency Club that any real doubt could exist of our willingness to take gold from them."[74] Fears regarding gold's future had receded in public; now was not the time to amplify them among governments. Paris responded similarly, having coordinated with London.[75]

Morgenthau forged ahead but heeded the advice. He directed H. Merle Cochran, the financial attaché in Paris, to present the letter to the Swiss but to do so informally. More important, Morgenthau stressed to Cochran that, so long as the Swiss agreed to the principles, he should tell them that the United States would "stand ready to accept any amount of gold they wish to send us."[76] In this way, Morgenthau could make his point clear – all Tripartite members needed to cooperate on the gold situation – without saddling the club with formalized rules and risking serious disagreement. Cochran made his way around Europe, visiting the three junior members, and attained their qualified acceptance. The Swiss stopped converting large amounts of gold into dollars; the Belgians and Dutch, while reserving ultimate discretion and expressing a desire for greater say in club affairs, affirmed their commitment to gold and the Tripartite Agreement.[77]

The Scare thus came to an end, in private and public. Chatter about gold continued in the ensuing months, but it receded from the front pages back to the world of expert opinion and then largely faded altogether. In September, when Phillips was in Washington for meetings set up in part

---

[73] Siepmann to Phillips, July 15, 1937, BoE C43/369.

[74] Simon to Morgenthau, July 19, 1937, BoE C43/369.

[75] "Message du Ministre des Finances à M. Morgenthau," July 19, 1937, SAEF B32325; Waley to Phillips, July 17, 1937, T 160/840/8.

[76] Morgenthau conversation with Cochran, July 19, 1937, MD 79/119–21.

[77] Cochran telegram to Morgenthau, July 24, 1937, MD 79/176–91. By time Cochran met with the Swiss, the latter had paused their conversion of gold into dollars. They expressed informal approval of the principles, pending further discussion, and later sent confirmation. While the Swiss then moved from dollars into gold, the conversion might have resulted more from the Dollar Scare discussed below rather than a desire to get into line. Cochran telegram to Morgenthau, September 20, 1937, MD 89/47–48; "Notiz über die Besprechung mit Cochran," July 21, 1937, SNB Zusammenarbeit der Notenbanken USA; "Auszug aus dem Protokoll des Direktoriums der Schweizerischen Nationalbank," July 29–30, 1937, SNB; Trip meeting with Cochran, July 23, 1937, NA 32.386/49260.

to confer on gold, the two sides discussed the matter but neither was interested in changing policy.[78] The visit was nevertheless a boon to Anglo-American relations: Morgenthau and Phillips conversed on many issues and got to know each other, even enjoying a day trip to Mount Vernon.[79] And in the next few months, as the United States went through a devastating recession, concerns about having too much gold faded entirely and Morgenthau started to reverse the sterilization policy and pump gold into the money supply to spur growth.[80] As for Britain, the notion that it had complained of too much gold would come to seem ludicrous in little over a year. Superabundance – of gold and just about everything else – disappeared from the British lexicon as the country went to war.[81]

What then to make of this episode? Einzig (1938, 41–42) deemed the Scare a "comedy of errors," resulting from frayed nerves, government indecision, and "scaremonger[ing]." Certainly, there seemed to be an inordinate focus on short-term issues to the neglect of long-term trends. For instance, while dehoarding was substantial and rapid, private gold holdings could not go below zero; as Keynes argued, it was a "non-recurrent event" and thus would wear itself out.[82] More important, what was a glut to Britain and America was a shortage to France and others. Observers and policymakers discussed mobilizing excess gold to assist countries lacking it – to let it, in Brand's words, "fructify" rather than lay "repos[ed] 'sterilized' in vaults in Kentucky or elsewhere" – but authorities were not yet ready to take that step.[83] America had been burned by war debts, Britain did not have faith in the economic program of France's Popular Front, and schemes to use gold to incentivize Germany and Italy to open

---

[78] Problems with the franc took up much of the discussion. See Drummond (1981, 233–35) and MD 89 for American records of the meetings.

[79] Mallet to Morgenthau, September 27, 1937, MD 90/215.

[80] Morgenthau alerted the British about the change in policy prior to announcing it, asking for their support. Morgenthau conversation with Butterworth, February 12, 1938, MD 110/1–11; Morgenthau conversation with Butterworth, February 14, 1938, MD 110/68–73.

[81] During the run-up to war and thereafter, London's loss was Washington's gain, forcing America to once again reckon with a "golden avalanche," as Graham and Whittlesey (1939) termed it. But there was no crisis as in 1937, and the mounting stockpile simply made Washington more intent on preserving gold's monetary role.

[82] "The Gold Problem," *The Times* (London), June 10, 1937.

[83] "Gold," *The Times* (London), June 17, 1937. Pierre Quesnay of the BIS suggested that all six members of the currency club contribute 1 percent of their gold to a joint fund administered by the BIS to help facilitate stabilization, the removal of exchange controls, and the financing of purchases of raw materials. Quesnay, "The Superabundance of Gold," June 24, 1937, BoE G1/7.

up their economies had far too many stumbling blocks. The failure to put gold to use in this way was not one of imagination but of political constraints. What was left was a very real sense that the two countries, at least for the time being, might not be able to keep absorbing gold.

Fundamentally, the Scare matters because it tested the Tripartite system, both its technical underpinning and its cooperative basis. By the end, gold's indispensability was reaffirmed, and consultation between Washington and London had reached new heights.[84] They were committed to acting in a way that upheld the system – to acknowledging, as the BoE put it, that "public responsibilities extended beyond national frontiers" – and not merely to pursuing short-term self-interest.[85]

WHIPLASH

Observers at the time did not know it, but the Gold Scare coincided with the onset of recession in America. This downturn, among the steepest of the century, threatened to erase the economic recovery. Its causes remain a matter of debate but were some combination of tighter monetary policy (higher reserve requirements and sterilization of gold imports) and tighter fiscal policy.[86] The downturn ricocheted around the world, contributing to a slowdown in Britain, but the United States was ground zero. Having been reelected for leading his nation out of depression, Roosevelt was determined not to let the country slip back into it. By October, just months after the Gold Scare had ended, rumors were spreading that he would devalue the dollar against gold in a bid to boost the economy. So swift was the change in public sentiment about the dollar price of gold – "it must fall" in the spring became "it must rise" in the autumn – that few paused to catch their breath.

Though not as intense as the Gold Scare or cause for as much soul-searching, the resulting "Dollar Scare" (also known as the "Inverted Gold Scare") nevertheless hung over markets during the last quarter of the year.[87] Throughout these months, club members cooperated to resolve

---

[84] Not to suggest that the monetary authorities walked in lockstep. Each country wanted the other to bear a larger part of the burden; neither revealed its entire hand. But both sides now operated under the assumption that collaboration was essential. .

[85] "Some Reflections on Dealing for Profit: A Rather Discursive Essay," October 7, 1937, BoE C43/77.

[86] Irwin (2012) discusses the role of sterilization in causing the recession.

[87] Einzig (1938, 243) sees the Inverted Gold Scare (resulting from a renewed demand for gold) and the Dollar Scare (resulting from fears of a dollar devaluation) as related but not identical events.

the situation. In doing so, an important technical debate took place on the rules of intervention. Britain wanted America to intervene more to shore up the dollar, while America increasingly considered the dollar the center of the international monetary system, a point around which other countries should manage their currencies. Herein was one root of the view that the dollar held a pivotal and thus asymmetric role, an attitude which persists to this day.

The devaluation rumors were a product of the sharp downturn in the autumn of 1937. Industrial production in the United States peaked in May and, after a few months of stagnation, contracted 24 percent from September to December. The Dow Jones plunged 32 percent in just three months, and commodity prices likewise fell.[88] Given Roosevelt's focus on prices four years earlier and his willingness to throw the World Economic Conference into disarray in order to halt a decline in prices, it was natural for observers to worry that this new slowdown would rouse pro-devaluation tendencies no matter what the one-year-old Tripartite Agreement might demand. After all, he retained the authority to increase the price of gold from $35 to up to $41.34 an ounce with just a day's notice. By the beginning of November, the *Financial Times* reported that "rumors [were] rife as to an imminent devaluation of the dollar."[89] The dollar depreciated as capital headed for the exits, and gold, which had been flung on the market in the spring as if it were borderline worthless, was once again bought by hoarders as a hedge against devaluation.

As it turned out, Morgenthau and Roosevelt did not give much consideration to devaluing the dollar and were, in fact, intent on maintaining the $35 price. To combat the rumors and live up to the Tripartite Agreement's spirit, the United States undertook its first large-scale, concerted effort to dampen a fall in the dollar since Roosevelt's inauguration.[90] From October to December, Morgenthau had the ESF sell $335 million (£67 million) of gold to monetary authorities. These sales included $115 million (£23 million) to Britain, $108 million (£22 million) to Switzerland, $61 million (£12 million) to France, and $51 million (£10 million) to the Netherlands.[91]

In some ways, this expenditure was easy for Washington to swallow since the Treasury's inactive gold account from the sterilization program

---

[88] "Industrial Production Index" (INDPRO) and "Dow-Jones Industrial Stock Price Index for United States" (M1109BUSM293NNBR), Federal Reserve Economic Database.

[89] "Hot Money and Gold," *Financial Times*, November 6, 1937.

[90] There had been sporadic intervention to strengthen the dollar in the past, such as against the franc in September 1934 (Brown 1942, 45–51).

[91] Ibid., 199.

had $1.2 billion (£240 million) at the beginning of October. The Treasury thus had a substantial buffer before gold sales would affect the domestic money supply.[92] And months earlier, Washington had wanted less gold anyway. But there was a difference between complaining of too much gold during a boom and actually selling gold during a bust. That Washington would work to counter depreciation in the depths of recession was by no means certain given recent history. That it did revealed just how much its attitude toward the responsibilities of monetary power had shifted.

And far from hiding gold sales, the Treasury publicized them. Morgenthau wanted the world to know that America intended to cooperate in good times and bad. He told reporters, "I want to say that we will let gold go willingly," emphasizing the Tripartite Agreement's centrality in US policy.[93] The press covered the loading of ships with gold, not as some crisis but as proof of commitment to the Agreement and as validation of the pact's importance.[94] Overall, sales of gold kept the dollar's depreciation rather minor, with the sterling-dollar rate rising from $4.94 to $5.02 during the second half of the year.

While publication of gold shipments helped rebut rumors of devaluation, it also brought to light an area of disagreement between Britain and America. On November 10, the US Treasury announced that it was shipping $5 million (£1 million) of gold to Britain for the EEA, which had purchased dollars to prevent sterling from appreciating.[95] Siepmann was furious at the press release. First, the statement revealed details about the EEA's actions without British approval. More important, its framing – Britain buying dollars to keep sterling from appreciating – placed the onus of intervention on London. "It had been our intention, at some stage, to make it clear that dollar depreciation should be the concern, primarily, of the U.S. Treasury," Siepmann grumbled. Morgenthau "now succeeds not only in ascribing the initiative to us but also in suggesting that we have voluntarily assumed it in this instance."[96] That is, by telling the world that the British had bought gold

[92] "Treasury Statement," *The New York Times*, October 8, 1937. The inactive account had $1.4 billion in September, at which point the Treasury decided to freeze sterilization and began monetizing $300 million from the account. "Treasury Frees 'Sterilized Gold' to Aid Easy Money," *The New York Times*, September 13, 1937.
[93] Press conference, November 8, 1937, MPC 9/207.
[94] "U.S. Stabilization Fund Ships $5,000,000 of Gold to London," *New York Herald Tribune*, November 11, 1937.
[95] "$5,000,000 of Gold Taken by England," *The New York Times*, November 11, 1937.
[96] Siepmann, "The Times," November 11, 1937, BoE C43/92.

to keep sterling from rising too much, Morgenthau implied that it was their responsibility to do so, rather than his job to prevent the dollar from falling.

On one level, the question of how to support the dollar was straightforward: Gold just needed to flow from the United States to Europe, whether on ships or through earmarks. But how to effect that movement was not obvious. In general, when currency A was under pressure, there were two options. Country B could buy currency A (against currency B) in the market and convert it into gold in country A, where it would be held under earmark. Alternatively, country A could sell gold to country B from its holdings there in exchange for currency B and then sell currency B (against currency A) in the market. In both cases, country A sold gold to country B, but the initiating country differed and the location of gold movements differed. Thus, Britain could purchase dollars and exchange them for gold in New York, America could sell gold held in London to Britain for sterling and then use it to buy dollars in the market, or there could be some combination of the two.

Each country felt the other should take the initiative. In a letter to Siepmann in December 1937, Allan Sproul of the Federal Reserve Bank of New York argued that the crucial distinction between the dollar and other currencies was that the dollar was fixed on gold. The British "seem to be the money managers," Sproul wrote, "while we merely provide the fixed points which help you to manage." When the dollar was under pressure, gold needed to move from America to Britain. The best way to facilitate this, Sproul argued, was for the price of gold in London to rise to the equivalent of $35.22, the point at which shipping gold from New York to London was profitable. "If and when the dollar equivalent of the London gold price reaches $35.22+, you can take gold here at $35.08 ¾ [$35 plus 0.25 percent handling charge], an ordinary operation which would seem to be right down the Tripartite alley," Sproul stated.[97] In other words, once the dollar price of gold in London was high enough, the British could purchase dollars and convert them into gold in New York, so that it bought gold on profitable terms and helped strengthen the dollar. Underlying this suggestion, and the entire letter, was the notion that the dollar was the anchor currency and that the system worked best when other countries took advantage of the fixed buying and selling prices for gold, with the United States employing the ESF on a more limited basis.

[97] Sproul to Siepmann, December 7, 1937, BoE C43/327.

Siepmann did not find the matter so simple. While the dollar certainly had unique properties, the key element for him was whether a currency was weak or strong. In his reply, Siepmann characterized Sproul's argument as placing the "initiative ... with us at all times because we are a 'control' and you, being on the gold standard, are passive," and then countered that "[o]ur primary duty is ... to look after and defend our own currency and we must avoid interfering with other people's."[98] Whatever the differences in monetary arrangements, each country should be responsible for defending its currency proactively, and "co-operation should be biased in favour of the side which is in difficulties," Siepmann continued. [99] Members should concentrate on strengthening weak currencies rather than weakening strong ones, an approach, Siepmann believed, conducive to a healthy monetary system that minimized the opportunities for seeking a competitive advantage. Finally, there were technical matters involving US policy for converting dollars into gold that Siepmann thought made it easier for America to support the dollar than for Britain to do so.[100]

In the end, Siepmann and Sproul, and thus Britain and the United States, did not reach any hard-and-fast agreement on who should intervene when. Soon enough, pressure on the dollar ceased, by which point the shoe was on the other foot. The deteriorating political situation in Europe sent the pound into a prolonged period of weakness. As Siepmann had argued, the British were willing, and believed it their obligation, to take the lead when the pound was under pressure. The matter thus became less prominent. But the underlying tension remained. Indeed, the issue of intervention initiative, dormant for some time, would reappear in the postwar years, with the United States taking a passive approach, often to the consternation of others.[101] The Tripartite years thus not only marked the

---

[98] Siepmann to Sproul, December 15, 1937, BoE ADM25/12.

[99] Siepmann to Sproul, November 12, 1937, BoE ADM25/12.

[100] The large spread on US gold prices made countries hesitant to convert dollars into gold. Moreover, while private arbitrageurs could purchase gold in London and ship it to New York, they could not purchase gold in New York and ship it to London since the US Treasury no longer offered export licenses. This asymmetry heightened the role of exchange funds when the dollar was weak, making the question of initiative all the more important. Siepmann, "Foreign Lending and Control of the Exchanges," December 11, 1937, BoE C43/77.

[101] After World War II, the United States did not begin intervening until 1961 (Bordo, Humpage, and Schwartz 2015, chapter 4). There were also intra-European tensions on splitting up intervention in the postwar decades (Mourlon-Druol 2012, chapter 3).

beginning of cooperative intervention but the start of debating how best to orchestrate it.

The Dollar Scare fizzled out with the new year. Kindleberger (1986, 273) is largely correct that it was "neither serious nor prolonged," but it was in part neither serious nor prolonged because the United States was willing to act – with words and money – to dispel the rumors and uphold the Tripartite Agreement. Though the British would have preferred it to act more forcefully, this difference of opinion in no way threatened the fundamental premise of the Agreement, to which both countries subscribed.

With the Gold Scare and the Dollar Scare, 1937 was certainly an odd year in monetary history. Summing up, *The Economist* remarked, "The gold scare of April and May was due to fears of impending reduction in the dollar price of gold, while, conversely, the dollar scare of November reflected the fear of a forthcoming increase in the dollar price of gold. To set these two scares side by side is sufficient to disclose their inherent absurdity."[102] Each crisis had a seed of reason: Both countries had absorbed record amounts of gold; Roosevelt had a history of altering the dollar's value. But the rumors ran far ahead of reality and ultimately collapsed in the face of government action. Throughout, Britain and America had been in constant contact, working to reduce volatility and determine a common policy on gold that reaffirmed its indispensable role. France had also been party to many of these conversations. But it had played a minor part because, as we turn to next, its focus had been inward on the incessant drain of gold that threatened the franc, the economy, the country, and the Tripartite Agreement.

---

[102] "Tripartite Agreement in Action," *The Economist*, December 25, 1937.

8

Keeping France Afloat, 1937–1938

The "burden" of having too much gold was a problem with which the French could not relate. More often than not during the Tripartite years, Paris was losing gold. At times, its exchange fund even ran completely out of reserves. The franc's managers could only wish they had gold to spare. Instead, they had to contend with a series of crises, resulting from economic malaise, political strain, and international tension. Budget deficits wrecked the country's finances, public discontent corroded its foundations, and war clouds imperiled its safety. Prices rose relentlessly – the wholesale price index went up 30 percent in the year after September 1936 and then 35 percent the following year – eroding the franc's competitiveness. Though the French fought to maintain their exchange rate, they lost the battle, repeatedly. The franc depreciated from 105 per pound in the days after the Tripartite Agreement to 147 at the end of 1937 and 179 by the spring of 1938. "So much," Drummond (1979, 32) exclaims, "for the stability of exchange rates under the Tripartite Agreement!"

Indeed, the trials of the franc posed an existential threat to the Tripartite Agreement. Such sharp falls in the franc made the Agreement prima facie a failure: Serial depreciation did not appear to fit with a commitment to exchange stability. The British Treasury feared the pact would become a "farce."[1] In addition, French troubles risked undermining the cooperative framework on which the Agreement rested. London and Washington were tired of uncertainty and volatility (unsympathetic to the fact that Paris was far more exhausted than both). Tempers flared. The British felt the French too often notified rather than consulted. The Americans thought the French were not always truthful. The French believed they deserved greater

[1] Hopkins to Simon, September 10, 1937, T 160/766.

187

support – moral and financial. At stake: the very existence of the currency club and the future of the international monetary system. Should the club crumble, monetary policymakers might revert to the antipathies of earlier years, jeopardizing broader relations just as war inched closer.

But the French were not read out of the Tripartite Agreement. The members stuck together. The commitment to cooperate persisted. On one level, French policy was not necessarily inconsistent with the Agreement's principles. Stable rates did not mean fixed rates. Forswearing "competitive exchange advantage" did not mean renouncing depreciation. The parties understood when drafting the Agreement in 1936 that exchange rate adjustment could be necessary at times, and French conditions seemed to merit some movement in the franc given the much higher rate of inflation. In early 1937, London and Washington actually encouraged Paris to let the franc fall.

Moreover, even though depreciation during these years went beyond what Britain and America desired, the French demonstrated their fidelity to the Tripartite Agreement by maintaining the free exchange of funds, abiding by the rules of the twenty-four-hour gold standard, and yielding enormous sums of gold to defend the franc. As *The Economist* argued in September 1937, France had not "broken the terms of the Agreement, for she has neither imposed exchange restrictions nor indulged in a wilful and competitive depreciation of her currency. To-day the chief need is to continue the Agreement, and to interpret it elastically."[2] London and Washington agreed, deeming it best to "stretch" the accord rather than allow it to shrivel on the basis of too strict an interpretation.[3] The true import of the Agreement was not that it specified precise rules on exchange rate variability, which it pointedly did not, but that it brought the members together so that disagreement triggered discussion and negotiation rather than seclusion and indignation.

The Tripartite Agreement also endured because it was as much political as economic. Morgenthau believed the "moral backing it gives to England and France" was "just as important as the stabilizing of the exchanges."[4] French leaders spoke often of being "bound to two great democracies by the tripartite agreement," convinced that deepening ties was imperative at a time of increasing danger on the continent.[5] Britain was not as explicit in

[2] "London and Washington," *The Economist*, September 25, 1937.
[3] Siepmann to Sproul, November 12, 1937, BoE ADM25/12.
[4] Treasury meeting, November 16, 1936, MD 45/45.
[5] Cochran telegram, November 12, 1938, MD 150/235.

its articulation but grew to share the sentiment.[6] To Norman, the Agreement had "become a declaration of international solidarity on which the world now counts."[7] Whether or not war eventually came, all the parties understood that the democracies had to work together, both to demonstrate cohesion and to show that liberalism could compete in a world careening toward totalitarianism. It was this combination of economics – getting countries to work toward stability even if not all could achieve it – and politics – understanding that the club had to remain united – that made the members so committed.

This chapter examines the problems of the franc and, in so doing, reveals how the club navigated questions about membership and rules. The Big Three generally shared the following hierarchy of priorities (in decreasing order of importance): maintain solidarity, uphold the Tripartite Agreement, forestall exchange control, and prevent excessive depreciation. They succeeded in achieving their top three priorities, a signal accomplishment. Yet confidence in the franc plummeted at times, and with French requests for financial support refused and capital fleeing at an unsustainable rate, depreciation seemed the only way out. The ensuing falls in the franc were larger than Britain or America wished, but both agreed that it was much better to manage them within the club than to eject France. As Whitehall told Washington, "A breakup of the Tripartite arrangement would be hailed everywhere by advocates of autocracy as a disaster for liberal ideas in international finance and business."[8] And such a result was to be avoided if the values cherished by democracies were to have a chance.

PAUSE THEN FALL

Britain's policymakers focused on two exchange rates: the dollar and the franc. Uncertainty about the former gripped officials and markets during the Gold and Dollar Scares, as discussed in Chapter 7. But in day-to-day matters, management of the sterling-dollar rate became rather mechanical as the Tripartite system matured: consult with the Federal Reserve Bank of New York (FRBNY), intervene to dampen fluctuations, inform the

---

[6] Though the Foreign Office was not involved in the negotiations leading to the Tripartite Agreement or subsequent developments, Drummond (1981, 218) notes that it was "inclined to see the declarations as a significant step in democratic cooperation, consultation, and solidarity."

[7] "Introductory Remarks," May 26, 1937, BoE C43/25.

[8] Note delivered by Bewley, May 4, 1938, MD 123/209; Draft telegram to Bewley, May 4, 1938, T 160/766.

FRBNY, and clear in gold. Experts at the Bank of England (BoE) had broad authority from Whitehall to act as necessary. From the Tripartite Agreement's announcement to the summer of 1938, the rate never went below \$4.87 or above \$5.04, and volatility was lower than during the corresponding period preceding the Agreement. Both countries had sufficient reserves to ensure that neither had to worry about market pressures draining them of gold and forcing substantial depreciation at a moment's notice.

Such was not the case with the franc.[9] Crises always seemed afoot. Club members fretted over the currency's prospects. And the rate fell repeatedly. In one regard, the British were less concerned with the franc than they had been prior to the Tripartite Agreement. Having shifted from managing the pound against the franc to the dollar, they now rarely intervened in the franc market on their own account. Indeed, they effectively ceded day-to-day control of the sterling-franc rate to Paris. But nonintervention in no way implied disinterest. Because of gold clearing, British reserves moved with French intervention: When the franc was weak, the French exchange fund yielded gold to Britain's to obtain sterling; when the franc was strong, the French fund bought gold from Britain's in exchange for sterling. These operations accounted for the bulk of the variation in the holdings of the Exchange Equalisation Account (EEA) and at times filled the fund with so much gold that Britain risked losing capacity to intervene on its own initiative. The franc also mattered given the trading relationship with France and the not-to-be-ignored interests of exporters. But, most of all, the franc was of prime concern because the Tripartite Agreement bound all three currencies together. Britain simply could not ignore its fate.

Unfortunately, the franc did not seem headed anywhere good. The postdevaluation honeymoon was brief and capital repatriation limited. Charles Cariguel, foreign exchange manager at the Banque de France (BdF), continued to hold the franc at 105 to the pound even as markets turned against the currency in late October 1936 and despite the monetary law permitting a range of 98 to 112. He kept the rate steady not because he thought a hard peg the best policy but because his superiors did. Unlike Harry Siepmann and the BoE, Cariguel did not have much discretion in running the French exchange fund. The Finance Ministry maintained tight control and believed that the public, still digesting the demise of the franc Poincaré, could not stomach a moving rate.[10] So Cariguel did what he

---

[9] This chapter builds on Drummond (1979) and Mouré (2002, chapter 8).
[10] Mouré (2002, 230).

could to defend the 105 rate – he sold a lot of gold. By January, the 10-billion-franc exchange fund ran dry and needed a public injection from the BdF.[11]

The obvious problem with this strategy, as Chancellor of the Exchequer Neville Chamberlain explained to Premier Léon Blum in early 1937, was that with gold flowing out, speculators knew that any break in the peg would be a depreciation toward 112 and thus kept doubling down on their bets against the currency.[12] And the more gold France lost the more Britain had to absorb. "Nothing could be worse," Siepmann commented, "as we have frequently protested, than to maintain a cast-iron peg at any rate whatever.... This is a situation in which French losses of gold are likely to be as high as they can possibly be, and the effect is to reduce the sterling resources of the E.E.A. to an alarming extent."[13] He tried at the end of January 1937 to coordinate a joint maneuver with Cariguel to break the franc out of its box and punish speculators, but the French government was not yet ready to act.[14]

The crux of the problem facing Blum was that the economy failed to reach escape velocity. The September devaluation gave a much-needed fillip, but it was not deep or sustained enough to alter the situation fundamentally. The Popular Front's social program, particularly the inflexible application of the forty-hour law, held the economy back. The reforms were, of course, about much more than economics: They provided many workers with a treasured sense of liberation and autonomy and redressed a long-standing imbalance between labor and capital. But there were economic consequences too. They increased the cost of production, thereby attenuating the boost to competitiveness from devaluation, and they drove up government expenditure. Moreover, international tensions necessitated rearmament, further straining the nation's finances. The situation was unsustainable. Pulled from every angle, Blum announced a "pause" in his reforms on February 13, 1937, so as to let the economy adjust to those on the books and create space for defense spending.[15]

The pause was not enough to make 105 sustainable, however, leaving Paris with a familiar choice: go the way of Germany and impose exchange controls or depreciate the franc. Blum ruled out the former course. Even though he thought exchange controls might be beneficial financially, he explained to the Finance Ministry's Jacques Rueff that they would have the

---

[11] Oye (1985, 196).   [12] Chamberlain to Blum, February 19, 1937, T 177/34.
[13] Siepmann, Untitled memo, January 28, 1937, BoE C43/343.
[14] Mouré (2002, 231–32).   [15] Colton (1987, 191–92).

"fatal effect of straining the ties which unite us to the Anglo-Saxon powers, ties which are essential to the coherent development of our foreign policy."[16] After all, paragraph four of the Tripartite Agreement called on members "to relax progressively the present system of quotas and exchange controls with a view to their abolition." Britain was convinced that French institution of controls would bring all of the negative aspects of centralization and restriction of trade without the success of the German system: In the end, France would still need to devalue, resulting in the worst of both worlds.[17] While Washington and London never reached agreement on precisely which restrictive measures would trigger expulsion from the club, it was clear to Paris that resort to financial coercion would jeopardize its membership. Blum informed Chamberlain that "the French Government firmly refuses to establish an exchange control which would in effect be contrary to the principles of the monetary agreement and to the requirements of close international co-operation."[18] The Tripartite Agreement was a pillar of Blum's foreign policy, and he understood that clamping down on the free movement of funds risked shattering it.

The other option was depreciation, which, far from opposing, club members supported. Chamberlain informed Blum in February that he saw no reason why the franc should remain stuck at 105 and suggested Paris "make use of the liberty given by the existing law."[19] The implication was that London would not view depreciation to 112 unfavorably. Morgenthau felt likewise and suggested as much to Georges Bonnet, Paris' ambassador to Washington.[20] As Morgenthau told a British representative – part of the continuous coordination on the French situation between the two countries – depreciation up to the limit of the monetary law would be "within the sacred circle of the Tripartite Agreement."[21]

---

[16] Quoted in Jackson (1988, 180).

[17] As Phillips told Butterworth, "We did not believe that exchange control in practice meant higher exchange rates; you would get both Exchange Control plus depreciated exchanges." Phillips, Untitled note, May 3, 1938, T 160/766.

[18] "Message from Monsieur Blum and Monsieur Vincent Auriol to the Chancellor of the Exchequer," February 17, 1937, T 177/34.

[19] Chamberlain to Blum, February 19, 1937, T 177/34. Opposition to controls by the Radicals in Blum's coalition also played a role. But even here the opposition resulted in part from international considerations. At a party congress in 1937, delegates resolved that the party "[r]esolutely rejects exchange control, which would result in isolating France from other countries and would definitely ruin the currency by the unlimited inflation which it would provoke." Cochran telegram, October 30, 1937, MD 93/268.

[20] Morgenthau conversation with Bonnet, March 5, 1937, MD 58/72.

[21] Morgenthau conversation with Mallet, March 5, 1937, MD 58/74.

Though Blum did not follow the advice to depreciate immediately, in early March he appointed a committee to oversee the stabilization fund, choosing conservative experts in the hopes of reassuring capital interests and seizing the initiative on the financial front.[22] The committee soon decided to allow the franc to move to 112, to which Chamberlain and Morgenthau raised no objection.[23] There was a temporary reflux of gold, but the outflow resumed in late April. Blum just could not catch a break. In mid-June, two members of the exchange committee resigned when their entreaties for fiscal retrenchment went unheeded. The blow to confidence was swift, the acceleration in capital outflows once again emptying the exchange fund of gold.[24] Blum sought decree powers to tackle the mounting crisis, but the Senate refused to grant him the authority, leading to his resignation on June 21. The balance of power in the Popular Front government then shifted away from the socialists. In the cabinet reshuffling, Camille Chautemps (Radical) became head of government, Blum deputy premier, and Bonnet (Radical) finance minister.

Bonnet rushed from Washington to Paris to assume his position, arriving at noon on June 28, 1937.[25] Within hours, the government decided that the franc could no longer remain bound by the monetary law and that it would seek decree powers to remove the gold limits. That night, the French informed British and American representatives of the plan to abrogate the law. London was not pleased with the procedure. Sir John Simon, who was now chancellor, wrote to Bonnet that, while Paris claimed "the communication was made under paragraph 3 of the Tripartite Agreement," he could "not see how there can be any effective consultation at this stage when a decision has been reached and is about to be communicated to the French Parliament."[26] Washington, on the other hand, tended to be more forgiving, with one official pleased that the notification "gave us very precise advance information as to what the French Government planned to do."[27] Both sides had a point. Prior warning was useful, but the presentation of a fait accompli left little room for other members to make their opinions

---

[22] The experts were Rueff; Charles Rist, an eminent economist and former BdF official; and Paul Baudouin, a banker.

[23] Colton (1987, 193).

[24] Rowe-Dutton, "Financial Situation in France," July 23, 1937, T 177/34. Rueff did not resign as, unlike the two other members, he was a government official. Nevertheless, he supported their move (Mouré 2002, 234).

[25] See MD 76 for a detailed discussion of events.

[26] Simon to Bonnet, June 29, 1937, T 160/689.

[27] Cochran to Morgenthau, July 7, 1937, MD 76/19.

clear. The central problem, by no means unique to the Tripartite Agreement, was that the chaos of exchange crises often impelled quicker decision-making and less deliberation than the parties thought ideal. This tension would remain throughout the Tripartite years.

June 29, 1937, was a day of intense discussions, within and between governments, as London and Washington worked together to determine their response and communicated with Paris to better understand its intentions. One concern was how the French plan would impact gold convertibility. Of all the components of the Tripartite system, gold convertibility was the most categorical: Either the central bank provided a daily price and agreed to yield gold or it did not, whereas competitive depreciation and exchange control were more nebulous concepts. The BdF had not quoted a gold price that day, raising alarms in Britain and America. As Simon wrote to Morgenthau:

I do not know whether we shall have any quotations or if so whether the French authorities will be ready to continue arrangement to turn daily surpluses of francs into gold. I am completely in the dark as to how we can operate. It is no doubt true that the French Government can continue to express concurrence in the very general declarations which were embodied in the tripartite agreement itself but I cannot help feeling that what has especially attracted notice and especially been approved by public opinion everywhere was the general character of the administrative arrangements concerted at the time of that declaration and continued since to give practical effect to the desire to maintain the greatest possible stability in exchanges.[28]

Convertibility not only facilitated intervention but also served as a manifestation of cooperation. Were France to stop providing gold, the Tripartite system would likely founder, with members no longer willing to work with the French and observers questioning the utility of the pact. Paris quickly responded that the absence of a quotation was due only to the turmoil engulfing the government and affirmed its intention to continue with the arrangements moving forward.[29]

In the end, with this assurance and after much back-and-forth, Simon and Morgenthau decided that French actions were consistent with the

---

[28] Butterworth telegram to Morgenthau, June 29, 1937, MD 74/275. Morgenthau also spoke with Simon about France via telephone, though the conversation was stilted as Simon did not enjoy transatlantic calls. In his earlier stint as foreign secretary, his calls with Secretary of State Henry Stimson on Manchuria in 1932 had led to a misunderstanding that became publicly embarrassing. Morgenthau conversation with Simon, June 29, 1937, MD 74/178–89; Morgenthau conversation with Simon, December 17, 1937, MD 103/63–74; Dutton (1992, 133).

[29] "Reponse a votre communication telephonique," June 29, 1937, T 160/689.

Tripartite Agreement. Expelling France would bring no benefit and would only make a stable franc more difficult to achieve. As Bonnet often emphasized, the Agreement was the "strongest argument" he had for defending the government's liberal policy in parliament and public.[30] The international stakes weighed heavily as well. "The whole world is on the brink," Morgenthau told staff, "and we are trying to save the only one agreement that is in existence between the countries."[31] Morgenthau similarly wrote to Simon, "In the present juncture of world affairs, I trust you will agree with me that it is of prime importance to preserve the beneficial effects which resulted from the Tripartite Declaration and its ensuing arrangement. It was thus demonstrated that great democratic nations could, with mutual confidence, create and carry out co-operative measures."[32] Simon "fully agree[d]," and the two countries coordinated the release of statements declaring the Agreement in force.[33] The other members of the club, which were not involved in these deliberations, "expressed great relief" when informed by the US Treasury that there would be no expulsion.[34]

Whether the franc's fall – it went from 112 to the pound on June 29 to 128 on July 1 and 133 by the end of the month – contravened the Tripartite Agreement's principles is in some sense simple to answer (see Figure 8.1 for the sterling-franc rate). France disclaimed any competitive intention and the other members accepted that; ipso facto, it was in compliance. The more illuminating question is how vigorously the French tried to defend the franc. The EEA's gold ledgers show that from October 1936 to June 1937, France sold £216 million of gold to Britain. This gold loss was more than double the original endowment of the French exchange fund. Total, the French parted with roughly 20 percent of their gold during these months.[35] Nobody doubted that Paris was putting up a fight. The

---

[30] Bonnet to Simon, June 30, 1937, BoE C43/90.

[31] Treasury meeting, July 1, 1937, MD 77/22.

[32] Telegram to Butterworth, June 30, 1937, MD 75/233.

[33] Simon did, however, send a personal message to Bonnet, with Morgenthau's cognizance, expressing his "apprehension both on the score of the level to which the franc may fall and on the difficulty of controlling it." If the franc became too erratic, Simon was unsure whether Britain "would be able to continue reciprocal arrangements on the lines which have been followed up to now." "Personal Message from the Chancellor of the Exchequer to Monsieur Bonnet," July 1, 1937, T 160/689; "Message for Mr. Morgenthau from the Chancellor of the Exchequer," July 1, 1937, T 160/689.

[34] Taylor to Morgenthau, July 6, 1937, MD 77.

[35] "French Exchange Fund," August 3, 1937, BoE C43/343; "Bankers' Gazette," *The Economist*, October 10, 1936, and July 3, 1937.

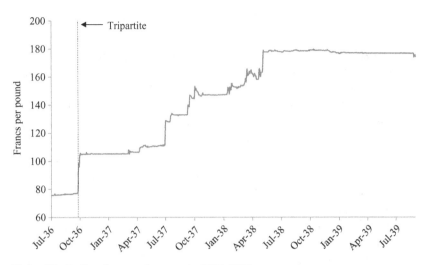

Figure 8.1 Sterling-franc exchange rate, 1936–1939.
Source: Global Financial Data

counterfactual is impossible to know, but one suspects that in the absence of the Agreement, the effort would have been more muted.

Abrogation of the monetary law meant that the franc was no longer anchored to a physical quantity of gold. The French explained to London that their aim was "to pursue a policy exactly similar to the policy of the United Kingdom" in ironing out exchange fluctuations but defending no parity.[36] There was certainly a similarity in that the pound also had no gold anchor. But London did not appreciate the comparison, believing that markets did not have the necessary faith in the underlying value of the franc to allow for such management. A miffed Siepmann declared the franc "rotten at the core." He thought that, at the very least, the government ought to give Cariguel "a free hand" in tactical decisions.[37] Bonnet did remove Émile Labeyrie as governor of the BdF, replacing him with the much more qualified Pierre Fournier. But with the exchange committee defunct, the Ministry of Finance resumed control over currency policy.

Even though the French disclaimed any intention of pegging, they held the rate at 133 through August. The currency then weakened in September and crossed 150 in early October. The renewed depreciation set off another flood of cables between capitals. Sir Frederick Phillips happened to be in

---

[36] Mönick statement, June 29, 1937, T 160/689; Morgenthau conversation with Butterworth, June 30, 1937, MD 75/20.
[37] Siepmann, Untitled memo, July 19, 1937, BoE C43/343.

Washington for previously scheduled discussions and conferred with Morgenthau on the matter.[38] Whitehall cabled Phillips that the French "ought to continue to be regarded as members of the Club as long as possible."[39] The US State Department's top economic official argued that French motivations were in the right place, even if the results were wanting: "The French Government has always shown an exceptional disposition to try to make the agreement work: firstly, in the extent of the gold losses; and secondly, in its stern avoidance of exchange control. There are extraordinarily few nations in the world that would have gone through what they have been going through without controlling exchanges."[40] Britain and America deemed it best – for the franc's future, for France's future, and for the currency club's future – to view the depreciation as in conformity with the Tripartite Agreement. After weakening to 153 on October 2, the franc finally found relief in the last quarter of the year, as the onset of recession in the United States and the concomitant Dollar Scare shifted market concern across the Atlantic, and the franc strengthened to 147 by December.

The Tripartite Agreement had survived its first year. Simon gave an appraisal of these months at his Mansion House address in October. Since the Agreement's announcement, "a welcome degree of stability has been maintained between the pound and the dollar. As regards the franc, our hopes have not been fulfilled to the same extent. The French Government has had to face great difficulties, and I desire to pay my tribute to the efforts which it is making to overcome these difficulties."[41] It was an apt assessment, though many in the audience probably wondered how the arrangement actually worked behind the scenes, free of any gloss added for public consumption. Intergovernmental relations were messy, and there had been no shortage of hurt feelings and harsh words, as members sought to take measure of one another, deal with pressing issues, juggle conflicting interests, and understand the limits of acceptable action. But there was also no question to those involved that it was far better to talk things out than retreat to the hostile silence of earlier years.

The benefits of dialogue were particularly evident in the relationship between London and Washington. Both were exasperated by the franc's

---

[38] See files in MD 89, especially Butterworth, Memorandum of meeting with Phillips, September 23, 1937, MD 89/18–20.

[39] Treasury telegram to Phillips, October 5, 1937, T 160/766.

[40] "Meeting re exchange of views with British on French situation," September 21, 1937, MD 89/118.

[41] "Rising Tide of Prosperity," *The Times* (London), October 8, 1937.

periodic crises, though the US government approached them with a greater affection for the Popular Front than did His Majesty's Government, which felt less ideological kinship. The two Treasuries spoke candidly with one another and developed a routine of conferring prior to formulating a position vis-à-vis France. There were drawbacks to this evolving two-power approach, with France appearing at times as a mezzanine member of the club, below the senior two and above the junior three.[42] The nature of the situation, however, made this inevitable. France would remain in good standing, but Britain and America would take the lead.

ROSTER AND RULES

From the end of 1936 to the beginning of 1938, discussion of the currency club's roster was not solely about whether France should remain. There was also talk about bringing in new members. The six countries adhering to the Tripartite Agreement made sense as a group – liberal economies, important and independent currencies – but there was no self-evident reason why the list should end there. The Big Three had, after all, "invite[d] the cooperation" of other nations in the Agreement's final paragraph, and perhaps more would like to join.

Indeed, Sweden expressed interest soon after the Agreement's announcement. The central banks of Denmark, Finland, and Norway then deputized Ivar Rooth, head of the Sveriges Riksbank, to find out more about the system's operation. Morgenthau was keen on bringing these countries in, as they were important economies that largely adhered to the club's principles. But toward the end of 1936 they decided against participating. As Rooth explained to H. Merle Cochran, Morgenthau's European envoy, the four central banks were committed to acting in unison and they felt that Denmark's system of exchange control precluded it, and thus all of them, from joining. London, for its part, was hesitant to admit them anyway.[43] The countries were part of the Sterling Area,

---

[42] Mönick complained to London that Phillips' visit to Washington "had unfortunately given rise to the impression that the French were, to some extent, being left in the cold and that the Tripartite Agreement was becoming bipartite." Morgenthau tried to arrange an unofficial visit with the French economist Charles Rist, but the plans fell through. Waley to Hopkins, September 23, 1937, T 160/766; Morgenthau conversation with Cochran, October 14, 1937, MD 92/118–26; Morgenthau conversation with Cochran, December 29, 1937, MD 104/187–92.

[43] Cochran to Morgenthau, December 28, 1936, MD 43/part II; Bingham telegram to Treasury, November 20, 1936, MD 46/6.

meaning that they already kept their exchange rates steady with the pound, and Britain wanted them to remain squarely in its sphere of influence. Scandinavia's self-disqualification thus saved the club from a potential confrontation.

With the most plausible new members no longer interested, the early momentum to expand the club petered out. But there were a few other preliminary discussions in the following years. The oddest case occurred in March 1937. As France lost gold and Blum's grip on power appeared tenuous, Morgenthau hit on what he thought was a brilliant plan. "There is one way to solve this French problem," he concluded. "[W]e should ask Soviet Russia to join the Tripartite Agreement. With their large holdings of gold it might make just the sufficient difference to tide the French across the present crisis."[44] Apparently he had forgiven Moscow for its supposed attempt to destroy the Tripartite Agreement several months earlier. In fact, he started to think that realpolitik necessitated moving closer to Moscow, as "Russia and we have the same common enemies," a perceptive judgment to be sure.

Morgenthau admitted that the scheme was not yet fully "crystallized," but even as a preliminary idea it was ill-judged.[45] Britain and America had more than enough gold to aid France; they just refused to use it. Morgenthau never articulated how Russian gold would make its way to the BdF's vaults, nor how drafting a communist country would strengthen a club predicated on liberal values. No doubt, as the Gold Scare set in that spring, the opacity of Russian gold production became more troublesome, and Morgenthau believed it imperative to gain insight into Moscow's thinking. But membership in the club was neither necessary nor sufficient for this aim. He mooted the idea to the British in April but realized, after much pushback from his incredulous advisors, that it was no masterstroke and dropped it, without ever having mentioned it to the Russians.[46]

A rather different episode occurred when Japan approached Britain about joining in May 1937.[47] Japan often conducted monetary operations in a less-than-transparent manner. The prospect of shining a light on these transactions was enticing, as was the possibility of getting Tokyo to relax its

[44] Dictation, March 3, 1937, MD 57/233.
[45] Treasury meeting, March 3, 1937, MD 57/281–82.
[46] Bewley, Untitled memo, April 14, 1937, T 177/35; Morgenthau conversation with Feis and Lochhead, April 22, 1937, MD 65/391. Morgenthau did, however, discuss Russian gold production with Soviet representatives and facilitated the opening of an account for the Russian State Bank with the FRBNY. "Soviet Russia," undated, MD 64/79–81.
[47] Untitled memo, May 27, 1937, T 160/840/8.

exchange controls and the slight chance of pulling it away from Berlin and Rome. Unlike with Morgenthau's Russia gambit, there was some genuine interest in including Japan and a fair amount of discussion between British and American representatives. Japan had raised the issue, after all, and so would perhaps be willing to make significant concessions to join.

But authorities decided not to extend an invitation. The benefits seemed "completely intangible," as W. Walton Butterworth, the US financial attaché in London, told Phillips during one of their regular conversations, while the risks of admitting a country with exchange controls were too large. France might then feel free to impose them as well. Phillips agreed.[48] There was no formal rejection because there was ambiguity as to whether Japan's financial attaché had specifically asked to join or was merely testing the waters. Anyway, the Japanese soon imposed additional exchange restrictions; as a result, London felt they had "blackballed themselves from the club."[49] And with Japan's invasion of China ratcheting up during the second half of 1937, talk of membership ceased completely, consideration of sanctions taking its place.

In addition to these abortive one-off attempts to expand the club, 1937 witnessed a sustained effort to figure out how best to build on the Tripartite Agreement's liberal principles, especially as the much hoped for unfettering of trade had yet to occur. Britain and France commissioned Paul van Zeeland, Belgium's prime minister, to conduct "an inquiry into the possibility of obtaining a general reduction of quotas and of other obstacles to international trade" in April 1937.[50] Van Zeeland undertook an intensive study, not only exploring how to improve economic conditions among the democracies but also how to bring Germany and Italy into the international economy. The final report, issued in January 1938, touched on many topics, from the goals of ending import quotas and abolishing exchange controls to the questions on raw materials and colonial holdings around which economic appeasement revolved.

In terms of monetary policy recommendations, Van Zeeland argued that the "best policy" would be the "re-establishment of the gold standard, though on a considerably altered basis." However, he conceded that such an outcome was unlikely at present and that focus should turn to

---

[48] Butterworth telegram to Treasury, May 28, 1937, MD 70/225.
[49] Butterworth telegram to Treasury, July 8, 1937, MD 78/63.
[50] Van Zeeland (1938, 48). See Crozier (1988, chapter 9) for a detailed discussion of Van Zeeland's mission.

"interim solutions," foremost "the revision and extension" of the Tripartite Agreement:

The parties interested would agree to define the reciprocal parities of their currencies, in relation to each other, and would pledge themselves to keep any eventual variations within certain limits. The undertaking should extend over a period long enough to free current commercial operations from any monetary risk; it should be for one year or at least for six months – proviso being made for quite exceptional circumstances, a character practically equivalent to that of *force majeure*. . . .

As for the form of such an agreement, there would be no objection to its retaining the very flexible one of joint declarations.[51]

Observers often faulted the Tripartite Agreement for not stabilizing rates within predetermined and public ranges. For those brought up on and nostalgic for fixed parities, the twenty-four-hour gold standard was not sufficient, and the French experience suggested that the general pronouncements in the Agreement needed to be supplemented by more stringent commitments. Van Zeeland shared this view, proposing a middle way between the present system and the gold standard. This reform would include setting ranges for rates, not through statute but through the "joint declarations" technique employed to great effect by the Tripartite Agreement. Van Zeeland's ultimate aim was to bring Germany, Italy, and other countries into this reformed arrangement as part of a grand settlement. But he also thought that getting the original members to commit to hold rates for longer periods would be an accomplishment in itself – and surely more achievable.

Policymakers in Britain and America, who were most insistent on the necessity of maintaining freedom of maneuver, did not reject the idea out of hand. They agreed that progress on the monetary front would best be funneled through the currency club. Nobody wanted to return to the practice of unwieldy conferences where anticipation ran so high as to make failure inevitable. The Tripartite Agreement's framework permitted more flexibility and allowed for discreet negotiations on an ongoing basis.[52] France favored stronger commitments on exchange rates, believing that the franc's instability was due in part to the flexibility of the dollar and sterling.[53] There was considerable back-and-forth on a range of proposals

---

[51] Van Zeeland (1938, 52).

[52] As for the specific idea of committing to rates for a preset period, the British worried that doing so would court speculation as the end date approached but did not reject the suggestion out of hand. Cochran telegram, February 15, 1938, MD 110/158.

[53] Paris approached London and Washington about the possibility of France returning to the gold standard and the group as a whole moving to more rigid rates, though by the

in the weeks after publication of Van Zeeland's report. There was even talk of approaching Germany and Italy. Though it was unclear what extension to the Tripartite Agreement, if any, would occur, and to what extent the democracies would seek rapprochement with the fascist powers under Van Zeeland's auspices, there was momentum behind doing something.

But then, on March 12, 1938, German tanks entered Austria. The Anschluss upended the international situation, shunting the Van Zeeland report to the side. As Sir Frederick Leith-Ross explained to a correspondent, the Treasury had been considering how to move forward with the proposals, but then "the Germans suddenly pounced on Austria" and the calculus changed.[54] Economic concessions would not bring world peace. Adding to the sense of chaos, the nine-month-old Chautemps cabinet had resigned on March 10, leading to Blum's resumption of the premiership on March 13. Any hope in Paris of returning to the gold standard or committing to stabilize the franc at its current rate faded. Just holding on was difficult enough. The various efforts at expanding the Tripartite Agreement had therefore come to naught: The currency club would have six and only six members. With the international scene darkening, it was now more imperative than ever to keep them all together.

FINAL DROP

The misfortunes of the franc, however, threatened one more time to rip the club apart. The currency depreciated from 147 per pound at the beginning of 1938 to 153 by the start of March and then weakened to 165 following the Anschluss. Blum, whose misery as premier was compounded by serving as his own finance minister, struggled to get a grip on the situation. Morgenthau offered to consider – should Paris express interest and only with London's concurrence – whether control of capital flows could be consistent with the Tripartite Agreement. The outflows of capital were the primary source of pressure on the franc, and restrictions on capital seemed of a different, and more permissible, kind than those on commercial transactions. Britain and America had both resorted to them in the past and still had some limitations on international investment.[55] Blum,

---

beginning of March the most likely outcome seemed to be a Tripartite statement in support of France rather than a return to fixed rates (Drummond 1979, 26–29).

[54] Leith-Ross to Jones, April 21, 1938, T 188/218.

[55] For instance, Britain prohibited funding new foreign issues in 1931, and while it relaxed the restriction over the years, it did not rescind the measure. Importantly, the embargo covered the financing of new capital issues abroad; nothing prevented investment in

however, did not take Morgenthau up on the offer, perhaps due to his sense that Britain would view implementing such controls as a slippery slope.[56] Anyway, he had far too little time in office to make much headway on financial problems. His second stint as premier lasted for just under a month, and the Radical Édouard Daladier replaced him on April 10, signaling the Popular Front's demise as the new government shifted to the right.

With the franc's prospects worsening, Daladier and Bonnet, now foreign minister, headed to London at the end of April. Bonnet met with Simon to discuss financial issues – very much in the spirit of the Tripartite Agreement – and submitted a series of questions. He wondered whether the governments could agree on a franc rate and then hold the rate through the "concerted assistance" of the exchange funds. Essentially, he was asking if the British would purchase francs without converting them into gold, an action equivalent to operating on joint account. Simon responded in the negative, "since such a use of the Account would be contrary to the understanding on which Parliament has provided the funds."[57]

This explanation was, of course, bogus. The British had bought and held francs in 1932 and 1933; there was no "understanding" that prevented them from doing so now. Rather, London worried that it would take a loss on such purchases. This concern was reasonable, but it also highlighted a weakness of the currency club: The members refused to provide financial support to one another. It was not that they were unaware that friendly financing was key to making the system more stable. The BoE had previously considered the possibility of setting up a "joint exchange fund to which all signatories to the Tripartite Agreement would contribute gold and on which any might draw."[58] But the British never proposed the plan, unwilling to take any responsibility – politically or financially – for other currencies.

Anticipating Simon's answer, Bonnet also inquired as to the chancellor's reaction should the French let the franc depreciate sharply, perhaps to 190 or 200, with the aim of catalyzing repatriation and then bringing the rate back to a suitable level. Simon replied that the Tripartite Agreement

preexisting securities. The US government spent much time in the second half of the 1930s studying ways to limit capital inflows. Sayers (1976, 3:284–302); Stewart (1938, 56–57); Bloomfield (1966, 178–86).

[56] Cochran telegram to Morgenthau, March 14, 1938, MD 114/377–80.

[57] "Questions Put by Monsieur Bonnet" and "Replies to Monsieur Bonnet's Questions," April 30, 1938, BoE G1/305.

[58] "The French Franc," September 3, 1937, BoE G1/304.

forbade such a maneuver. Indeed, the British could see no reason why the current rate of 160 should not be maintained. As Siepmann had noted the previous week, "Hitherto the Tripartite Agreement has been interpreted with great laxity, in favour of the French. This was only reasonable, because the franc was obviously undergoing a process of natural adjustment. No such arguments can be adduced in defence of any further move. A rate of 180 would represent serious undervaluation, in present conditions."[59]

Bonnet left empty-handed. Simon made the British position clear, but he ought to have known that doing so did not settle the matter. The French could not continue to lose gold indefinitely. Reserves not only backed up the currency: They constituted the war chest. As Daladier proclaimed, "National Defence is bound up with the solidity of the currency and the integrity of the gold reserve."[60] The country's safety, more and more in doubt, could not permit selling gold without end.

And so, on May 2, 1938, just days after the Anglo-French conversations, Paris informed London and Washington that it intended to depreciate to "around 175" and urgently requested that they judge the action in conformity with the Tripartite Agreement.[61] Morgenthau was furious lest the Agreement become a "laughing stock."[62] He responded that he needed more time to review the request and consult the British, effectively forcing the French to keep selling gold in the interim. Two days of discussions followed. Whitehall found the depreciation excessive but informed the US Treasury that "it was felt that it would be the wrong policy to take any step which would result in France leaving the currency club."[63]

A key factor was the menacing situation on the continent. On May 3, the day after Morgenthau raged about the Tripartite Agreement becoming a joke, Mussolini welcomed Hitler to Rome on a state visit full of fascist pomp. Some three hundred thousand spectators lined the route, cheering the motorcade as it made its way from the train station – specially built for the Fürher's arrival – along the new Via Adolf Hitler to the royal palace.[64] Ejecting France at the very moment that the world was watching this totalitarian spectacle would give the autocrats too much to celebrate. "The British maintain," Butterworth cabled Morgenthau, "that they are just as annoyed as we are about the French action, but they are prepared to

[59] Siepmann, Untitled memo, April 22, 1938, BoE C43/343.
[60] "Stabilisation of the Franc," undated, T 160/766.
[61] Cochran telegram to Morgenthau, May 2, 1938, MD 122/30.
[62] "Treasury meeting re French monetary situation," May 2, 1938, MD 122/95.
[63] Note delivered by Bewley, May 4, 1938, MD 123/210.
[64] "Mussolini Greets Hitler in a Resplendent Rome," *The New York Times*, May 4, 1938.

overlook it because they are profoundly convinced that it would be a grave mistake for political as well as financial reasons to break up the Tripartite Agreement, particularly on the occasion of Hitler's visit to Mussolini."[65] London had been least enthusiastic about attaching political values to the Tripartite Agreement at first, but it had grown to appreciate that the financial could not be separated from the political. France also assured the two countries that this depreciation would be the last. On May 4, they begrudgingly approved the action and affirmed that the Agreement remained in "full operation."[66]

They did not, however, hold back on expressing their displeasure. During parliamentary question time, Simon declared that the move was "not inconsistent" with the Tripartite Agreement, hardly a ringing endorsement and a signal that the next depreciation might not receive such grace.[67] When the French opened the sterling-franc rate at 179 on May 5, after having based discussions on 175, Morgenthau hit the roof. At one point, he protested with such temper to the French ambassador that, at the meeting's conclusion, Morgenthau burned the stenographic record in the fireplace, presumably to reassure the frightened envoy that details of the dressing-down would not leak.[68] Morgenthau pressured Paris to start bringing the rate up immediately. London likewise did not appreciate the weaker-than-expected quotation and believed consultations needed "to be more timely and honest."[69]

Were the political stakes not so high, France very well might have had its membership revoked. But they were and authorities concluded that expulsion would have served little purpose. Observers largely agreed. The *Financial Times* ran the numbers on purchasing power parities and concluded that the franc was likely undervalued. But "it is necessary to take the broad view and not regard the Tripartite Agreement as the law of the Medes and Persians. The real need of the world to-day is a strong and prosperous France, with a revived home production and reconstituted gold reserve."[70] *The Economist* considered Anglo-American acceptance "a valuable decision, both in itself and as a gesture of goodwill."[71] Paris, for its

---

[65] Butterworth telegram to Treasury, May 3, 1938, MD 122/188–89.
[66] Note given to Le Norcy, May 4, 1938, T 160/766.
[67] 335 Parl. Deb. H.C. (5th ser.) (1938) col. 1037. Simon also used this language directly in his communication to Paris. Note given to Le Norcy, May 4, 1938, T 160/766.
[68] Morgenthau conversation with French ambassador, May 6, 1938, MD 123/397.
[69] Untitled memo, May 18, 1938, T 166/760.
[70] "Pound, Franc & Dollar," *Financial Times*, May 9, 1938.
[71] "Background of the Franc," *The Economist*, May 14, 1938.

part, now knew that the boundary of permissible action had been reached, arguably breached, and could not be pushed further without repercussion.

As was becoming routine, depreciation sparked momentary capital repatriation and then the franc once again came under duress.[72] By August 1938, the situation seemed critical. Morgenthau was on his summer holiday in Antibes, chosen in part so that he could travel around the continent to meet club counterparts. Cochran suggested to the secretary that exchange funds start purchasing and holding spot francs as a way to support the currency. Morgenthau did not immediately reject the proposal. But there was a misunderstanding: Morgenthau thought the idea was to have the Exchange Stabilization Fund buy *forward* francs with the French posting gold as collateral and guaranteeing the gold value of those francs, ridding the scheme of much of its merit by tying up French gold. When Cochran corrected him, Morgenthau rehearsed the many reasons why he would not follow his aide's plan, emphasizing that he could not hold spot currencies nor could he neglect the role of profit in exchange management (forward purchases offering a greater likelihood of making a buck).[73]

Morgenthau remained intrigued by the notion of buying forward francs, however. He had earlier requested that Phillips cross the channel for confidential talks, resuming their dialogue from September, and the secretary used the opportunity to sound him out on the idea in Rouen. Few would have expected these two men – one an ambassador's son, the other a teacher's; one with authority due to his famous friend, the other earned after decades in the civil service – to develop a rapport. But, as Morgenthau later said, "I like that man. I suspect he's a little slow of speech as I am myself."[74] Their working relationship, built on few words, served each country well.

In Rouen, Phillips reiterated Britain's opposition to buying spot francs while remaining open to the proposal to purchase forward ones. It was, Phillips thought, "all to the good that Mr. Morgenthau should be trying to be helpful," even though he doubted the scheme's benefits.[75] The next day,

---

[72] The EEA sold £79 million of gold to the French fund in the two weeks following devaluation, nearly 60 percent more than the EEA had gained from it in the first four months of the year.

[73] For a detailed account of these meetings, see Cochran, Untitled memo, August 25, 1938, MD 135/266–91.

[74] Quoted in Skidelsky (2001, 109).

[75] In Phillips' memorandum of his conversations with Morgenthau, Phillips wrote that "from an abstract point of view Cochran's idea is the right one. If the three main financial powers were really firmly joined together, then the obvious remedy for a run on one

Morgenthau explained the idea to Rueff, who was delighted at the effort to help but was unsure how such measures would improve the situation. The British and French then discussed the matter in London, eventually concluding that the plan would not work. The United States required too many layers of security.[76] The two countries coordinated a gentle response turning down the offer, and the Americans dropped the idea.[77] Morgenthau wanted to assist the French but refused to take on the risk necessary to help meaningfully. A shortcoming of the Tripartite Agreement, yes, but also a reflection of the historical burden of earlier depreciations and an indictment of the political atmosphere that prevented him, dedicated as he was to the Agreement and democratic unity, from taking the leap.

Though the French received no aid, they made it through the summer holding the rate around 178–79. In October, Morgenthau again suggested that they clamp down on capital transactions. He used the French envoy Jean Monnet, visiting the United States to discuss aircraft production, as his conduit. The Americans drafted a statement with Monnet deploring "flight capital," which "hangs at present as a Damoclean sword" and threatens to "gradually undermine the basis of the Tripartite accord." The parties would share information on foreign holdings in their countries and then consult on methods to bring about repatriation.[78] But the French, likely aware that the British would object and hesitant to take a step on capital controls that could lead to a tumble toward full-blown commercial restrictions, did not avail themselves of the offer.[79]

At any rate, Daladier had already decided on a different course, installing Paul Reynaud as finance minister at the beginning of November and enacting decrees modifying the forty-hour week and imposing economies on the budget. "The week of two Sundays," Reynaud announced, "is

---

currency is for the other two partners to buy *and hold* that currency for the time being. . . . The objection to this range of ideas is that it is suited to an ideal world and not to the world we live in. Neither here nor in the United States is there any confidence in France's financial future as would reconcile public opinion to 'their' money being invested in francs with a view to helping France." Phillips, "Talk with Mr. Morgenthau, Mr. Cochran and Mr. Butterworth," August 24, 1938, BoE G1/305.

[76] Siepmann argued that "from the technical point of view there is nothing to be made of it," and Cariguel feared that it was "a trap, not assistance," because the guarantees would "double our losses" in the event of a crisis. Siepmann to Norman, August 26, 1938, BoE G1/305; "Note of Conversation with Monsieur Cariguel," August 29, 1938, BoE G1/305.

[77] Rueff, "Note sur les conversations avec M. Morgenthau, les 24 et 25 août 1938," undated, SAEF B21848; Cobbold conversation with Cochran, October 12, 1938, BoE G1/305.

[78] Draft statement, October 29, 1938, MD 148/194.   [79] Drummond (1979, 45–48).

over."[80] This shift to the right – and the ensuing failure of protest strikes at the end of the month – made complete the Popular Front's disintegration. But it also helped restore confidence in the economy. Pressure on the franc receded, and Daladier upheld his promise not to devalue further, the currency hovering around 177–78 until the outbreak of war. It had finally reached a level that the French could comfortably hold.

What to make of Britain's response to these depreciations? "While France was reasonably clearly in breach of the 1936 understandings," Drummond (1979, 53) argues, "Britain and the United States were prepared to swallow almost any French action rather than announce that the Agreement was dead." Political necessity thus trumped economic integrity. On some level this view is accurate, though it in no way undermines the Tripartite Agreement's centrality during these years, as members clearly regarded the club's survival essential.

But the description misses the bigger picture on the evolution in international monetary relations. As the *Financial Times* insisted in May 1938, "The Tripartite Agreement has been badly strained from time to time, but international commerce, as well as finance, owes a debt of gratitude to our own country and America for the sympathetic and accommodating attitude which has permitted the pressing demands of France to be met without disrupting the framework of the pact."[81] What mattered most was not that France might have depreciated more than members thought justified, but that they did not allow the franc's fall to infect the rest of the club. There was no retaliation. The "framework of the pact" remained intact, guiding members' monetary policy. That exchange rates were a topic for multilateral discussion was now accepted without second thought, even if crises constricted the scope for consultation. Indeed, at a time as charged as the last years before the war, a "sympathetic and accommodating attitude" among the democracies was surely for the better. And with the focus turning to sterling in the late summer of 1938, such goodwill was what London now hoped to receive.

---

[80] Cochran telegram, November 12, 1938, MD 150/237–38.
[81] "Adjusting the Franc," *Financial Times*, May 5, 1938.

9

Battle for Sterling, 1938–1939

The interwar era was a time of transition for monetary policy. It is fitting, then, that it was also a time of transition at Threadneedle Street. Throughout the 1920s and 1930s, an extensive rebuilding project turned what had been a three-story headquarters into one that today rises seven floors above ground with an additional three hidden below, all set within the City's cramped medieval streets. The vast increase in office space accommodated the expanding workforce at the Bank of England (BoE), which during these years included professional economists for the first time.[1] And the excavation below – no easy task with Tube tunnels winding around – enabled the construction of an elaborate series of gold vaults.

This new storage capacity came in handy. In 1937, staffers wheeled more and more gold down to the vaults as Britain's reserves reached record highs. The Exchange Equalisation Account (EEA) started 1938 with £280 million of gold, and experts estimated that the fund might have to absorb another £100 million or perhaps £200 million in that year alone. The metal was so plentiful that officials even discussed using some of it to make good on the nation's (previously defaulted on) war debt to the United States.[2]

---

[1] Walter Stewart, an American economist, joined as an economic adviser in 1927. Henry Clay, a professor at the University of Manchester, then joined in 1930. The BoE remained skeptical of economists, however, and continued to be for some time. Capie (2010, 33) notes that the BoE's "attitude to the role of economics . . . had not changed from the 1930s to the 1950s, where it was still a case of being able to defend themselves against economists rather than in using them in the pursuit of improved policymaking." For details on the rebuilding, see Sayers (1976, 3:338–42).

[2] Norman, Untitled note, January 9, 1938, BoE G1/488; Siepmann, "E.E.A. Position and Prospects at the End of 1937," January 5, 1938, BoE G1/488; Clay, "Gold," January 18, 1938, BoE G1/488. There was also some discussion of settling the war debt in November

But these plans were not to be. At the end of January 1938, the EEA's gold holdings reached their peak at just over £300 million, and within four months, they began a persistent decline that would continue, almost without interruption, until the onset of war. This outrush of gold – propelled by capital flight – was at times so rapid that it overwhelmed the staff, who not only had to lug bars from the vaults and pack them but also had to handle the immense amount of accompanying paperwork.[3] Of course, losing reserves had a host of negative repercussions, foremost reducing the war chest. There was, however, one silver lining to freeing up vault space in the autumn of 1938. With aerial bombardment a near certainty in the event of combat, underground facilities were at a premium. The BoE thus put its newly empty vaults to good use, retrofitting them with everything from a canteen to a gas decontamination center and even an operating room.[4]

As BoE staff began conducting gas attack drills during the Czechoslovakian crisis in September 1938, capital bolted from London in ever greater amounts. Despite massive sales of reserves, sterling plummeted. From a high of $5.04 in February 1938, the pound fell below its old parity of $4.86 at the end of August and reached a low of $4.61 on September 28, when war over the Sudeten problem seemed imminent. The settlement at Munich temporarily boosted sterling, but as the gloss on that agreement wore off and the reality that war was merely delayed, not avoided, set in, capital flight resumed, with sterling closing the year at $4.64. Throughout these troubling times, the Tripartite Agreement remained the centerpiece of international monetary relations, guiding Britain's efforts to support the pound and preventing the currency's depreciation from triggering reprisals.

The pound's tumble did, however, usher in a fundamental revamping of the British monetary system. Ever since Britain had suspended gold convertibility in 1931, its monetary policy had in many ways been on a temporary footing. The government had suspended, not terminated, the gold standard, and there was an implicit potential – among some, an explicit desire – to return. Indeed, it was the government's formal goal as articulated in the declarations at Ottawa in 1932 and the World Economic

---

1938 after the Anglo-American Trade Agreement, but the proposals did not advance far. "Bank of England: 1939-1945," undated, BoE M5/533/1025–26.

[3] The British were also shipping their own gold to safety. The BoE at times reached the limit of its capacity to process gold outflows in the autumn of 1938. See, for instance, Knoke conversation with Hawker, September 28, 1938, FRBNY C261.

[4] Hennessy (1992, 5–6).

Conference in 1933. But the incessant drain on London's reserves nearly depleted the EEA's gold holdings by the end of 1938. In order to continue supporting the pound, authorities transferred most of the gold held in the BoE to the EEA in January 1939; in September, they moved all of the remaining gold. Since this gold had backed the note issue, there was no longer any pretense of a gold-based currency. The metal now mattered solely for international transactions and balance of payments adjustments. The final remnants of the domestic gold standard were gone and there would be no return.

This chapter studies these developments in Britain's monetary system and relations during the harrowing run-up to war. The sheer pressure on the pound created friction among currency club members, which could have led to the reemergence of a crippling animus. However, a middle ground developed whereby Britain made good faith efforts to support the pound and other members – most importantly, the United States – acquiesced to its decline. The Tripartite Agreement continued to embody democratic solidarity. It deepened the bond between London and Washington and survived all the way up to the eruption of hostilities in fact and for some time thereafter in name, falling into abeyance due to the necessities of war finance rather than any disagreement between the parties. The chapter then explores the techniques of management. While the Tripartite system provided the essential architecture, the methods of intervention evolved in response to circumstances, notably with Britain's turn to forward markets. In the final section, the chapter shows how the effort to support the pound resolved Britain's monetary limbo. The decision to transfer gold from the BoE to the EEA severed the remaining threads that had tied sterling to the metal and readied monetary policy for battle in what would become a total war.

CROSSING THE RUBICON

In March 1938, George Bolton, manager of the BoE's foreign exchange section, contemplated the future of the international monetary system. While he "unfortunately" was not yet "in a position to determine what general set of conditions represent twentieth century financial normality" – especially when evaluating whether the autarky and exchange control prevalent in much of the world would last – it was also "slowly becoming clearer that the present and continually modified form of gold and exchange policy carried out by Exchange Funds under the loose international Agreement known as the Tripartite Monetary Arrangement is tending to become a permanent feature of the world's monetary struc-ture."[5] It was difficult to tell in the moment whether the Tripartite para-digm would define the system for the indefinite future, but for the time being it certainly did. After all of the reversals and confusion in monetary relations earlier in the decade, there was finally a mutually recognized structure, at least among the six adherents.

Hitler annexed Austria just days after Bolton finished his memo, initiat-ing a new phase of suspense that would dominate international politics and capital markets. But for the most part, the daily working of the currency club did not change much in 1938. Responsibility for control of the exchanges shifted from the Banque de France (BdF) and the BoE to the Federal Reserve Bank of New York (FRBNY) as markets closed in Europe and opened in America. Daily gold clearing remained the norm since members did not want to amass foreign exchange. The financial authorities of the Big Three continued to communicate by cable, telephone, and even the occasional personal trip, orchestrating intervention, reviewing market movements, interpreting political developments, and conferring on mon-etary policy broadly.[6] Consultation had become so commonplace that it seemed almost natural, even though this new state of affairs marked a momentous change from just a few years prior.

While Anglo-American discussions had often focused on France during the Tripartite Agreement's first year and a half, club attention shifted to London and the pressure on the pound in the summer of 1938. By August, the pound was nearing the old parity of $4.86 as capital fled for the safety of US shores. When Henry Morgenthau secretly met with Sir Frederick Phillips in Rouen that month, the secretary expressed his "hope that sterling would not fall below $4.86 as it would lead to unsettlement."[7] He worried that the psychological significance of the old parity was such that crossing it could lead to a rout. This concern was widespread, the governor of the BdF telling an American interlocutor that "the prestige of the

---

[5] Bolton, "Some Aspects of Forward Exchange in Relation to Control," March 7, 1938, BoE C43/101.

[6] In addition to Phillips' visit to Washington in the autumn of 1937, Morgenthau's trip to Europe in the summer of 1938, and Cochran's frequent travels around Europe, central bank officials also visited one another. While such visits had occurred prior to the Tripartite Agreement, they had added importance in these years: They were not just efforts at collegiality but attempts to discuss ideas for the currency club's improvement. For memoranda from some of these visits, see Schnorf, "Besuch von Herrn. L. Werner Knoke," undated, SNB Korrespondenzen und Akten betr Zusammenarbeit Tripartite/ Sixpartite; Baudewyns, "Résumé des entretiens," August 14, 1938, NBB Y190.

[7] Phillips to Norman, August 24, 1938, BoE G1/305.

Tripartite Agreement would be irreparably injured" if sterling fell below the old par.[8]

British officials, however, did not place much store in the "magic par," as Bolton derisively termed the rate.[9] If the pound fell below $4.86, the situation would not suddenly become uncontrollable, Phillips reassured Morgenthau; London would defend the rate at a more fitting level given the circumstances, perhaps $4.80.[10] Indeed, the authorities seem to have wanted to get $4.86 in the rearview mirror. On August 30, with apparently little internal debate, they allowed the rate to dip below the old parity for the first time under the Tripartite Agreement.[11] As *The Economist* reported, the pound's crossing of the "Rubicon" laid to rest any idea of "the sanctity of $4.86" as the floor. The Tripartite Agreement was not meant to force "precise and rigid limitations upon the fluctuations of the exchanges" like the gold standard, the newspaper argued. Rather, its spirit was that "the three countries will keep their currencies within the range that represents a fair equilibrium."[12]

Not everyone was as sanguine as *The Economist*. Emmanuel Mönick, the French financial attaché in London, thought the British should have defended the rate more strongly and had opened the floodgates by failing to do so.[13] Yet there was no immediate collapse, the pound remaining above $4.80 for the first half of September. It was also difficult to argue against some movement in the exchange rate given Britain's worsening balance of payments and comparatively high prices. Washington soon announced that it did not place much significance in the old parity – after all, it had had no official meaning since 1931 – and did not view the decline as competitive in intent, thereby reassuring the public that the Agreement remained in force.[14]

The trouble, however, was that sterling's biggest battles were yet to come. The deteriorating situation in central Europe that autumn battered the pound, as shown in Figure 9.1. Ministers and officials in London, no matter how optimistic that war could be averted, agreed that they needed to take into account the possibility of armed conflict when determining

---

[8] Cochran to Morgenthau, August 20, 1938, MD 136/107; Cochran, Untitled memo, August 5, 1938, MD 136/13.

[9] Bolton, "Bank for International Settlements Memorandum," November 7, 1938, BoE C43/77.

[10] Cochran, Untitled memo, August 25, 1938, MD 135/283–84.

[11] "Pound under Parity," *Financial Times*, August 31, 1938.

[12] "The Pound and the Dollar," *The Economist*, September 10, 1938.

[13] Parker (1983, 267). [14] "City Notes," *The Times* (London), September 2, 1938.

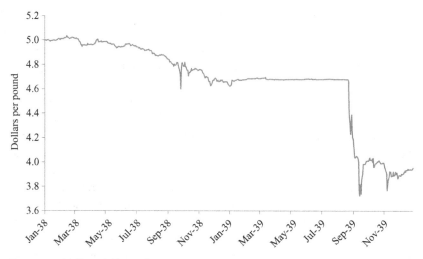

Figure 9.1 Sterling-dollar exchange rate, 1938–1939.
Source: Global Financial Data

exchange rate policy. Indeed, the prospect of war influenced all of economic policy. When considering how best to respond to this potential for hostilities, authorities faced a spectrum bounded by laissez-faire on one end and command and control on the other. The former would let the economy and financial markets operate with little government intervention; the latter would direct production to rearmament and impose rigid exchange controls. The consensus, as expressed in a report to the Cabinet in 1937 that largely guided policymakers until 1939, was to delay heavy regulation. Economic stability, the report argued, was the "fourth arm of defence" – complementing the navy, army, and air force.[15] To wage a long war successfully, Britain would need to raise money, and according to this framework, imposing a command economy and resorting to exchange controls too soon would reduce the country's exporting power (necessary for financing imports) and investor confidence (necessary for borrowing funds). The government thus wanted the economy to remain on a peacetime footing for as long as possible.

---

[15] Whether or not the fourth arm policy was prudent is a matter of debate, with many scholars criticizing policymakers for refusing to accept the inevitable and arguing that it would have been preferable to subordinate the economy to the coming war by adopting exchange control sooner regardless of the implications for international monetary relations. Price (2001); Peden (2007, chapter 3).

A key dimension to this policy was sterling. World confidence in the currency was an indispensable element in Britain's defense strategy. Though members of the currency club did not hold sizeable sterling balances, countries in the Sterling Area held almost all of their reserves in sterling. If the latter feared a sterling depreciation, they would hesitate to accept the currency. And if sterling were to fall considerably, they might sell their existing holdings, exacerbating the decline. A fall in sterling would make it harder to import necessities and wage war. As a senior official in the Foreign Office observed in October 1938, "We have to import the greater part of our food, and consequently to maintain the value of the £ on the foreign exchanges."[16] All of these factors pointed toward supporting the pound. To be sure, there were conflicting objectives. Sterling's strength depended in part on the expenditure of reserves; the expenditure of reserves lessened the country's future purchasing power for materiel. Trade-offs would have to be made. And the application of the fourth arm strategy to the exchange rate was vague: It precluded exchange control and an inordinate drop in sterling, but it was not clear how low sterling should be allowed to go.

Whereas war strategy merely provided a general orientation for managing the pound, the Tripartite Agreement – consonant as it was with the broad outline of the fourth arm – supplied the thrust. It appeared in almost all internal discussions. When pressure was acute in October 1938 and some questioned whether the BoE should retreat, Harry Siepmann observed that, however tantalizing it might seem to let the market operate on its own and exhaust itself, "the Tripartite Agreement and our own essential function of moderator [of the market], forbid us to take refuge in any such comfortable doctrine of laisser faire."[17] All agreed that upholding the Agreement was nonnegotiable, both to keep exchange markets orderly and to remain on good terms with other members. At the same time and by design, there was no set rate for sterling that would trigger the disbandment of the pact. As such, there had to be a back-and-forth between parties, which, after all, was one of the motivations behind and benefits of the Agreement.

And talk they did. Sterling's slide – falling 5 percent against the dollar from August through December – affected all club members. Belgium, France, the Netherlands, and Switzerland discussed the matter among themselves and with Britain. The French were "very much

---

[16] Quoted in Peden (1984, 23).
[17] Siepmann, "Exchange Policy and Tactics," November 9, 1938, BoE C43/463.

perturbed."[18] On several occasions, these countries warned London that too steep a fall could lead them to alter their policies, potentially setting off a chain reaction of depreciations and threatening the Tripartite Agreement.[19] But in the end, there was no break. Paris largely held on to its peg with sterling, permitting a slight appreciation of around 1 percent over the final five months of 1938, while the three junior currencies appreciated between 4 and 5 percent against sterling and thus clung closer to the dollar.

Then there was the United States, by far the most important party from Britain's perspective. As sterling fell, the US Treasury convened many meetings on the topic and often publicized them, both to appease domestic audiences and signal the severity of political agitation to the British.[20] Some officials advocated a forceful stance against Britain so as to prevent it from gaining a competitive advantage. Harry Dexter White drafted a flurry of memos criticizing London's efforts to halt the pound's decline and even suggested that Washington should hold out the possibility of declaring Britain in violation of the Tripartite Agreement.[21] The situation was further complicated in November by the impending conclusion of negotiations on a trade agreement between the two countries, itself a manifestation of the improvement in economic relations in recent years. False rumors spread that the agreement contained a clause that would fix sterling at \$4.50, causing the pound to slide. Days before the signing, a State Department official related to the British ambassador how "gravely alarmed" Roosevelt was at the recent fall in sterling and the president's hope that something could be done to scuttle the rumors and support the pound.[22]

For all of these reasons, Parker (1983, 261) concludes that Washington "compelled the British Treasury to reduce its 'war chest,'" thereby hampering "British ability to fight a long war against Germany." After all, the EEA's gold holdings fell from £210 million at the end of August to £139 million in

---

[18] Cobbold, Untitled note, December 22, 1938, BoE C43/344.

[19] Trip to Norman, January 13, 1939, BoE G14/133.

[20] See, for instance, "Treasury meeting re Sterling Exchange Rate," October 21, 1938, MD 147/74–129; "Treasury meeting re Sterling Exchange Rate," November 10, 1938, MD 150/97–117; "Treasury Studies Decline in Pound," *The New York Times*, October 22, 1938.

[21] See the memos in HDWP B1F7.

[22] However, the official "emphatically repudiat[ed] any suggestion that United States would refuse to sign trade agreement if such fall occurred." Lindsay telegram, November 14, 1938, T 188/232. For a history of negotiations on the Anglo-American Trade Agreement, see Drummond and Hillmer (1989).

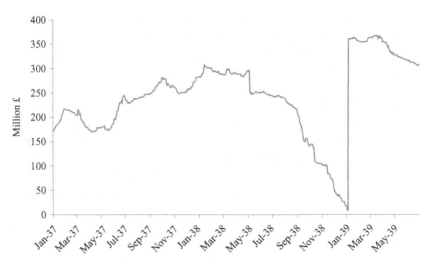

Figure 9.2 EEA gold reserves, 1937–1939 (million £, at cost).
Source: BoE C139/1 and author's calculations

September, £100 million in October, £62 million in November, and £19 million in December in what must have made for dreadful accounting work, as shown in Figure 9.2. And Washington did discuss the matter with London throughout these months, repeatedly emphasizing its concern.

Yet, while American pressure might have had some impact, there is a tendency to assign too much importance to the views of the most hawkish advisers. Morgenthau was decidedly calmer than White. Though by no means nonchalant about the depreciation – neither were the British for that matter – Morgenthau cared most about the bigger international picture and viewed the Tripartite Agreement as one of his best tools for supporting the democratic world. He thus favored a measured approach. In September, Morgenthau told subordinates that, as to "the English operation of their funds ... they've gone the absolute limit to cooperate with us to keep the thing—nobody could go further than they have." In November, he told T. K. Bewley, London's financial representative, "as far as the operations of the British Treasury are concerned, all through these difficult times I have felt that they have done everything that they could to maintain the price of sterling."[23] The daily conversations between the BoE and FRBNY, relayed to Morgenthau, revealed the enormous efforts to

---

[23] "Treasury meeting re gold policy," September 21, 1938, MD 142/16; Morgenthau meeting with Bewley, November 22, 1938, MD 152/316.

which London went to soften the fall, as did his frequent discussions with Bewley. Morgenthau pushed London to take more action, sought add-itional information as to its intentions, and expressed his displeasure, but he did not go beyond that.[24] Most important, he never threatened to read Britain out of the currency club.

As sterling fell, the fourth arm policy, the Tripartite Agreement, and the importance of getting along with America all pushed London to counter the decline. The many conversations with Washington in the last months of 1938, far from suggesting that there was no unity of purpose between the leaders of the club, reflected just how much the Tripartite Agreement had altered international monetary relations. The two nations were discussing exchange rates as a matter of mutual concern, hearing each other's side so that the issue did not fester and infect the broader relationship. As Morgenthau told Bewley, he was there to help, for "it was of the greatest importance that the democracies should stand together."[25]

SQUEEZING THE BEARS

Discussing the pound was one thing; actually managing it was quite another. In broad terms, the British leaned against the wind, spending reserves to check the fall. But this designation brushes over the host of decisions that needed to be made on a day-to-day basis over the course of 1938 and into 1939: when to fight, when to retreat, what facilities to use, what markets to enter. According to Sayers (1976, 2:563), since capital would likely keep flowing out, the general strategy in the autumn of 1938 was "to let the rate drop a little whenever the pressure was intensified, but to take, and if possible to make, opportunities for getting the rate up a trifle when pressure was relaxed." As Figure 9.1 shows, sterling strengthened slightly in the middle of October 1938 and the end of November even as the trend was clearly downward.

As for the mechanics of intervention, while daily gold clearing remained the foundation, there were a couple of modifications that went beyond the standard operations explained in Chapter 6. The first had to do with gold transfers. The EEA supported sterling in large part by selling dollars in London. It obtained these dollars by providing gold to the FRBNY mostly

---

[24] As Price (2001, 104) aptly concludes, "It has been suggested that Morgenthau coerced Britain into a full-blooded support of sterling. . . . This assertion is beside the point, as the British monetary authorities were already fully committed to the defence of sterling."

[25] Bewley telegram to Treasury, December 22, 1938, T 160/871.

through the facility established in 1935, whereby the Americans bought gold in London against dollars, up to prespecified weekly limits. To the extent that the Americans intervened in New York in support of the pound, its sterling purchases were converted into gold in London as well, further stuffing its account there. With war possible at any moment, however, more gold in London did not appeal to US officials. Morgenthau wanted to bring much of the gold home as the crisis over the Sudetenland intensified and, with private shipping infeasible due to the difficulty in obtaining war risk insurance, he arranged for US naval carriers to transport the metal from London to New York.[26]

One way to lessen accumulation of US gold in London while still intervening in the New York market was for the FRBNY to operate for the BoE's account.[27] On September 16, Bolton suggested this option to his counterpart at the FRBNY, L. Werner Knoke, who reported that Bolton "would give us two sterling rates, buying and selling, against which we could operate for his account if we felt so disposed and if we didn't want to take any more gold in London."[28] Operating for the BoE's account allowed the FRBNY to support sterling by selling dollars created from the BoE's gold holdings in New York rather than selling its own dollars and then converting the sterling into gold in London. The BoE was already in the process of shipping gold to North America in order to shore up its New York account and ensure the safety of its war chest. This additional means of intervention would allow the continued support of sterling in New York while taking account of American sensitivities on foreign gold holdings.

Knoke found the idea "splendid" and was sure the Treasury "would appreciate this proof of their desire to even the burden between the two of us." He nevertheless expressed his hope to operate as much as possible on the daily gold price underlying the Tripartite system because "there was no intention whatever on the part of our Treasury not to continue as heretofore but on the contrary to do whatever we possibly could do."[29] The BoE provided sterling limits for two weeks, until the resolution at Munich calmed markets. It then seems to have resumed the practice when it began pegging the sterling-dollar rate in 1939.[30] While the magnitude of

---

[26] Knoke conversation with Hawker, September 29, 1938, FRBNY C261.

[27] The FRBNY often operated for the BdF's account in this manner. See, for instance, Knoke conversation with Cariguel, March 5, 1937, FRBNY C261.

[28] Knoke conversation with Bolton, September 16, 1938, FRBNY C261.   [29] Ibid.

[30] Knoke conversation with Hawker, September 30, 1938, FRBNY C261; Knoke conversation with Bolton, January 6, 1939, FRBNY C261; McKeon conversation with Bolton, February 16, 1939, FRBNY C261.

intervention under this order is not clear, the adjustment demonstrates the flexibility inherent in the currency club as well as the cooperative manner in which the two sides worked. The arrangements were loose enough to allow innovations during crisis but strong enough to serve as a foundation for normal times.

A more consequential change in intervention techniques was Britain's foray into forward exchange markets beginning in the autumn of 1938. Forward transactions – the purchase or sale of foreign exchange at a price set now for delivery in the future – became more prevalent after the First World War with the currency instability of the 1920s and collapse of fixed rates in the 1930s.[31] The BoE's experts viewed forward markets warily, however, convinced that speculative forces were predominant.[32] Though there had been sporadic interventions in forward markets in the years preceding the Tripartite Agreement, there was no inclination to undertake sustained action to influence forward rates.[33] France and America shared this hesitancy, Knoke recalling decades later that had he operated heavily in forward markets, he would not have been able to sleep at night given the risks of an open position.[34]

But in 1938, the BoE started to reappraise forward intervention. Bolton was the point person on the subject, and in March 1938 he finished a 25-page memorandum outlining his thoughts. Still skeptical about relying on intervention in forward markets, Bolton nevertheless argued that these markets could no longer be ignored: Exchange managers had "been forced by the logic of the situation to change their policy and outlook and while intervention in spot exchange forms the basis of exchange control the

[31] Atkin (2005, 45–47 and 67–69).

[32] Bolton believed that "it is doubtful whether genuine trade requirements have been responsible for more than 10% of the activity in the forward markets of the leading exchanges." Bolton, "Some Aspects of Forward Exchange in Relation to Control," March 7, 1938, BoE C43/101.

[33] For instance, the British had ventured into forward markets when they sold forward francs to cover the usance risk prior to the Tripartite Agreement as well as when they sold forward dollars in the immediate aftermath of the Agreement. Ibid.

[34] Knoke also recalled telling Bolton, "a central bank does not operate in the forward market." Nevertheless, the Americans and French intervened in forward markets at times. As Bolton commented, "No Central Bank has been more opposed to forward transactions than the Bank of France but since the inception of the Tripartite Monetary Arrangement no Central Bank has been more continuously active in forward exchange." Sayers interview with Knoke, March 11, 1971, BoE ADM33/31; Bolton, "Some Aspects of Forward Exchange in Relation to Control," March 7, 1938, BoE C43/101; Bordo, Humpage, and Schwartz (2015, chapter 3).

influence of the forward markets has become so powerful that it cannot be neglected." Preventing a depreciation in forward rates could signal to the market the authority's intention to hold the spot rate stable and thus instill confidence. Consistent with London's general views on when club members should act, Bolton felt that the "initiative for forward intervention will in the majority of cases come from the Control of the weak currency." In addition, the case for forward intervention was strengthened when weakness in the forward rate was "due to some external phenomenon rather than internal rot." He regarded intervention in forward markets as treating "symptoms," and this action made more sense when the disease – the underlying reason for sterling's weakness – was due to international factors rather than domestic policy.[35]

Both of these conditions were satisfied starting in September 1938. Not only was the pound weak, but exchange managers believed much of the weakness was due to the international situation rather than fundamental economic causes. The widening forward discount against the dollar, nearly quintupling from 0.1 percent in June to almost 0.5 percent by the end of September, as shown in Figure 9.3, elicited much commentary. John Maynard Keynes suggested to the Treasury that the EEA "support the forward exchange (without bothering too much about the spot exchange)."[36] Moreover, the British were now losing reserves, so the ability to intervene without the immediate expenditure of gold became more attractive. For these reasons, the BoE began selling dollars forward in September. By the end of November, it had contracted for roughly £40 million in forward dollar sales – far beyond any previous intervention – with the majority maturing before the end of the year.[37]

These forward interventions were in part a reflection of sterling's sorry state, but they also offered the potential for a technical coup.[38] When the forward contracts matured, the BoE could either renew them or let them run off. Renewing them would continue to provide support to the forward rate but would leave a lot of sterling in the system, thereby pushing toward a weaker spot rate. Letting them run off would end support of the forward rate but would deprive the market of sterling and flush it with dollars,

---

[35] Bolton, "Some Aspects of Forward Exchange in Relation to Control," March 7, 1938, BoE C43/101.

[36] Keynes to Hopkins, September 6, 1938, BoE C43/101.

[37] "Forward position at the close of business on the 29th November 1938," November 30, 1938, BoE C43/67; "The Depreciation of Sterling," November 22, 1938, BoE C43/100.

[38] Sayers (1976, 2:563–64) provides additional detail on the operation's planning, which involved obtaining the cooperation of the clearing banks.

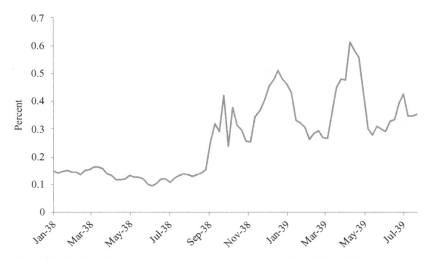

Figure 9.3 Sterling three-month forward discount on the dollar, 1938–1939 (percent of spot rate).
Source: Financial Times

forcing the bears to scramble for pounds and helping to strengthen the spot rate. In an attempt to bring sterling up temporarily, the BoE decided in November to let the sales run off rather than renew the contracts, selling gold to the United States to obtain the requisite dollars. As a memorandum outlining the plan declared, "*The Scheme* is simple—to squeeze the bears, reduce the sterling available for speculation and make what is left dear."[39] The timing was doubly conducive for a squeeze, as banks often scrambled for sterling during the end of the year for window-dressing purposes and market participants already held a sizeable short position in sterling.

Dollars were, of course, necessary to execute the scheme, and the BoE's best option was to sell gold to the United States. Selling gold to the FRBNY for such a big operation made "nonsense of the '24-hour basis'" at the heart of the system, Siepmann thought, since transactions were supposed to occur on a daily basis for daily interventions rather than on a massive sale to close out a record number of forward contracts. "We must not fail to give them warning in advance, and so preserve what is really the essence of the Tripartite Agreement," he advised.[40] The British informed the Americans and received their blessing and pledge of cooperation, with

---

[39] "The Depreciation of Sterling," November 22, 1938, BoE C43/100.
[40] Siepmann, "Notes on the Proposal for Dealing with the Foreign Exchange Position," November 28, 1938, BoE C43/100.

Morgenthau "plainly gratified," indeed "damned glad," and offering to assist in any way possible.[41] The operation proceeded as planned and helped sterling stay stable against the dollar at around \$4.65 throughout December when other forces were pushing it down. "The limited objective of gaining time had been achieved," Sayers (1976, 2:564) concludes. Thereafter, forward intervention remained a part of the BoE's regular toolkit, though there was no attempt to stage another squeeze.

Forward intervention broke the symmetry between the day of intervention and the day of gold movements that formed the foundation of the Tripartite system. When the BoE sold dollars forward, the aim was to affect rates immediately, while gold (to obtain the requisite dollars) did not move until the contract matured. It should be noted that the BoE sometimes sold dollars forward in conjunction with a spot purchase, and in so doing increased its dollar holdings – at least temporarily – without converting them into gold.[42] These dollars were cover for future sales, however, and they did not represent a desire to build up a long position in foreign exchange. The system continued to be predicated on gold, and the ability to incorporate forward interventions within the framework reflected its versatility.

The changes that did not occur in the club are equally important. In particular, the parties did not establish a facility for longer-term support. Though the British had repeatedly refused French entreaties to operate on joint account, pooling reserves suddenly became more palatable to London once the pound started to depreciate. Siepmann brainstormed a joint operation that "could be presented as an extension of the Tripartite Agreement." He explained in December 1938: "We should, in reality, be asking for just such a partial pooling of gold resources as we have so often refused to the French. But we are in a better position than the French to make such a request—and our need is now no less—because the fate of sterling matters to the U.S.A. much more than the fate of the franc."[43] Some American officials were pushing for the Exchange Stabilization Fund to purchase and hold sterling, as the British had "proven their willingness

---

[41] Bewley telegram to Treasury, December 1, 1938, BoE C43/100; Morgenthau conversation with Knoke, November 28, 1938, MD 153/145.

[42] For instance, on June 30, 1939, the EEA held £20 million in foreign exchange. However, it had £23 million in forward commitments, leaving the fund short. Table, undated, T 276/6.

[43] Siepmann, "The New Year," December 13, 1938, BoE C43/100. A subsequent version of the memo took out this explicit language on pooling reserves but continued to favor "a major operation, dressed up in technical garb," whereby the United States would support sterling. Siepmann, "The New Year," December 15, 1938, BoE C43/100.

to support their currency" and American assistance would "prevent questions being raised as to the usefulness of the tripartite arrangement."[44] Again, however, the two sides did not take the jump. London does not appear to have suggested any plan to Washington, and Morgenthau remained convinced that the politics was not right.[45]

Thus, while the Tripartite system had space for innovation, its principle of minimizing risk remained nonnegotiable. There would be no pooling of reserves or joint intervention. Members had the moral support of the club, but they never received financial support. Britain would have to fight for the pound using its own ever-dwindling resources.

PREPARING FOR WAR

The awful truth as 1938 came to a close was that there was little basis to believe the new year would be any better. And there was plenty of reason to think it would be far worse. On December 22, the British Treasury sent Bewley briefing instructions for Morgenthau: Barring a reduction in continental tensions, "the outlook is gloomy and we fully anticipate general pressure on the £ in the early part of January."[46] Several days later, Sir Frederick Phillips and the BoE's deputy governor huddled with W. Walton Butterworth, financial attaché at the American embassy in London, feeling it their duty to elaborate on the anticipated peril and "let Mr. Morgenthau know of our fears." Sterling was going to fall: They would attempt to moderate it – "we should continue to fight while there is a shot in our locker" – but no promises could be made.[47]

---

[44] "Sterling," November 22, 1938, MD 152/370. At a Treasury meeting on the subject, "There was some discussion of establishing a joint fund for supporting sterling, but the Secretary was very reluctant to undertake that, and most of those present were not favorable to it on the ground that it would be chiefly a gesture; might result in weakening sterling psychologically, and would be entirely inadequate against a fundamental movement." Goldenweiser to Eccles, November 29, 1938, MEP B9F9.

[45] Washington often cited the Johnson Act of 1934, which prohibited loans to governments in default, as a reason for not holding foreign exchange. Of course, the ESF held working balances of foreign exchange, so the Act did not impose a blanket prohibition. It seems that the American public interpreted the Act broadly, however, and while a top Treasury official hinted to the British financial attaché that the Treasury "was not bound by the Johnson Act," the political obstacles were such that it would "find it difficult to justify buying spot sterling [to hold] except possibly as part of a larger scheme." Bewley telegram to Treasury, November 22, 1938, T 188/232.

[46] Treasury telegram to Bewley, December 22, 1938, T 188/232.

[47] Untitled memo, December 29, 1938, T 188/232.

Ministers and officials could not permit their pessimism to become paralyzing. There were immediate issues that had to be handled. For one, the EEA was full of sterling and out of gold, leaving it without resources to support the currency. The bear squeeze was complete, and there were no more tricks in the bag. To further complicate matters, war was likely but not yet imminent, so policymakers had to figure out how to manage the pound in a state of constant near-war.

Policymakers chose to defend the pound indefinitely, spending gold to prop it up until either war arrived or peace seemed certain. Doing so required putting more gold into the EEA. That the fund would need replenishing was obvious during the last months of 1938. The account had £62 million in gold at the end of November and just £19 million at the end of December. At its low, the EEA had only £9 million on January 5, 1939. Any new gold would have to come from the Issue Department, which had £326 million, all earmarked as gold cover for BoE notes as prescribed under the 1844 act and all valued at the old statutory value (at current prices, the gold was worth £575 million.)[48] By law, the BoE's note issue had to be backed by gold in the Issue Department and securities in the Fiduciary Issue. The Fiduciary Issue could go as high as £260 million, but increases above that level were temporary and required parliamentary approval to become permanent. Since the Fiduciary Issue was £200 million at the beginning of the year, there was only £60 million of gold that could be transferred to the EEA without any further action being necessary.

Whitehall originally favored transferring the relatively small amount of £60 million and doing nothing more. Should that amount prove insufficient, the authorities would deal with the matter again later on. London informed Washington in early December that it would likely implement such a transfer in January.[49] But as the gold drain continued, the band-aid approach seemed increasingly unsatisfactory. At the end of the year, experts wondered about upping the amount to £160 million. Threadneedle Street then argued for £200 million, convinced that the EEA would need a lot of ammunition in the coming months. Such a transfer would require parliamentary approval for increasing the Fiduciary Issue, but rather than being put off by the need to go to Parliament, the BoE wanted to take this opportunity to enact a range of reforms, including the removal of the

---

[48] See Chapter 1 for a discussion of the Issue and Fiduciary Departments.
[49] Cochran, Untitled memo, December 3, 1938, MD 154/232.

anachronistic statutory price for gold and the adoption of a new process for valuing the metal.[50]

Quite at the last minute, Whitehall decided on the grand gesture coupled with reform.[51] On January 6, ledgers recorded a transfer of £200 million of gold from the Issue Department to the EEA, the metal entering the latter's books at its current value of £350 million. The BoE's deputy governor explained that the "[o]bject of this measure is to strengthen Exchange Equalisation Account beyond possibility of question." The magnitude of the act certainly made a splash.[52] Market participants figured a transfer could be in the offing, but they were surprised by the size. Part of the shock might have resulted from their underestimation of just how dire the EEA's situation was, as many thought the EEA had about £100 million prior to the transfer as opposed to the dismal reality of less than £10 million. Gratified City operators deemed the replenished fund a "Maginot Line" for the pound – a comparison that at the time was more complimentary than it would soon be.[53] Washington was pleased as well. Upon receiving advance notice of the infusion, Archie Lochhead called Morgenthau, on vacation in Florida, to fill him in: The secretary considered it "the best news that's come my way in a long while" and sent word to Chancellor of the Exchequer John Simon of his delight.[54]

As for the reforms to gold policy, the Currency and Bank Notes Act of 1939, passed in February, put an end to much of the monetary dissonance set off by the suspension of gold in 1931. The historical parity disappeared from the statute books, and there would be no new parity. The BoE would now value its gold at the market price every week, the frequent updating helpful for "avoid[ing] any appearance of stabilisation."[55] The gold remaining in the Issue Department, some £126 million at the old parity, in an instant became worth £226 million, its value thereafter changing as the market price of gold changed. While the reform maintained the trappings of a gold-backed currency and Simon told Parliament that the

---

[50] In addition, should the value of assets in the Issue Department fall short of (exceed) the desired note issue, the EEA would make up (receive) the difference each week, further severing the connection between the note issue and the remaining gold. Hopkins, Untitled memo, January 5, 1939, T 188/232.

[51] It seems that a decision was not reached until January 5. Hopkins, "Dollar Exchange EE Fund," January 5, 1939, T 188/232.

[52] Catterns telegram to Towers, January 6, 1939, BoE C43/26.

[53] "Exchange Fund Fortified," *Financial Times*, January 7, 1939; "Britain Bolsters Equalization Fund," *The New York Times*, January 7, 1939.

[54] Morgenthau conversation with Lochhead, January 5, 1939, MD 159/123.

[55] Hopkins, Untitled memo, January 5, 1939, T 188/232.

Act had "no bearing whatever upon the question of the time or the manner of our ultimate stabilisation on gold," there was no way to interpret it as anything other than a move away from the gold standard.[56] The nation's reserves were now concentrated in the EEA, and they would be used according to the dictates of international developments, not the necessities of the note issue. The altering of the "statutory tie between gold and the note issue" was a "long-term measure already overdue," according to Sayers (1976, 2:566), but it was no less important for having taken so long.

In addition to replenishing the EEA at the beginning of 1939, Britain imposed some restrictions on markets and solicited support from the club members in limiting speculation against sterling.[57] Now better armed against the bears, the British pursued a policy of pegging the pound near its December level, settling on $4.68. Though a momentous decision that ran in the face of years of opposition to a strict peg, there is remarkably little extant documentation on the deliberations behind the move. It is likely that the impetus to peg came from the Treasury. Besides the fact that the matter was of high enough import to merit attention from Whitehall, a BoE memorandum at the beginning of the year described the Treasury, with a touch of exasperation, as viewing the peg as "the laziest and best of all solutions," thereby suggesting at the very least that the Treasury was a strong proponent.[58]

There is even less light on the reasoning behind choosing $4.68, though pressure from currency club members surely played a part in avoiding a rate lower than December's.[59] Nor is it clear how strict of a peg policy-makers intended. Siepmann would later explain, somewhat cryptically, that the "pegging of sterling, which we have always opposed in principle, would be inexcusable if it were not for two facts: first, a state of increasing weakness which we, for our part, could do nothing but confess and, secondly, the existence of what amounts to a state of war."[60] Whatever the rationale, the initial results were promising, as the EEA lost only a little bit of gold in January, gained gold in February, and continued to gain for much of March.

Then, once again, German military action trampled over monetary policy. On March 15, 1939, Hitler invaded what remained of Czechoslovakia,

---

[56] 343 Parl. Db. H.C. (5th ser.) (1939) col. 676.
[57] Knoke conversation with Bolton, January 3, 1939, FRBNY C261.
[58] Untitled memo, January 4, 1939, BoE C43/100.
[59] Minutes of the Committee of Treasury, January 1939, BoE G14/133.
[60] Siepmann, "E.E.A. Memorandum on Policy," August 9, 1939, C43/26.

flouting the promises made at Munich. War seemed ever more likely and the pound's fortunes ever bleaker. The British lost gold and debated lowering the peg. They considered a plan to reduce the price overnight to $4.50, but the BoE thought that such a policy was "a war measure which should be reserved for zero hour."[61] London would not break the Tripartite Agreement until war forced it to, even though, by this point, it was just emptying its war chest. As a Treasury memorandum for Cabinet discussion concluded several months later, a "further small depreciation of the £ would be ineffective; a large depreciation, even if it were on balance desirable, is not at present practical politics."[62] In the meantime, the British made sure their gold holdings were in secure locations. During the previous year, officials worked out a plan for building up stocks of gold in Ottawa, Pretoria, and Bombay for safe keeping, as well as New York for intervention purposes. The task became all the more urgent as 1939 progressed.[63]

The prospect of hostilities also sparked a reassessment of what had become the decade's guiding monetary principle: Gold was safe and foreign exchange was risky. Because reserves would actually need to be spent on supplies and many of these supplies would invariably come from the United States, the disadvantages of gold vis-à-vis the dollar became more salient. As early as August 1938, the French had expressed concern to the British that "there is a danger that some countries might decline to take gold in exchange for armaments, war material etc."[64] By March 1939, Siepmann shared this anxiety, arguing that "gold is less certainly equivalent to purchasing power" than dollars – after all, the United States could alter its gold buying policy at any time – "and it carries no interest." "Has not the time come," he asked, "when we should consider holding securities as well as gold?"[65] He wanted North American assets to include £50 million of gold in Ottawa, £50 million of gold in New York, and £50 million in US Treasury bills or dollar balances. For Siepmann, gold was the ideal reserve asset when the purpose of reserves was to manage exchange rates, but it lost some of its sheen when the purpose was to finance purchases. In the end, his proposal failed to gain traction, and gold remained Britain's predominant reserve asset. His thinking marked, however, the beginning of a turn to the dollar over gold that would last well into the Bretton Woods era.

---

[61] Siepmann, "Sterling-Dollar Rate," April 24, 1939, BoE C43/463.
[62] "Note on the Financial Situation," July 3, 1939, CAB 24/287/32.
[63] "Gold Held Abroad," February 27, 1939, BoE C43/26.
[64] Wilson, Untitled note, August 15, 1938, BoE G1/305.
[65] Siepmann, "E.E.A. Assets Abroad," March 17, 1939, BoE C43/26.

As war approached, policymakers started considering what would become of the currency club. In the run-up to Munich, Morgenthau had his team, under Roosevelt's instructions, draft proposals to give club members preferential treatment on monetary transactions to help in case of war, but the president ultimately decided to hold off.[66] Then in April 1939, Morgenthau reached out to the Tripartite members, arguing that it was "desirable that there be prompt consultation directed toward protecting the security, commodity and money markets in the event of war in Europe.... Our joint interest in this problem, together with the record of satisfactory cooperation among the members adhering to the Tripartite Accord should assure the success of such consultations."[67] Britain was particularly interested in talks. Butterworth and Phillips met in London and Morgenthau and Bewley met in Washington to discuss each country's financial plans for zero hour, including regulation of exchange markets and the conversion of dollar securities into cash.[68] Though the talks were oriented more toward sharing information with each other than proactive coordination, they surely helped develop the working relationship.[69]

On August 21, 1939, news of a German-Soviet nonaggression pact shocked a world accustomed to seeing fascists and communists as implacable enemies. The next day, His Majesty's Government recalled Parliament into session from its summer break, and on August 24, Parliament passed emergency powers granting the government immense discretion to prosecute the coming war. That same day, London "decided that, in view of the international outlook, the central gold reserves of the nation and the Empire must be conserved intact."[70] The BoE increased Bank Rate from 2 percent to 4 percent as a crisis measure – the first change in over seven years – but as of the next day, the EEA would no longer sell gold for intervention purposes.[71] A timetable set out when and how to notify the Tripartite members. Since the US Treasury would be informed before

---

[66] Blum (1959, 514–17).

[67] Morgenthau telegram to Butterworth, April 12, 1939, MD 178/18–19; "Antwoord aan den Heer Cochran," April 15, 1939, NA 32.386/49623.

[68] See, for example, Butterworth telegram to Morgenthau, April 14, 1939, MD 179/63–67; Butterworth to Morgenthau, April 14, 1939, MD 179/25–30; Morgenthau telegram to Butterworth, April 16, 1939, MD 179/323–25.

[69] The BoE started preparing for war as early as 1937. Hennessey (1992, 5).

[70] Draft telegram, August 24, 1939, BoE C43/26; Treasury conference, April 28, 1939, MD 181/326–29.

[71] The hike in Bank Rate was temporary, and by November, it was back at 2 percent, where it would remain until 1951.

markets closed, it was imperative that Morgenthau "not blab."[72] The notifications went smoothly, and word did not leak. Now unsupported, the pound fell to $4.51 on August 25 and continued to drop thereafter. On September 1, Germany invaded Poland, and two days later, Prime Minister Neville Chamberlain informed the public by radio that Britain was at war. On September 4, the government issued regulations forcing residents to sell their foreign assets to the Treasury and imposing a host of provisions on exchange transactions. And on September 5, authorities made $4.03 the wartime rate, which would last through the war and beyond.[73]

To further retool the monetary system for war, Parliament approved the Currency (Defence) Act, which removed the statutory limit on the EEA's size and broadened its remit. The EEA's original mandate had been "checking undue fluctuations in the exchange value of sterling" – a phrase that governments around the world had interpreted as code for currency war. After the passage of the new act, its purpose now included "securing defence of the realm and the efficient prosecution of any war" – a directive for aiding in a real military conflict.[74] On September 6, the EEA absorbed the remaining gold in the Issue Department. Gold no longer backed BoE notes, and the EEA was now responsible for all of the nation's reserves. "Thus," the BoE's Henry Clay recorded, "the revolution initiated by the suspension of the Gold Standard in 1931 was carried to its logical conclusion."[75]

France imposed exchange controls shortly thereafter. Even though the belligerents had contravened the currency club's principles, the US Treasury declared the Tripartite Agreement still in effect, "recogniz[ing] the emergency conditions which impelled this action."[76] There was much interest in the first weeks of war about the Agreement's status given its symbolism, with questions abounding whether Washington considered London and Paris as members in light of the radical change in their policies. Publicly, at least, Morgenthau reaffirmed its continuance for months. As late as April 1940, he told reporters that "the spirit of the

---

[72] "Time-Table," August 24, 1939, BoE C43/26.

[73] BoE officials calculated that a rate of $4.00 seemed defensible. Norman accepted the general argument but thought it best not to use a round figure: "A round figure such as 4 would be very difficult to break and could become a figure of tribal significance; a broken figure does not look so final." Thus the rate became $4.03. There was also a free market for sterling in New York during the first months of the war where the rate traded below the official rate as depicted in Figure 9.1. Quoted in Atkin (2005, 77).

[74] Currency (Defence) Act, 1939, 2 and 3 Geo. 6. c. 64.   [75] Clay (1957, 436).

[76] US Treasury (1940, 456–57).

tripartite has not been affected to date."[77] But already in September 1939 he was calling these pronouncements of the Tripartite Agreement's health a "joke" within the Treasury's walls. "The only thing that is left in the Tripartite Agreement," he complained, "is that Treasury should exchange information," but even that pillar was collapsing under the pressure of events. "I am having difficulty enough convincing the President there is a Tripartite."[78]

Wartime exigencies led to new arrangements and regulations that simply could not be consistent with the Agreement. Exchange control replaced market forces, and reserves were earmarked for purchasing materiel. Nevertheless, the charade continued for a while on all sides – democratic solidarity, even if just verbal support, was more necessary than ever. London argued, for good measure, that the new rate of $4.03 was not a competitive deprecation, and the other club members did not dissent. The worsening cataclysm soon made the Agreement recede from the spotlight, however, and after the fall of France, focus was not on past agreements but the potential for future ones.

By May 1941, Morgenthau told Congress, "Since the outbreak of the war, the machinery set up by the Tripartite accord has been inactive." While the war put an end to the arrangement, he hoped the spirit of September 1936 would live on: "I venture to predict that the experience in international monetary cooperation gained through the Tripartite accord will prove of permanent value. I believe that that machinery, which functioned in a spirit of cooperation and equality, promises more for future international economic organization than any of the aggressive monetary devices which now hold sway."[79]

It would take some years for monetary cooperation in a peacetime setting to reappear. But London and Washington were already working together on more pressing issues. Two months before Morgenthau's statement, the US Congress had passed the Lend-Lease Act to enable American support of Britain's fight. Sir Frederick Phillips – now Treasury representative in Washington – was laboring tirelessly with Morgenthau to carry it out. The two men had first met in 1937 to discuss monetary matters as part of the Tripartite Agreement and, despite their patent differences, took well to each other. In 1943, an American official emphasized to the British

---

[77] Press conference, April 8, 1940, MPC 14/213.

[78] "Meeting re publicity release on value of pound sterling," September 15, 1939, MD 211/221.

[79] Morgenthau statement, May 8, 1941, MD 396/59–60.

economist Lionel Robbins, "Phillips is worth his weight in gold to the British Empire. If you recalled Phillips, Morgie would almost call off the war. They sit and talk to one another, about ten sentences to the hour; and everything is grand."[80] The Tripartite Agreement had gotten Britain and America talking again. Indeed, it had helped bring an end to years of monetary animosity. More broadly, it had been an attempt to "safeguard peace," to shore up democracy against fascism. As it fell into abeyance with the outbreak of war, the members faced the much greater task of defeating the fascists outright.

---

[80] Quoted in Skidelsky (2001, 306).

10

From Bretton Woods to Today

Successful though the Tripartite Agreement was in putting an end to the monetary chaos of the early 1930s, it could not survive the demands of total war. Soon after Britain and France imposed exchange controls with the outbreak of the Second World War, it became an agreement in name only and then faded from view. Policymakers were intent, however, on avoiding a relapse to the economic conflagration of the 1930s and began planning for a postwar world early on in the conflict. These efforts culminated in the 1944 conference at Bretton Woods, where the allies established the International Monetary Fund (IMF), World Bank, and a system of fixed-but-adjustable exchange parities. Ever since, Bretton Woods has become the key landmark of international monetary cooperation, forming the historical backdrop for policymakers today. The Tripartite Agreement, on the other hand, is largely forgotten, product of a decade whose lessons many assume to be only in the negative.

Yet the Agreement's principles live on, embedded in so much of the postwar push for collaboration. The sentiments articulated in those five paragraphs of September 1936 – refrain from competitive depreciation, work toward exchange stability, avoid exchange control, consult and inform – reappear time and again, from the IMF's Articles of Agreement in 1944 to G20 communiqués today.[1] In fact, the Tripartite Agreement first recognized the dual concept that countries should not sacrifice their domestic economies just to maintain their exchange rates but neither should they ignore the effect of their international monetary actions on

---

[1] For instance, the July 2013 G20 communiqué of finance ministers and central bank governors declared, "We will refrain from competitive devaluation and will not target our exchange rates for competitive purposes. We will resist all forms of protectionism and keep our markets open" (Group of Twenty 2013).

others. Cooperation was essential precisely because those two principles tugged at each other. Intellectually, then, the accord was not a blip in monetary history but a milestone. And practically, many aspects from the Tripartite system carried over to the Bretton Woods years as well.

Flash forward, and today's international monetary system is vastly different from those of the 1930s and postwar decades. Advanced economies rarely intervene in exchange markets or target exchange rates, focusing instead on prices and economic activity. Gold no longer serves as the foundation of the monetary system. Capital flows are much larger. And sterling's role as a reserve currency is a shadow of what it once was. Yet, at the system's core, many of the same tensions still pull. Worries of a currency war frequently make the news, as the United States and China trade barbs over monetary policy. Economic nationalism seems ascendant once again. And just as policymakers in the 1930s had to navigate a new monetary world, so too we find ourselves at the threshold of one – with questions not only about which currencies will reign supreme but also about what it even means to be a currency in a digital age.

The monetary problems faced by Harry Siepmann, Henry Morgenthau, Charles Cariguel, and all of the other policymakers roaming the halls of finance ministries and central banks in the 1930s thus remain as relevant as ever. A full discussion of contemporary monetary issues and their relation to that decade is far beyond the scope of this book, but three points stand out. First, opaque foreign exchange operations continue to raise suspicion. But just as the sharing of intervention information under the Tripartite Agreement helped build trust in the 1930s, so too greater transparency in intervention data may help ease tensions today. Second, the daily consultation required for the twenty-four-hour gold standard to function fostered personal connections and working relationships that came in handy during times of crisis. Building such technical relations, say by expanding swap facilities, could serve countries well today. Finally, the Tripartite Agreement's success shows that informal monetary arrangements can be effective. With the monetary system potentially at the verge of a new era, such incremental steps may be the best route to making progress today.

This chapter sketches some of the connections between the Tripartite system and developments in the postwar period. It in no way aims to be comprehensive. Rather, it brings to light many of the links between the Tripartite Agreement and Bretton Woods, arguing that what made the latter possible was not so much an intellectual breakthrough – many of the ideas had circulated within the currency club – but a new political will. This is not to downplay the results of Bretton Woods or the brilliance of its designers. The institutionalization and universality at its heart were monumental steps, and the sheer doggedness with which its framers worked to hammer out details and corral so much of the world into joining continues to inspire. But illuminating prewar antecedents place these achievements in the proper context. The chapter concludes with a brief discussion of how the Tripartite Agreement can inform some of today's problems. Transparency in foreign reserves, routinization of technical collaboration, and a willingness to consider small steps can all help prod policymakers onto a more cooperative path.

NEW WORLD, OLD IDEAS

The Tripartite system's machinery became defunct with the outbreak of war. Belligerents imposed exchange controls, ditching the principles of 1936 as they battled for survival. While molding their monetary systems for war, London and Washington also began to think about what to do after the peace. John Maynard Keynes and Harry Dexter White independently put pen to paper, brainstorming new systems to make the future better than the past. Both schemes centered on fixed exchange rates and a multilateral institution, White's an international stabilization fund and Keynes' a more daring international clearing union. Negotiations commenced in 1943, the ultimate result of which was approval of Articles of Agreement for the IMF and World Bank – largely following White's plan – by representatives of forty-four allied nations at the Mount Washington Hotel on July 22, 1944.[2]

Though just under eight years after the Tripartite Agreement's pronouncement, the signing ceremony at the hotel must have felt like an eternity later. After all, in-between the two was a cataclysmic war that seemed to wipe away all that had come before. The world needed to be built anew. It is not surprising then that scholars often glide over the link between the Tripartite Agreement and Bretton Woods, sometimes granting the former ancestral status but not much else.[3] The 1930s began with

---

[2] Excellent histories covering Bretton Woods include Horsefield (1969, part I), Skidelsky (2001), and Steil (2013).

[3] For instance, Drummond (1981, 251) writes, "it is really not correct to see this short and confused period as a 'bridge to Bretton Woods.'" To be sure, some scholars have noted connections between the 1930s and the Bretton Woods era. Urban and Straumann (2012) argue that, in the last years of the 1930s, exchange rates were for the most part fixed on a de facto basis; as such, the "1930s should be viewed as a key link between the gold standard and Bretton Woods rather than as a temporary digression from fixed exchanges rates."

depression and culminated in war: Surely, the new monetary system would bear little resemblance to the old.

And in a narrow sense, Bretton Woods was a repudiation of the Tripartite system. Whereas the White and Keynes plans focused on establishing an enduring structure for the postwar world, an alternative proposal building on the Tripartite Agreement argued for a more flexible and temporary approach. This "key currency" program, whose main proponent was John Williams of Harvard, suggested that the victors concentrate on the crucial sterling-dollar rate and delay formalizing anything else.[4] Williams thought it best to deal with the key currencies that underpinned the monetary system and eschew the universalism inherent in the leading proposals. The postwar world would be too uncertain and too fragile to force countries, each requiring varying levels of political and economic reconstruction, to declare parities so soon. As Bordo (1993, 33) summarizes, Williams' idea was to "follow the experience of the Tripartite Agreement," whereby "the monetary authorities of the United States and Britain would have set up a joint Exchange Stabilization Fund to stabilize the dollar-pound exchange rate." Better to start from a known basis – Anglo-American cooperation through exchange intervention – than risk constructing a system so ambitious that it might never take off.[5]

But the moment called for more. White, Keynes, and other leading officials believed that rules had to be made and institutions set up while the opportunity existed: There might not be another time with so much space for action and such concentrated power to chart the course. Informality would not suffice. Williams' plan, as a result, did not gain much support. The terms set forth at Bretton Woods required all members of the IMF, not just a select few, to declare par values for their currencies and keep their exchange rates within 1 percent on either side, going well beyond the more pliable aim of achieving the "greatest possible equilibrium in the system of international exchange" of the Tripartite years. Members would place funds with the IMF, which would then lend them to countries at times of crisis. A member could alter its parity only in the

---

Mundell (2000) characterizes the Tripartite Agreement as a "precursor of the Bretton Woods agreement." Helleiner (2016) describes the connection between the ESF's stabilization loans to low-income countries and the IMF.

[4] Williams (1943) explained that the Tripartite Agreement would not be "the model, however, unless it can be greatly strengthened in its provisions for external collaboration and supplemented by provisions for cooperation on internal policies, to which it made no reference."

[5] The BoE favored such an approach (Fforde 1992, 39).

case of a "fundamental disequilibrium" – never explicitly defined – and the IMF would have to approve large alterations. Compared to the experience of the late 1930s – no fixed rates, no central institution, no long-term funding for imbalances – Bretton Woods appears to be a sharp departure.

However, that the proposal most directly associated with the Tripartite Agreement did not become the basis for Bretton Woods does not mean that planners spurned the Agreement. In the broadest sense, the underlying thrust of the Tripartite Agreement – exchange rates were matters of international concern – suffused the planning. The officials working in the 1940s were not novices: They had lived through and often influenced the monetary events of the 1930s. The IMF was in many ways an institution designed to achieve the Tripartite Agreement's goals. As outlined in its Articles of Agreement, the IMF's purposes included "to promote international monetary cooperation;" "to facilitate the expansion and balanced growth of international trade;" "to promote exchange stability, to maintain orderly exchange arrangements among members, and to avoid competitive exchange depreciation;" and "to assist in the establishment of a multilateral system of payments in respect of current transactions": all aims articulated in the statements of September 1936.[6]

On a technical level, moreover, many characteristics of Bretton Woods originated in the late 1930s. The hallmarks of the postwar system were the official US gold price of $35 per ounce and the maintenance of fixed nominal exchange rates with the dollar. As we have seen, Washington implemented the $35 price in 1934 when Roosevelt formally devalued. Congress had granted Roosevelt the authority to further alter the price within limits, leading to concern – sometimes panic – in markets that there could be changes. But as early as 1936, when setting up the reciprocal gold facilities in the Tripartite Agreement's first weeks, the Americans spoke of the $35 price as the "pivot" around which all would revolve, and pivot it would remain for decades (until Nixon's closing of the gold window in 1971).[7] Moreover, while the requirement for fixed parities was certainly stricter than anything under the Tripartite Agreement, the underlying concept was similar. The Tripartite Agreement called for members to work toward stability without sacrificing "internal prosperity;" Bretton Woods

---

[6] Quoted in Horsefield (1969, 3:187–88).

[7] Treasury meeting, October 5, 1936, MD 37/212. The president's power to alter the gold value of the dollar lapsed in 1943; the legislation ratifying the Bretton Woods Agreements then explicitly forbade the president from altering it without congressional approval (Friedman and Schwartz 1963, 509).

took that stability one step further by mandating fixed rates but included the fundamental disequilibrium escape clause so that domestic economies were not held hostage to international dictates.

Just as in the 1930s, exchange intervention remained essential. Keeping currencies within bands required constant intervention, so that the EEA and other funds established during the depths of the Depression were as active as ever. To be sure, some of the architecture had changed. The United States allowed conversion of official dollars into gold no matter when they were acquired during Bretton Woods, in contrast to the currency club rules of converting balances obtained through intervention each day only.[8] This change mattered because countries now held dollars as reserves, so the potential drain on US gold holdings became larger. In addition, countries other than the United States no longer converted official holdings of their currencies into gold; rather, operations worked through the dollar. But these modifications to convertibility should not obscure the many similarities.

Of course, the Bretton Woods negotiations did more than build on the Tripartite legacy: They took account of the pact's shortcomings in order to create a better system. The most consequential improvement involved the financing of payments imbalances. The Articles of Agreement specified that the IMF would "give confidence to members by making the Fund's resources available to them . . . to correct maladjustments in their balance of payments," thus providing the longer-term support lacking in the 1930s.[9] Back then, club members had not been able to overcome their fear of loss on exchange holdings to help finance each other during crises. There had been much discussion on the topic throughout the Tripartite era – from direct loans to intervention on joint account to the pooling of gold reserves into a shared fund. Siepmann mocked up a plan for an "International Gold Fund" as a means to aid France in 1937.[10] But the political and financial risks appeared too large throughout this period. The achievement of Bretton Woods in endowing an institution with funds to lend to one another was of immense consequence. The devastation of war, by enabling such action, allowed a giant step forward.

---

[8] However, the United States at times put pressure on other countries, notably France, not to convert their dollars into gold (Bordo, Monnet, and Naef 2019).

[9] Quoted in Horsefield (1969, 3:188).

[10] Siepmann, "The French from the point of view of the Exchange Equalisation Account," August 27, 1937, BoE C43/463.

In the event, the international monetary system did not begin to resemble the plan set forth at Bretton Woods until the late 1950s. Attempts to end controls on current transactions and install fixed parities ended disastrously, most notably Britain's failed implementation of current account convertibility in 1947 and the wave of devaluations in 1949.[11] Policymakers had to make due in the meantime. Many of the protagonists from the 1930s remained in positions of influence. George Bolton and L. Werner Knoke continued consulting by phone into the 1950s. Allan Sproul took the helm at the FRBNY, and Cameron Cobbold did so at the BoE. Siepmann remained at Threadneedle Street into the 1950s. Emmanuel Mönick, one of the Tripartite Agreement's framers, led the Banque de France during the second half of the 1940s. And H. Merle Cochran, Morgenthau's peripatetic financial emissary, became the IMF's deputy managing director in 1953.

Other leading players from the 1930s were no longer in the arena. Morgenthau left office in 1945 after eleven years as secretary but not before shepherding the Bretton Woods agreements through Congress.[12] Neville Chamberlain died in 1940, his reputation, forever connected to appeasement, already in tatters. The British Treasury also lost its monetary knights – Hopkins, Leith-Ross, and Phillips – the first two having retired from government at the war's end and the last having passed away in 1943. But clearly the operators of the Bretton Woods system were not working from a blank slate: They had experienced far too much to forget the tragedies and triumphs of the past.

At times in the succeeding decades, policymakers referred wistfully to the Tripartite Agreement. In 1954, when Bretton Woods as conceived still remained a distant dream, BoE officials recirculated old memoranda on the Agreement. Cobbold commented to Bolton: "When I negotiated the Tripartite Agreement with M. Fournier I repeated like a parrot, 'Ni accord, ni entente, uniquement coopération journalière,' until it became a joke between us. We ought to go on the same basis and work for as much de facto stability as possible."[13] Later, in 1960, some in France wondered whether the Agreement could be reactivated to better coordinate intervention among the major powers, though nothing came of the proposal.[14]

---

[11] Fforde (1992, chapters 3 and 4); Schenk (2010, chapter 2).

[12] Rauchway (2015, 227–29).

[13] Quoted in Fforde (1992, 501). The BIS also published a note on the Tripartite Agreement in 1955 that seemed to broach the possibility of reinstating the intervention protocols. "The Tripartite Agreement of 1936," July 8, 1955, BISA 9.1 003 HS 375.

[14] Monnet (2017).

By the 1970s, the protagonists of the Tripartite era were no longer in power, their experience consigned to history. The collapse of the system of fixed parities at the beginning of the decade, however, reignited interest in the accord. In 1973, the BoE's governor asked for a report on the Tripartite Agreement and its norms for intervention. Staff dug into the BoE's "innermost secrets."[15] The study concluded that the Agreement "signalled a new era of co-operation in international monetary affairs" and "seems in the main to have been a success."[16] There was so much talk of the Agreement that one official thought it was taking on the role of a "new nostrum."[17] Yet this dive into the past does not seem to have gone any further in influencing the policymaking process, and the Tripartite Agreement returned to obscurity. The 1980s then saw the Plaza and Louvre Accords, informal arrangements to bring about a more sustainable equilibrium in exchange rates.[18] With the archives for those years only recently beginning to open, it is not yet clear whether policymakers found any inspiration in the Tripartite Agreement. It seems safe to assume, however, that the then fifty-year-old arrangement was long forgotten.

LESSONS FOR TODAY

In many ways, the Tripartite Agreement's relative obscurity is a testament to its success. The Agreement's principles of cooperation and consultation have become so ingrained as to seem commonplace. That is not to suggest that countries always act according to these principles. The multilateral system is under attack from within and without. Tension between the world's two largest economies is at an all-time high. The reasons for this setback to the liberal order are manifold; the actions necessary to right the ship will likely be as well. Looking at the transition from monetary war to peace in the 1930s provides some insight into just a few steps policymakers can take to shift toward a more cooperative stance once they are ready to do so.

Exchange Intervention Transparency: Today, Britain no longer intervenes in exchange markets to influence the value of the pound. Since the collapse of the European Monetary System in 1992, it has stayed out of

---

[15] Handwritten note, November 8, 1973, BoE C43/463; "Tripartite Agreement," November 1, 1973, BoE C43/463.

[16] Smeeton, "Tripartite Currency Agreement," November 21, 1973, BoE C43/463.

[17] "Your note of 7th December," December 12, 1973, BoE OV53/75.

[18] Bergsten and Green (2016) is a valuable collection of essays on the Plaza Accord.

exchange markets, save for a couple of one-off, coordinated interventions at moments of crisis (most recently the G7 effort to steady the yen after the deadly Japanese tsunami in 2011). The United States likewise has not intervened in recent decades except for such isolated events. Indeed, most central banks in advanced economies, including the European Central Bank (ECB), do not systematically intervene anymore.[19] Freely floating rates are now the norm for this group; central banks operate by adjusting interest rates in pursuit of an inflation target rather than following an exchange rate target, and finance ministries maintain exchange funds but do not employ them to influence rates.

Other countries, however, still intervene, often substantially. China grabs the headlines, but the group of interveners is large and diverse, from Turkey to Switzerland to Singapore.[20] Intervention per se, as this book makes clear, is neither good nor bad. There can be ample justification for managing exchange rates.[21] Leaning against the wind can help make markets more orderly. It may make sense for a small country to peg its currency to that of a large trading partner. Natural resource exporters can reasonably accumulate foreign reserves to build a buffer for when export prices fall. But intervention can also involve manipulation. Countries may seek a competitive advantage through excessive purchases of foreign exchange, usually the dollar. The United States is thus keenly interested in the actions of others.[22] Condemnation of currency interveners – sometimes merited, sometimes not – is frequent. So strong is the concern in some corners that proposals for countermeasures, including a return to intervening or even blatant manipulation of the dollar, have become common of late in Washington.[23]

Secrecy only magnifies the suspicion. Many countries are less than forthcoming in reporting their purchases and sales of foreign exchange. The US Treasury's semi-annual report on foreign exchange intervention regularly implores for more disclosure.[24] Though there has been progress in recent years, a veil continues to cover up much of what is going on. In some ways, the haze has even gotten thicker recently, because, as Setser

---

[19] See Neely (2011) for a review of G7 intervention practices.　　[20] US Treasury (2020).

[21] Indeed, Ilzetzki, Reinhart, and Rogoff (2019) show that most countries do not allow their currencies to float freely.

[22] See Bergsten and Gagnon (2017) and Setser (2019) for comprehensive discussions of currency manipulation and potential policy responses.

[23] "Strong U.S. Dollar Prompts Speculation of Trump Intervention," *The Wall Street Journal*, September 15, 2019.

[24] US Treasury (2020).

(2019, 5) explains, countries can "mask their interventions" by working through state banks or other outlets rather than official exchange funds. The Treasury's push for greater transparency thus remains a worthy goal even as it must now be more encompassing.

The experience under the Tripartite Agreement adds historical weight to the Treasury's argument. The wall separating London and Washington that so harmed relations during the first half of the 1930s derived in part from their refusal to inform each other of their activities in exchange markets – even when they were expending reserves to lessen depreciation rather than accumulating reserves to hasten depreciation. Once they began sharing information in 1936, trust started to develop. As Morgenthau raved to an advisor, "that kind of information we never received and never gave" prior to the Agreement, but now "the ice is broken, and they [the British] give us enough to work with and we give them enough to work with, so we can work together."[25]

Exchanging information can thus remove an unnecessary hindrance to better relations, creating room for discussion in a less heated atmosphere. Since what matters most is reducing tensions between countries, officials should focus first on the confidential exchange of information between authorities – as in the 1930s – without insisting on public disclosures. Transparency may be just the first step, but it is an imperative step nonetheless.

Routine Collaboration: The twenty-four-hour gold standard required central banks to be in touch daily. Exchange managers discussed market developments and interventions, sharing insights and soliciting advice. The technical facilities for gold conversion also gave the public a sense that authorities were working together and not at cross-purposes. One consequence of the increase in communication was that exchange managers came to know one another – their moods, skills, and biases. As Siepmann explained in 1937, "the continuous dealings between the different controls leads inevitably to an intimacy of contact and a continuous exchange of market information which would have been impossible without the [Tripartite] Agreement."[26] And at times of crisis, these relationships proved useful in navigating turmoil in the markets, allowing for frank conversation and contributing to greater understanding of one another's viewpoints.

---

[25] "Conference on Question of Transfer of Earmarked Gold," January 26, 1937, MD 53/19.
[26] Siepmann, "The Tripartite Agreement," September 3, 1937, BoE G1/304.

Today, there is no need to reinstate reciprocal gold facilities. But an analogy can be made to central bank liquidity swap lines: arrangements between central banks to exchange currencies for a specified period of time. A liquidity swap line between the Federal Reserve and the ECB works as follows: If the ECB needs dollars – perhaps because European banks have trouble getting access to dollars – the Federal Reserve can provide dollars to the ECB in exchange for euros. The ECB will then reverse the transaction at a later date by giving the Federal Reserve dollars in exchange for euros at the same exchange rate. Many central banks created swap lines during the financial crisis in 2007.[27] Though temporary at first, they have since become permanent, with the Federal Reserve, BoE, ECB, Bank of Canada, Bank of Japan, and Swiss National Bank all extending reciprocal facilities to one another. Unlike the gold arrangements in the 1930s, the swap lines are not used daily. Nevertheless, they represent to the public a united front to combat financial instability and serve as a safety net in times of need, demonstrated most recently by their employment during the coronavirus crisis.[28]

Missing from this system of swaps is an arrangement between the United States and China, the two ends of the axis around which the world economy revolves.[29] As China's economy grows, the potential benefits of establishing such a swap line will likely increase. In fact, the BoE and ECB have already established arrangements with the People's Bank of China. Besides providing access to emergency liquidity, the facility would promote better relations at a technical level. Setting the swap line up and conducting operational testing would lead to greater contact between personnel and pierce some of the barrier separating the two countries. In the current geopolitical environment, it is difficult to see such an agreement in the near future, but there is conceivably space for the United States to use a swap line as a lever to extract greater cooperation on other fronts, such as transparency in exchange intervention.

Informal Agreements: Discontent with the current monetary system sometimes leads to calls for a "new Bretton Woods," the hope being that a grand conclave can bring the world together and set out new rules for the

---

[27] Swap lines had previously existed during the Bretton Woods years to facilitate exchange intervention. Bordo, Humpage, and Schwartz (2015); McCauley and Schenk (2020).

[28] "Fed Expands Dollar Swap Lines with Central Banks," *Financial Times*, March 19, 2020.

[29] To help combat the economic fallout from coronavirus, the Federal Reserve created a new facility to lend dollars to central banks against Treasury securities, which China and other countries without swap lines qualify for. "Fed Launches New Lending Facility for Foreign Central Banks," *The Wall Street Journal*, March 31, 2020.

next quarter century.[30] That new rules will be needed is clear. Technology may redefine what a currency is, making it incumbent on the international community to reach agreement on which forms of innovation are permissible and which threaten monetary stability. The dollar remains unrivaled as a reserve currency for now, but its very power may contribute to the slow erosion of its status as Washington imposes financial sanctions and incentivizes a move away from the greenback. The rise of China, with its still heavily controlled financial sector, makes it all the more important to secure agreement on rules that promote an open international economy. And the growing weight of emerging markets necessitates reforming international governance.

Worthy though these goals are, a reincarnation of Bretton Woods appears too lofty a vision for the moment. Bretton Woods was in large part possible due to a political dynamic – American hegemony – in conjunction with general agreement on the structure of a new system, neither of which currently exists. The United States, while preeminent, no longer exerts such overwhelming power, and uncertainties and disagreements abound about the consequences of digital currencies, the future of reserve currencies, and the role of the state in the economy. Rather than focus on recreating a unique moment in history, it is better to move cautiously. The incremental, informal nature of the Tripartite Agreement thus serves as a more suitable precedent for the moment.[31] It worked because it homed in on what governments could agree on and left space to build on it.

As Morgenthau explained, "the beauty of the thing is—there are no signatures.... I would ten times rather shake hands than have all the signatures in the world."[32] Though he never actually got to shake Chamberlain's hand, the point stands. Especially at a time such as now when the aim is to reduce tensions and make sense of what could turn into a monumental transformation of the monetary system, a handshake may be better than a signature. Policymakers should resist the urge to seek formalization for its own sake and accept that provisional agreements have a role to play.

---

[30] Calls for a second Bretton Woods were particularly frequent during the global financial crisis and the run-up to the G20 meeting in November 2008. "Brown, Sarkozy seek 'new Bretton Woods,'" *Financial Times*, November 2, 2008.

[31] There is a vast literature on the role of informal agreements. See Lipson (1991) and Raustiala (2005).

[32] Treasury meeting, September 25, 1936, MD 34/53.

Transparency, routine collaboration, and informality: Heeding the lessons from the Tripartite years will not lead to a perfect system, but it can contribute to a better one. While these topics barely scratch the surface of debates about the contemporary monetary system, they demonstrate that, despite the vast institutional changes of the past seventy-five years, the experience from the 1930s still matters. Of course, the connections to that decade go well beyond economics. Nationalism, not just of the economic variety, is spreading and poses an acute challenge to the rules-based international system. One can only hope that the world, as it enters the centenary of the interwar period, will apply the many lessons from that time rather than fling itself once more into the depths of depression, dissension, and disintegration.

Conclusion

In February 1939, Chancellor of the Exchequer John Simon praised the Exchange Equalisation Account (EEA), telling the House of Commons that "the reputation" of the account "is one of our great sources of strength. We were the first country to show the world how to do it. It is being done with great skill, and we owe a great deal to the devoted men, whose work is never published, who watch this matter and serve the country so well in trying to maintain our currency value."[1] While the EEA's reputation had not always been so high – foreign observers likened the account to a weapon of war in its early days – by the time of Simon's address it was admired at home and abroad as a protector of monetary peace and the nation's prestige. As for the men who managed it and indeed all those involved in sterling policy, they witnessed and contributed to immense changes in the monetary system, the consequences of which reverberate to this day. They were born under the gold standard, worked to reconstruct it after the First World War, started to dismantle it in 1931, and then created a new method of management that sought to balance exchange stability with internal prosperity.

Economic historians have too often ignored much of this narrative, treating Britain's suspension of convertibility as the end of the story. But as this book has aimed to show, it was just as much the beginning of another. In the eight years after 1931, officials managed the pound in unfamiliar circumstances and in novel ways. Previously, when Britain had suspended convertibility it had done so during war. Once the fighting ceased, resumption had been widely expected, and the main question was at what time it would occur. But Britain was not at war when it made the

---

[1] 343 Parl. Deb. H.C. (5th ser.) (1939) col. 1173.

fateful decision in September 1931. There were therefore no battles to watch in order to gauge when suspension would end. The Treasury's formal policy was that it intended to return to the gold standard in some form at some time, but these routine statements lost meaning over the years. By 1939, they were no more than "eschatological hot air," in the words of one Bank of England (BoE) adviser.[2]

The real policy was to make the best of the situation as it was. The government's insistence on cheap money meant that Bank Rate stuck to 2 percent for nearly the entire decade. The EEA thus became the prime tool for managing the exchange rate. Intervention was a daily occurrence and determining how much to buy or sell required balancing a host of priorities pulling in a variety of directions. Target rates incorporated many conditions that changed with time: ideas of the equilibrium rate, the desire for a trade advantage, the need to maintain purchasing power. All the while, the relationship between the Treasury and BoE morphed, as the former became supreme in monetary affairs. To be sure, the BoE was still a private corporation and retained a good deal of discretion: Harry Siepmann applauded the "remarkable liberty, accorded to officials of the Treasury by their Ministerial chiefs, to divest themselves of any active control over E.E.A."[3] But the old days of operating without the Treasury's consent were long gone.

As the years went by, the ancestral totems of monetary policy fell to expediency. At first, all that changed was the ability to convert pounds into gold: The statutory price of the metal remained the same, as did the statutes underlying the backing of the note issue. Yet the requirement for the note issue to depend on the amount of gold in the Issue Department – valued at the old statutory price – became increasingly outmoded. When the crisis in the autumn of 1938 emptied the EEA's holdings, the necessity of replenishing the fund provided the opportunity to repeal the statutory price. Soon thereafter, the outbreak of hostilities resulted in the transfer of nearly all of the Issue Department's remaining gold to the EEA and the end of any connection between the note issue and gold. This protracted evolution reflected the government's caution. Policymakers had to grope their way forward one step at a time and leap when circumstances demanded action. Far from an abrupt end, then, the gold standard came apart piece by piece.

---

[2] Clay, Untitled memo, January 5, 1939, BoE C43/100.
[3] Quoted in Sayers (1976, 2:469).

The EEA filled the vacuum left by suspension of convertibility. From its creation in 1932, it was both omnipresent and elusive, seemingly lurking in the exchange markets at all times yet undetectable. Other countries did not take well to this new force. The United States created the Exchange Stabilization Fund (ESF) in 1934 explicitly to even the playing field. When Archie Lochhead, the ESF's first manager, passed away in 1971, *The New York Times* reported that his task had been particularly demanding during the fund's early years, when "lacking official connections with the British and French monetary authorities, Mr. Lochhead had to keep guessing what they might do next. It was not only the speculators he had to contend with, but big foreign central banks as well." His "job had its most difficult moments" until "1936, when the Tripartite Agreement was signed," and the monetary powers pledged to work with rather than against one another. The newspaper added that he insisted on a "daily settlement of foreign accounts and gold on hand to cover the Treasury if it should be caught in an emergency with a quantity of depreciated foreign currency."[4]

This description quite accurately summarizes exchange rate relationships during the decade. Britain's suspension, coupled with the establishment of the EEA, embittered relations. The US decision to embark on eleven months of monetary experimentation in March 1933 – and Roosevelt's gratuitous denunciation of the World Economic Conference in July – effectively brought Anglo-American communication on monetary matters to a halt. The installation of a modified gold standard in the United States in January 1934 stabilized the situation somewhat, but there was no truce. Nations explained little to nothing about the actions they took. London and Washington remained so suspicious of one another that the occasional feeler seemed more like a threat. Paris viewed both as apostates, and the constant turnover in governments hampered its ability to right the economy and serve as a reliable partner.

As each country navigated the fragmented system from 1934 to 1936, there was a continued emphasis on gold. Precisely because nations were either off gold (Britain), on it in a constricted form (United States), or on it in an unsustainable way (France), officials considered gold the only suitable reserve asset: Every exchange manager wanted to avoid being caught with "a quantity of depreciated foreign currency." In this way, the decline of gold as the fundamental base of the monetary system led to its rise as the

---

[4] "Archie Lochhead is Dead at 78," *The New York Times*, January 16, 1971.

unrivaled reserve asset. This shift in gold's role in turn influenced intervention strategies. For example, because US regulations prevented Britain from exchanging dollars for gold, the British stopped intervening in dollars and instead operated in francs. The lack of transactions between the two powers deepened the breach between them. With each of the Big Three countries on a different system – and each considering its system superior – the future was unclear, save for its bleak outlook. These were the dark years of monetary relations, made darker still by the proliferation of totalitarian controls on trade and exchange dealings in Central Europe.

Only with the imminent collapse of the franc in 1936 could the three countries overcome the bad blood of the first half of the decade. If the franc were to fall, London and Washington did not know how the other would react, and the fear of the unknown brought them together. They agreed that neither would depreciate in response to a French devaluation. This promise smoothed the way for Paris to act: It did not need to worry that its devaluation would be negated, and Anglo-American support would help sell the move to the French public. The resulting Tripartite Agreement offered a new way forward, where the monetary powers did not have to "contend" against one another but could cooperate. They vowed to promote stability, abjure competitive depreciations, and avoid exchange control. The exchange funds would work toward this end. As Nurkse (1944, 159) emphasizes, "Exchange Stabilization Funds are instruments of control and cooperation, but they may equally be used for attack and currency warfare." The Tripartite Agreement heralded the shift from the latter to the former: They were no longer objects of mistrust but necessary tools in a cooperative effort to achieve stability.

Soon after the Tripartite Agreement's promulgation, the members negotiated gold convertibility facilities to enable intervention, and Belgium, the Netherlands, and Switzerland joined several weeks later. Each country set a buying and selling price for gold in terms of its currency every day, and it cleared the exchange interventions of other members at this price. Fund managers had the assurances they needed to intervene in any member currency, since they could convert any purchases of foreign exchange into gold. There was no risk of suffering a loss on foreign exchange holdings because there were none. The daily system required frequent contact among the central banks operating the funds, and Treasuries, which had taken over control of monetary policy, consulted and negotiated regularly.

Members relied on the currency club to confront the monetary crises that plagued the last years of peace. From the Gold Scare in the spring of 1937 to the Dollar Scare that autumn, from France's habitual emergencies to Britain's plight during Munich and its aftermath: The responses to all of these episodes were based on cooperation rather than confrontation, on the need for upholding the Tripartite Agreement even as these pressures threatened it. The system was far from perfect. Most notably, it lacked mechanisms for long-term support, leading to rather absurd situations where some members desperately wanted to borrow gold while others had more than they wanted yet refused to lend it. Nevertheless, a profound shift had occurred. The six countries now thought of exchange rates as matters of international concern. The instinctive response to exchange rate developments was no longer how to gain the greatest advantage: It was how to minimize the disturbance to the system. The adherents discarded the monetary nationalism that had been so destructive during the early part of the decade. And at a time when the world was split between democracies and dictatorships, the Tripartite Agreement was a vital force bringing the former closer together and demonstrating to the world a fundamental solidarity.

Not all have judged the Tripartite Agreement positively. One American economist in the 1930s brushed it aside as "a collection of vagaries, pious platitudes, and affable nothing."[5] Later scholars have often expressed similar sentiments, dismissing the Agreement and arguing that its lack of detail and enforceable provisions necessarily made it ineffective. Ambiguity, however, can prevent a framework from becoming overly rigid and destroying itself, and monetary accords frequently employ indefinite language for this reason.[6] Informal agreements also bring many advantages, speed of enactment and flexibility foremost among them. All of these attributes helped in 1936: Governments negotiated the Tripartite Agreement during a time of crisis, and the pervasive uncertainty of what lay ahead made flexibility a necessity for all. The gold facilities established soon thereafter and the radical change in relations were testaments to the Agreement's very real effects.

Speaking at a conference of imperial central bankers in May 1937, Montagu Norman, governor of the BoE, commented that the "history of how" the Tripartite Agreement "actually came to pass, and of what it was thought to amount to by the different participants, will make curious

---

[5] The quotation comes from Walter E. Spahr, who was chairman of the economics department at New York University and a forceful advocate of returning to the gold standard. Bloomfield, "The Tripartite Agreement of 1936 as an alternative to the Keynes and White Plans," May 8, 1943, FRBNY FF4608.

[6] See, for instance, Best (2005).

reading if it is ever written."[7] Indeed, the Agreement came to life in the midst of crisis, and the parties patched over disagreements with ambiguities. Yet the three statements of 1936, in reaching for something better, in pivoting away from confrontation to cooperation, improved international monetary relations well beyond initial expectations. In a decade full of sorrow, this shift was no small feat. Forty years later, looking back on a long career at the intersection of finance and politics, the BoE's George Bolton remembered the Tripartite Agreement as "the first sign of monetary sanity," which, "like a candle in a window, threw a flickering light on the gloomy scene of international monetary and political convulsions."[8] Today, we would do well to keep that flame of cooperation alive.

[7] "Introductory Remarks," May 26, 1937, BoE C43/25.
[8] Bolton, "Memoirs," undated, BoE C160/179.

Appendix A: Exchange Intervention Empirics

When studying exchange intervention empirically, one of the key questions is what motivated exchange managers to act. In particular, did they try to moderate volatility by leaning against the wind or did they try to reinforce movements?[1] In this appendix, I describe the methodology for assessing Britain's motivations during the Tripartite years, the available data, and the results. I then conclude with a note about the data on EEA holdings cited throughout this book.

Reaction Functions: The methodology follows the standard approach in the literature.[2] I calculate reaction functions that relate Britain's intervention to changes in exchange rates:

$$Int_t = \beta_0 + \beta_1 Int_{t-1} + \beta_2(s_{t-1} - s_{t-2}) + \beta_3(s_{t-1} - \bar{s}) + \epsilon_t$$

where Int_t represents the intervention at time t (purchases of foreign exchange measured in millions of pounds), s_t is the log exchange rate (local currency per unit of foreign currency), $\bar{s}$ is the log of the target exchange rate, and ϵ_t is the residual. Though there was no official target rate during the Tripartite years, the old parity of \$4.86 remained salient and is taken as $\bar{s}$ in this exercise.

The coefficients of interest are β_2 and β_3. Negative coefficients suggest stabilizing motivations. β_2 reflects the influence of daily changes, so that a negative coefficient is consistent with leaning against the wind; β_3 measures the impact of deviations from target, so that a negative coefficient suggests

---

[1] Other empirical studies of the EEA in the 1930s include Whitaker and Hudgins (1977), which uses a proxy of intervention to determine whether intervention impacted exchange rates and finds a moderate effect, and Broadberry (1987), which uses quarterly data on reserves to assess the impact of intervention on exchange rate volatility and finds no effect.

[2] See, for instance, Bordo, MacDonald, and Oliver (2009).

a desire to move closer to the target. And the larger these coefficients are in absolute value, the more responsive exchange managers were to changes in rates.

Ideally, there would be a clean series of daily interventions during the Tripartite years, in particular purchases and sales of dollars, with which to calculate these reaction functions. However, data on exchange intervention in the 1930s, for Britain and other club members, come in bits and pieces. In some cases, the data are no longer extant; in other cases, they are not yet public.[3] The EEA's records are the most comprehensive among the Big Three club members, yet even these do not contain a complete daily series of intervention.

There are several sources for EEA interventions during the Tripartite years. George Bolton's retrospective on the EEA (BoE C160/78) provides monthly holdings of gold, foreign exchange (in aggregate), and sterling at cost for the entire decade. Harry Siepmann's quarterly reports (BoE C14/1-14) contain daily holdings of gold, foreign exchange (in aggregate), and sterling for 1936 to 1939. Neither of these sources, however, document the underlying intervention. That is, they do not provide insight into whether a change in gold holdings reflected a direct transaction in the gold market or whether it reflected clearing with another central bank after intervening in exchange markets.

To differentiate between these transactions, I use the EEA's gold ledgers (BoE 2A197/2 and C139/1). These ledgers document every gold transaction from 1936 to 1939: the counterparty, the currency against which the gold was bought or sold, the value of the gold in sterling terms, and the weight of the gold in ounces. Ordinarily, gold transactions would represent just one part of intervention. But because policymakers followed the twenty-four-hour gold standard during the Tripartite years, gold flows between club members shed light on exchange intervention. The system revolved around central banks clearing exchange interventions in gold with one another, and so it is reasonable to assume that each gold transaction between club members offset an exchange intervention and that each exchange intervention was offset by a gold transaction. For instance, on March 8, 1937, the EEA sold £520,000 of gold to the Banque de France (BdF) against francs. To estimate daily intervention, I assume that this transaction implies that the EEA sold £520,000 worth of francs in the

---

[3] Records for the ESF during the 1930s are largely nonexistent, though Brown (1942) contains valuable information. Records for the French stabilization fund can be found in BdF 1463200401/66–67.

market (against sterling) and obtained the requisite francs by selling gold to the BdF. That same day, the EEA also sold £2 million of gold to the BdF against sterling. Here I assume that the French purchased sterling in the market (against francs) and then converted it into gold.

Gold transactions thus map directly to interventions in exchange markets.[4] Anytime Britain bought gold against a foreign currency from another club member, I record that as Britain having purchased that foreign currency in the market; anytime Britain sold gold against a foreign currency, I record that as Britain having sold that foreign currency in the market. Applying this procedure to all gold transactions between club members results in estimates of all of Britain's interventions in club currencies as well as all interventions by other club members in sterling. These estimates are not perfect since some intervention occurred through working balances (meaning that there was no offsetting gold transaction) and by late 1938 forward intervention became significant, leading to a mismatch between the day of intervention and gold transactions. But there is a high correspondence between these estimates and references to intervention in contemporaneous conversations between exchange managers.

Using this intervention data, along with data on exchange rates from Global Financial Data, I calculate reaction functions for Britain's interventions in the dollar market for two periods. The first is from October 13, 1936 – the opening of the reciprocal gold facilities – to July 31, 1938. By ending in July, this period does not include the crisis set off by Munich. The second period extends from October 13, 1936 to November 30, 1938. I end prior to December so that Britain's large reserve losses associated with the bear squeeze in the forward market do not distort the measured daily responsiveness (indeed, the estimates are a lower bound on responsiveness since they do not take into account forward sales of dollars at the time.) Table A.1 depicts the results with standard errors in parentheses.

In both periods, the reaction function suggests that British intervention was consistent with leaning against the wind. Using the period 2 coefficient, a 1 percent depreciation of sterling at time $t-1$ relative to $t-2$ led to the expenditure of £1.5 million of reserves. Reaction functions calculated for US intervention in sterling similarly show results consistent with leaning against the wind, but the coefficient on β_2 is approximately −15, suggesting that a 1 percent depreciation of the dollar led to the expenditure

---

[4] That is, gold transactions between club members map to exchange interventions. Other gold transactions, such as selling in the market or buying from South Africa, did not have a direct counterpart in exchange intervention.

Table A.1 *EEA reaction functions*

	Period 1	Period 2
	10/13/36–7/31/38	10/13/36–11/30/38
Constant	−0.16***	−0.35***
	(0.05)	(0.06)
Beta 1	0.14***	0.30***
	(0.04)	(0.04)
Beta 2	−62.55***	−149.84***
	(22.84)	(24.20)
Beta 3	−6.92***	−16.12***
	(2.54)	(2.98)
Number of observations	455	541
Adjusted R-squared	0.06	0.26

Note: $*p < 0.1$, $**p < 0.05$, $***p < 0.01$
Source: Author's calculations

of £150,000 of reserves, a response lower by an order of magnitude. This estimate is in line with the discussion in Chapter 7: The United States viewed the dollar as the pivot of the international monetary system and thus believed the burden to intervene fell more heavily on other nations.

In conclusion, for all of the talk of beggar-thy-neighbor policies in the 1930s, during the Tripartite years, Britain and America worked to reduce exchange volatility.

Data on EEA Holdings: Reserves can be measured at cost or at value. Unless stated otherwise, the figures cited throughout this book are cost measurements from BoE C160/78, 2A197/2, and C139/1. There are several benefits to reporting holdings at cost. First, the records are most complete for holdings at cost. Second, looking at cost permits measuring intentional changes in reserves, whereas looking at value includes valuation effects.

However, there are shortcomings to cost data. The BoE's cost accounting often did not include forward transactions, which became significant in the second half of 1938. In addition, cost data overplay the importance – slight as it was – of foreign exchange in the EEA's holdings after 1933 due to sterling's appreciation. Figure A.1 presents estimated holdings at value net of forward liabilities (so that negative values mean that the EEA was short of the currency). This series is based off data from Howson (1980), which contains an invaluable though incomplete series of monthly data for

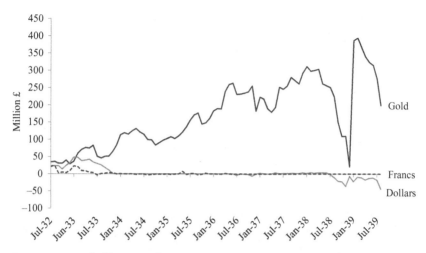

Figure A.1 EEA holdings at value, 1932–1939 (million £, current prices).
Source: Howson (1980), BoE 2A197/2, C139/1, C43/67, and author's calculations

Britain's total reserves (reserve holdings for most of 1937 and 1938 are missing). To fill in the missing months, I do the following:

- Gold holdings come from the EEA's gold ledgers (BoE 2A197/2 and C139/1).
- Dollar spot holdings come from BoE C160/78 and forward commitments from BoE C43/67. I assume that forward commitments prior to July 1938, when the data start, were zero.
- Franc holdings are assumed to be zero. There is no evidence of any substantial spot holdings or forward commitments during 1937 and 1938.
- Holdings of other currencies were minimal throughout these years and are excluded to improve the chart's readability.

This modified series reaffirms that the EEA essentially became a gold fund after 1933. The value of foreign exchange relative to the total value of the EEA's assets declined from an average of 52 percent for July 1932–February 1933 to just 0.2 percent for January 1934–June 1938.

Appendix B: Data Sources

Unless stated otherwise, data cited in text come from the following sources:

Bank of England balance sheet:	Huang and Thomas (2016)
Bank of England Bank Rate:	Huang and Thomas (2016)
British unemployment:	Boyer and Hatton (2002, table 6)
Exchange Equalisation Account:	BoE C14/1-14, C160/78, 2A197/2, C139/1
Exchange rates:	Global Financial Data
GDP:	Thomas and Dimsdale (2017)
Industrial production:	League of Nations (1937, table 106)
Inflation:	Global Financial Data
Trade:	Thomas and Dimsdale (2017)
US gold reserves:	Board of Governors of the Federal Reserve System (1943)
World gold reserves:	Bank for International Settlements (1933–1939)

Appendix C: Tripartite Statement

Text of the British statement, issued September 26, 1936.[1]

1. His Majesty's Government, after consultation with the United States Government and the French Government, join with them in affirming a common desire to foster those conditions which will safeguard peace and will best contribute to the restoration of order in international economic relations, and to pursue a policy which will tend to promote prosperity in the world and to improve the standard of living.

2. His Majesty's Government must, of course, in its policy towards international monetary relations, take into full account the requirements of internal prosperity of the countries of the Empire, as corresponding considerations will be taken into account by the Governments of France and of the United States of America. They welcome this opportunity to reaffirm their purpose to continue the policy which they have pursued in the course of recent years, one constant object of which is to maintain the greatest possible equilibrium in the system of international exchanges and to avoid to the utmost extent the creation of any disturbance of that system by British monetary action. His Majesty's Government share with the Governments of France and the United States the conviction that the continuation of this twofold policy will serve the general purpose which all Governments should pursue.

3. The French Government inform His Majesty's Government that, judging that the desired stability of the principal currencies cannot be ensured on a solid basis except after the re-establishment of a

[1] Bank for International Settlements (1937).

261

lasting equilibrium between the various economic systems, they have decided with this object to propose to their Parliament the readjustment of their currency. His Majesty's Government have, as also the United States Government, welcomed this decision in the hope that it will establish more solid foundations for the stability of international economic relations. His Majesty's Government, as also the Governments of France and of the United States of America, declare their intention to continue to use the appropriate available resources so as to avoid as far as possible any disturbance of the basis of international exchanges resulting from the proposed readjustment. They will arrange for such consultation for this purpose as may prove necessary with the other two Governments and the authorised agencies.

4. His Majesty's Government are moreover convinced, as are also the Governments of France and the United States of America, that the success of the policy set forth above is linked with the development of international trade. In particular, they attach the greatest importance to action being taken without delay to relax progressively the present system of quotas and exchange controls with a view to their abolition.

5. His Majesty's Government, in common with the Governments of France and the United States of America, desire and invite the co-operation of the other nations to realise the policy laid down in the present declaration. They trust that no country will attempt to obtain an unreasonable competitive exchange advantage and thereby hamper the effort to restore more stable economic relations which it is the aim of the three Governments to promote.

References

Archival Sources

Bank for International Settlements (BISA)
Bank of England (BoE)
Banque de France (BdF)
Cabinet Papers, National Archives of the United Kingdom (CAB)
Federal Reserve Bank of New York (FRBNY)
Franklin Roosevelt Master Speech Files, Roosevelt Library Digital Collections (RMSF)
Franklin Roosevelt Press Conferences, Roosevelt Library Digital Collections (RPC)
Harry Dexter White Papers, Mudd Manuscript Library, Princeton University (HDWP)
Henry Morgenthau Diaries, Roosevelt Library Digital Collections (MD)
Henry Morgenthau Press Conferences, Roosevelt Library Digital Collections (MPC)
Jacob Viner Papers, Mudd Manuscript Library, Princeton University (JVP)
Marriner Eccles Papers, Federal Reserve Archival System for Economic Research (MEP)
Morgan Library, New York (ML)
Nationaal Archief, The Hague (NA)
National Bank of Belgium (NBB)
Service des Archives Économiques et Financières, Savigny-le-Temple (SAEF)
Swiss National Bank (SNB)
Thomas W. Lamont Papers, Baker Library, Harvard University (TWLP)
Treasury Papers, National Archives of the United Kingdom (T)

Data Sources

Board of Governors of the Federal Reserve System. 1930–1936. *Federal Reserve Bulletin.* Federal Reserve Archival System for Economic Research. https://fraser.stlouisfed.org/title/62. Accessed March 31, 2020.

1943. *Banking and Monetary Statistics: 1914-1941.* https://fraser.stlouisfed.org/title/38. Accessed May 25, 2020.

Federal Reserve Bank of St. Louis. *Federal Reserve Economic Data.* https://research.stlouisfed.org. Accessed March 31, 2020.

Global Financial Data. www.globalfinancialdata.com. Accessed March 31, 2020.

Huang, Huaxiang and Ryland Thomas. 2016. "The Weekly Balance Sheet of the Bank of England 1844-2006." OBRA dataset, Bank of England.

League of Nations. 1937. *Statistical Year-Book of the League of Nations*. Geneva: League of Nations.

Thomas, Ryland and Nicholas Dimsdale. 2017. "A Millennium of UK Data." OBRA dataset, Bank of England.

Newspapers

The Baltimore Sun
Chicago Daily Tribune
The Daily Telegraph
The Economist
Financial Times
New York Herald Tribune
The New York Times
The Times (London)
The Wall Street Journal

Secondary Sources

Accominotti, Olivier. 2009. "The Sterling Trap: Foreign Reserves Management at the Bank of France, 1928-1936." *European Review of Economic History* 13: 349–76.

2020. "International Monetary Regimes: The Interwar Gold Exchange Standard." In *Handbook of the History of Money and Currency*, edited by Stefano Battilossi, Youssef Cassis, and Kazuhiko Yago, 633–64. Singapore: Springer.

Ahamed, Liaquat. 2009. *Lords of Finance: The Bankers Who Broke the World*. New York: Penguin Books.

Albers, Thilo N. H. 2020. "Currency Devaluations and Beggar-My-Neighbour Penalties: Evidence from the 1930s." *Economic History Review* 73 (1): 233–57.

Aldcroft, Derek H. 2004. "Exchange Rate Regimes and Economic Performance in the Inter-War Years." In *Exchange Rates and Economic Policy in the 20th Century*, edited by Ross E. Catterall and Derek H. Aldcroft, 17–70. Burlington: Ashgate.

Atkin, John. 2005. *The Foreign Exchange Market of London: Development since 1900*. New York: Routledge.

Balogh, Thomas. 1947. *Studies in Financial Organization*. Cambridge: Cambridge University Press.

Bank for International Settlements. 1933–1939. *Annual Report*. Basle: Bank for International Settlements.

1937. *The Tripartite Agreement of September 25, 1936 and Subsequent Monetary Arrangements*. Basle: Bank for International Settlements.

Bank of England. 1968. "The Exchange Equalisation Account: Its Origins and Development." *Quarterly Bulletin* 8 (4): 377–90.

2020. "How Much Gold is Kept in the Bank of England?" www.bankofengland.co.uk/knowledgebank/how-much-gold-is-kept-in-the-bank-of-england. Accessed May 25, 2020.

Bergsten, C. Fred and Russell A. Green, eds. 2016. *International Monetary Cooperation: Lessons from the Plaza Accord after Thirty Years*. Washington, DC: Peterson Institute for International Economics.

Bergsten, C. Fred and Joseph E. Gagnon. 2017. *Currency Conflict and Trade Policy: A New Strategy for the United States*. Washington, DC: Peterson Institute for International Economics.

Bernanke, Ben and Harold James. 1991. "The Gold Standard, Deflation, and Financial Crisis in the Great Depression: An International Comparison." In *Financial Markets and Financial Crises*, edited by R. G. Hubbard, 33–68. Chicago: University of Chicago Press.

Best, Jacqueline. 2005. *The Limits of Transparency: Ambiguity and the History of International Finance*. Ithaca: Cornell University Press.

Birnbaum, Pierre. 2015. *Léon Blum: Prime Minister, Socialist, Zionist*. Translated by Arthur Goldhammer. New Haven: Yale University Press.

Blaazer, David. 2005. "Finance and the End of Appeasement: The Bank of England, the National Government and the Czech Gold." *Journal of Contemporary History* 40 (1): 25–39.

Bloomfield, Arthur I. 1959. *Monetary Policy under the International Gold Standard: 1880-1914*. New York: Federal Reserve Bank of New York.

1966. *Capital Imports and the American Balance of Payments, 1934-39*. New York: A. M. Kelley.

Blum, John Morton. 1959. *From the Morgenthau Diaries: Years of Crisis, 1928-1939*. Boston: Houghton Mifflin.

Bordo, Michael D. 1993. "The Bretton Woods International Monetary System: A Historical Overview." In *A Retrospective on the Bretton Woods System: Lessons for International Monetary Reform*, edited by Michael D. Bordo and Barry Eichengreen, 3–108. Chicago: University of Chicago Press.

Bordo, Michael D., Owen F. Humpage, and Anna J. Schwartz. 2015. *Strained Relations: US Foreign-Exchange Operations and Monetary Policy in the Twentieth Century*. Chicago: University of Chicago Press.

Bordo, Michael D., Ronald MacDonald, and Michael J. Oliver. 2009. "Sterling in Crisis, 1964-1967." *European Review of Economic History* 13 (3): 437–59.

Bordo, Michael D. and Anna J. Schwartz, eds. 1984. *A Retrospective on the Classical Gold Standard, 1821-1931*. Chicago: University of Chicago Press.

Bordo, Michael, Eric Monnet, and Alain Naef. 2019. "The Gold Pool (1961-1968) and the Fall of the Bretton Woods System: Lessons for Central Bank Cooperation." *Journal of Economic History* 79 (4): 1027–59.

Boris, George. 1936. "Reforming the Bank of France." *Foreign Affairs* 15 (1): 155–64.

Boyce, Robert. 2009. *The Great Interwar Crisis and the Collapse of Globalization*. London: Palgrave Macmillan.

Boyer, George R. and Timothy J. Hatton. 2002. "New Estimates of British Unemployment, 1870-1913." *Journal of Economic History* 62 (3): 643–75.

Broadberry, S. N. 1987. "Purchasing Power Parity and the Pound-Dollar Rate in the 1930s." *Economica* 54 (213): 69–78.

Brown, William Adams. 1929. *England and the New Gold Standard, 1919-1926*. New Haven: Yale University Press.

1940. *The International Gold Standard Reinterpreted, 1914-1934*. New York: National Bureau of Economic Research.

1942. "Operations of the Exchange Stabilization Fund: 1934-1939." Unpublished draft, National Bureau of Economic Research. https://fraser.stlouisfed.org/title/6022. Accessed March 31, 2020.

Cairncross, Alec and Barry Eichengreen. 1983. *Sterling in Decline: The Devaluations of 1931, 1949, and 1967*. Oxford: Basil Blackwell.

Capie, Forrest. 2010. *The Bank of England: 1950s to 1979*. New York: Cambridge University Press.

Cesarano, Filippo. 2003. "Defining Fundamental Disequilibrium: Keynes's Unheeded Contribution." *Journal of Economic Studies* 30 (5): 474–92.

Chamberlain, Neville. 2002. *The Neville Chamberlain Diary Letters. Volume 3: The Heir Apparent, 1928-33*. Edited by Robert Self. Burlington: Ashgate.

2005. *The Neville Chamberlain Diary Letters. Volume 4: The Downing Street Years, 1934-1940*. Edited by Robert Self. Burlington, VT: Ashgate.

Chandler, Lester V. 1971. *American Monetary Policy, 1928-1941*. New York: Harper and Row.

Choudhri, Ehan U. and Levis A. Kochin. 1980. "The Exchange Rate and the International Transmission of Business Cycle Disturbances: Some Evidence from the Great Depression." *Journal of Money, Credit, and Banking* 12 (4): 565–74.

Clarke, Stephen V. O. 1967. *Central Bank Cooperation: 1924-31*. New York: Federal Reserve Bank of New York.

1977. "Exchange-Rate Stabilization in the Mid-1930s: Negotiating the Tripartite Agreement." Princeton Studies in International Finance no. 41.

Clavin, Patricia. 1996. *The Failure of Economic Diplomacy: Britain, Germany, France and the United States, 1931-36*. New York: St. Martin's Press.

2013. *Securing the World Economy: The Reinvention of the League of Nations, 1920-1946*. Oxford: Oxford University Press.

Clay, Henry. 1957. *Lord Norman*. New York: St. Martin's Press.

Colton, Joel. 1987. *Léon Blum: Humanist in Politics*. Durham: Duke University Press.

Crabbe, Leland. 1989. "The International Gold Standard and U.S. Monetary Policy from World War I to the New Deal." *Federal Reserve Bulletin* 75 (6): 423–40.

Crozier, Andrew J. 1988. *Appeasement and Germany's Last Bid for Colonies*. London: Macmillan.

2018. "Chamberlain, (Arthur) Neville (1869-1940), Prime Minister." *Oxford Dictionary of National Biography*. https://doi.org/10.1093/ref:odnb/32347. Accessed April 4, 2020.

Dam, Kenneth W. 1982. *The Rules of the Game: Reform and Evolution in the International Monetary System*. Chicago: University of Chicago Press.

1983. "From the Gold Clause Cases to the Gold Commission: A Half Century of American Monetary Law." *University of Chicago Law Review* 50: 504–32.

Drummond, Ian M. 1979. "London, Washington, and the Management of the Franc, 1936-1939." Princeton Studies in International Finance no. 45.

1981. *The Floating Pound and the Sterling Area, 1931-1939*. New York: Cambridge University Press.

Drummond, Ian M. and Norman Hillmer. 1989. *Negotiating Freer Trade: The United Kingdom, the United States, Canada, and the Trade Agreements of 1938*. Waterloo: Wilfrid Laurier University Press.

Dutton, David. 1992. *Simon: A Political Biography of Sir John Simon*. London: Aurum Press.

Edwards, Sebastian. 2017. "Keynes and the Dollar in 1933: The Gold-Buying Program and Exchange Rate Gyrations." *Financial History Review* 24 (3): 209–38.

2018. *American Default: The Untold Story of FDR, the Supreme Court, and the Battle over Gold*. Princeton: Princeton University Press.

Eichengreen, Barry. 1990. *Elusive Stability: Essays in the History of International Finance, 1919-1939*. Cambridge: Cambridge University Press.

1992. *Golden Fetters: The Gold Standard and the Great Depression, 1919-1939*. New York: Oxford University Press.

2008. *Globalizing Capital: A History of the International Monetary System*. 2nd ed. Princeton: Princeton University Press.

2013. "Currency War or International Policy Coordination?" *Journal of Policy Modeling* 35 (3): 425–33.

2015. "Before the Plaza: The Exchange Stabilization Attempts of 1925, 1933, 1936, and 1971." In *International Monetary Cooperation: Lessons from the Plaza Accord after Thirty Years*, edited by C. Fred Bergsten and Russell A. Green, 173–92. Washington, DC: Peterson Institute for International Economics.

Eichengreen, Barry and Jeffrey Sachs. 1985. "Exchange Rates and Economic Recovery in the 1930s." *Journal of Economic History* 45 (4): 925–46.

Eichengreen, Barry and Marc Flandreau. 1997. "Editors' Introduction." In *The Gold Standard in Theory and History*, edited by Barry Eichengreen and Marc Flandreau, 1–21. New York: Routledge.

Eichengreen, Barry and Peter Temin. 2000. "The Gold Standard and the Great Depression." *Contemporary European History* 9 (2): 183–207.

Einaudi, Luca. 2001. *Money and Politics: European Monetary Unification and the International Gold Standard (1865-1873)*. New York: Oxford University Press.

Einzig, Paul. 1937. *Will Gold Depreciate?* London: Macmillan.

1938. *World Finance, 1937-1938*. London: K. Paul, Trench, Trubner & Co.

Feinstein, Charles H., Peter Temin, and Gianni Toniolo. 1997. *The European Economy between the Wars*. New York: Oxford University Press.

Fforde, John. 1992. *The Bank of England and Public Policy, 1941-1958*. New York: Cambridge University Press.

Flandreau, Marc. 1997. "Central Bank Cooperation in Historical Perspective: A Sceptical View." *Economic History Review* 50 (4): 735–63.

Friedman, Milton and Anna J. Schwartz. 1963. *A Monetary History of the United States, 1867-1960*. Princeton: Princeton University Press.

Friedman, Milton. 1992. "Franklin D. Roosevelt, Silver, and China." *Journal of Political Economy* 100 (1): 62–83.

Fratzscher, Marcel, Oliver Gloede, Lukas Menkhoff, Lucio Sarno, and Tobias Stöhr. 2019. "When is Foreign Exchange Intervention Effective? Evidence from 33 Countries." *American Economic Journal: Macroeconomics* 11 (1): 132–56.

Graham, Frank D. and Charles R. Whittlesey. 1939. *Golden Avalanche*. Princeton: Princeton University Press.

Group of Twenty. 2013. "Communiqué of the G20 Meeting of Finance Ministers and Central Bank Governors, Moscow, July 20, 2013." *G20 Information Centre.* www .g20.utoronto.ca/2013/2013-0720-finance.html. Accessed May 25, 2020.

Helleiner, Eric. 2016. *Forgotten Foundations of Bretton Woods: International Development and the Making of the Postwar Order.* Ithaca: Cornell University Press.

Henning, C. Randall. 1999. *The Exchange Stabilization Fund: Slush Money or War Chest?* Washington: Institute for International Economics.

Hennessy, Elizabeth. 1992. *A Domestic History of the Bank of England, 1930-1960.* New York: Cambridge University Press.

Horsefield, J. Keith. 1969. *The International Monetary Fund, 1945-1965: Twenty Years of International Monetary Cooperation.* Washington: International Monetary Fund.

Howson, Susan. 1974. "The Origins of Dear Money, 1919-20." *Economic History Review* 27 (1): 88–107.

  1975. *Domestic Monetary Management in Britain: 1919-38.* Cambridge: Cambridge University Press.

  1980. "Sterling's Managed Float: The Operations of the Exchange Equalisation Account, 1932-39." Princeton Studies in International Finance no. 46.

Ilzetzki, Ethan, Carmen M. Reinhart, and Kenneth S. Rogoff. 2019. "Exchange Arrangements Entering the Twenty-first Century: Which Anchor will Hold?" *Quarterly Journal of Economics* 134 (2): 599–646.

Irwin, Douglas A. 2012. "Gold Sterilization and the Recession of 1937-1938." *Financial History Review* 19 (3): 249–67.

Jackson, Julian. 1985. *The Politics of Depression in France, 1932-1936.* Cambridge: Cambridge University Press.

  1988. *The Popular Front in France: Defending Democracy, 1934-38.* New York: Cambridge University Press.

James, Harold. 2001. *The End of Globalization: Lessons from the Great Depression.* Cambridge: Harvard University Press.

Keynes, John Maynard. 2010. *Essays in Persuasion.* 3rd ed. New York: Palgrave Macmillan.

Kindleberger, Charles Poor. 1986. *The World in Depression, 1929-1939.* 2nd ed. Berkeley: University of California Press.

Kunz, Diane B. 1987. *The Battle for Britain's Gold Standard in 1931.* London: Routledge.

Kynaston, David. 2017. *Till Time's Last Sand: A History of the Bank of England, 1694-2013.* London: Bloomsbury.

Leith-Ross, Frederick. 1968. *Money Talks: Fifty Years of International Finance: The Autobiography of Sir Frederick Leith-Ross.* London: Hutchinson.

Lindert, Peter. 1969. "Key Currencies and Gold, 1900-1913." Princeton Studies in International Finance no. 24.

Lipson, Charles. 1991. "Why are Some International Agreements Informal?" *International Organization* 45 (4): 495–538.

Martin, William McChesney. 1965. "Does Monetary History Repeat Itself?" Address before the Commencement Day Luncheon of the Alumni Federation of Columbia University, New York City. Federal Reserve Archival System for Economic Research, https://fraser.stlouisfed.org/title/448/item/7898. Accessed May 25, 2020.

McCauley, Robert N. and Catherine R. Schenk. 2020. "Central Bank Swaps Then and Now: Swaps and Dollar Liquidity in the 1960s." *BIS Working Papers* 851.

Meltzer, Allan H. 2003. *A History of the Federal Reserve, Volume 1: 1913-1951*. Chicago: University of Chicago Press.

Meyer, Richard Hemmig. 1970. *Bankers' Diplomacy: Monetary Stabilization in the Twenties*. New York: Columbia University Press.

Middleton, Roger. 2008. "Ross, Sir Frederick William Leith- (1887-1968), Civil Servant and Authority on International Finance." *Oxford Dictionary of National Biography*. https://doi.org/10.1093/ref:odnb/34489. Accessed April 4, 2020.

Mitchener, Kris James and Kirsten Wandschneider. 2015. "Capital Controls and Recovery from the Financial Crisis of the 1930s." *Journal of International Economics* 95 (2): 188–201.

Moggridge, D. E. 1972. *British Monetary Policy, 1924-1931: The Norman Conquest of $4.86*. Cambridge: Cambridge University Press.

Monnet, Eric. 2017. "French Monetary Policy and the Bretton Woods System: Criticisms, Proposals and Conflicts." In *Global Perspectives on the Bretton Woods Conference and the Post-War World Order*, edited by Giles Scott-Smith and J. Simon Rofe, 73–87. New York: Palgrave Macmillan.

Moran, Charles McMoran Wilson. 1966. *Churchill Taken from the Diaries of Lord Moran: The Struggle for Survival, 1940-1965*. Boston: Houghton Mifflin.

Morrison, James Ashley. 2015. "Shocking Intellectual Austerity: The Role of Ideas in the Demise of the Gold Standard in Britain." *International Organization* 70 (1): 1–33.

Mouré, Kenneth. 1991. *Managing the Franc Poincaré: Economic Understanding and Political Constraint in French Monetary Policy, 1928-1936*. New York: Cambridge University Press.

 1992. "The Limits to Central Bank Co-operation, 1916-36." *Contemporary European History* 1 (3): 259–79.

 1996. "Undervaluing the Franc Poincaré." *Economic History Review* 49 (1): 137–53.

 2002. *The Gold Standard Illusion: France, the Bank of France, and the International Gold Standard, 1914-1939*. New York: Oxford University Press.

Mourlon-Druol, Emmanuel. 2012. *A Europe Made of Money: The Emergence of the European Monetary System*. Ithaca: Cornell University Press.

Mundell, R. A. 2000. "A Reconsideration of the Twentieth Century." *American Economic Review* 90 (3): 327–40.

Neely, Christopher J. 2005. "An Analysis of Recent Studies of the Effect of Foreign Exchange Intervention." *Federal Reserve Bank of St. Louis Review* 87 (6): 685–717.

 2011. "A Foreign Exchange Intervention in an Era of Restraint." *Federal Reserve Bank of St. Louis Review* 93 (5): 303–24.

Nichols, Jeannette P. 1951. "Roosevelt's Monetary Diplomacy in 1933." *The American Historical Review* 56 (2): 295–317.

Nurkse, Ragnar. 1944. *International Currency Experience: Lessons of the Inter-War Period*. Geneva: League of Nations.

Officer, Lawrence H. 1996. *Between the Dollar-Sterling Gold Points: Exchange Rates, Parity, and Market Behavior*. New York: Cambridge University Press.

Oye, Kenneth A. 1985. "The Sterling-Dollar-Franc Triangle: Monetary Diplomacy 1929-1937." *World Politics* 38 (1): 173–99.

Parker, R. A. C. 1974. "Great Britain, France and the Ethiopian Crisis, 1935-1936." *English Historical Review* 89 (351): 293-332.

1983. "The Pound Sterling, the American Treasury and British Preparations for War, 1938-1939." *The English Historical Review* 98 (387): 261–79.

2002. *Chamberlain and Appeasement: British Policy and the Coming of the Second World War*. Basingstoke: Palgrave Macmillan.

Peden, G. C. 1984. "A Matter of Timing: The Economic Background to British Foreign Policy, 1937-1939." *History* 69 (225): 15–28.

2000. *The Treasury and British Public Policy, 1906-1959*. New York: Oxford University Press.

2007. *Arms, Economics and British Strategy: From Dreadnoughts to Hydrogen Bombs*. New York: Cambridge University Press.

2008. "Phillips, Sir Frederick (1884-1943), Civil Servant." *Oxford Dictionary of National Biography*. https://doi.org/10.1093/ref:odnb/74786. Accessed April 4, 2020.

Price, Christopher. 2001. *Britain, America, and Rearmament in the 1930s: The Cost of Failure*. New York: Palgrave.

Pumphrey, Lowell M. 1942. "The Exchange Equalization Account of Great Britain, 1932-1939: Exchange Operations." *American Economic Review* 32 (4): 803–16.

Rauchway, Eric. 2015. *The Money Makers: How Roosevelt and Keynes Ended the Depression, Defeated Fascism, and Secured a Prosperous Peace*. New York: Basic Books.

Raustiala, Kal. 2005. "Form and Substance in International Agreements." *The American Journal of International Law* 99 (3): 581–614.

Reti, Steven P. 1998. *Silver and Gold: The Political Economy of International Monetary Conferences, 1867-1892*. Westport: Praeger.

Richardson, J. Henry. 2019. *British Economic Foreign Policy*. London: Routledge.

Ritschl, A. O. 2001. "Nazi Economic Imperialism and the Exploitation of the Small: Evidence from Germany's Secret Foreign Exchange Balances, 1938-1940." *Economic History Review* 54 (2): 324–45.

Roberts, Richard. 2013. *Saving the City: The Great Financial Crisis of 1914*. Oxford: Oxford University Press.

Sayers, R. S. 1953. "The Bank in the Gold Market, 1890-1914." In *Papers in English Monetary History*, edited by T. S. Ashton and R. S. Sayers, 132–50. Oxford: Clarendon Press.

1960. "The Return to Gold, 1925." In *Studies in the Industrial Revolution*, edited by L. S. Pressnell, 313–27. London: Althone Press.

1976. *The Bank of England, 1891-1944*. New York: Cambridge University Press.

Schenk, Catherine R. 2010. *The Decline of Sterling: Managing the Retreat of an International Currency, 1945-1992*. New York: Cambridge University Press.

Schlesinger, Arthur. 2003. *The Age of Roosevelt, Volume II: The Coming of the New Deal, 1933-1935*. Boston: Houghton Mifflin.

Schwartz, Anna J. 1997. "From Obscurity to Notoriety: A Biography of the Exchange Stabilization Fund." *Journal of Money, Credit, and Banking* 29 (2): 135–53.

Self, Robert. 2006. *Neville Chamberlain: A Biography*. New York: Routledge.

2007. "Perception and Posture in Anglo-American Relations: The War Debt Controversy in the 'Official Mind,' 1919-1940." *International History Review* 29 (2): 282–312.

Setser, Brad W. 2019. "Policy Innovation Memorandum: Make the Foreign Exchange Report Great Again." Council on Foreign Relations.

Silber, William L. 2007. *When Washington Shut Down Wall Street: The Great Financial Crisis of 1914 and the Origins of America's Monetary Supremacy.* Princeton: Princeton University Press.

2009. "Why Did FDR's Bank Holiday Succeed?" *FRBNY Economic Policy Review* 15 (1): 19–30.

Skidelsky, Robert. 1994. *John Maynard Keynes: The Economist as Saviour, 1920-1937.* New York: Penguin.

2001. *John Maynard Keynes: Fighting for Britain, 1937-1946.* New York: Viking.

Siepmann, Harry. 1987. *Echo of the Guns: Recollections of an Artillery Officer, 1914-18.* London: Hale.

Steil, Benn. 2013. *The Battle of Bretton Woods: John Maynard Keynes, Harry Dexter White, and the Making of a New World Order.* Princeton: Princeton University Press.

Stewart, Robert B. 1938. "Great Britain's Foreign Loan Policy." *Economica* 5 (17): 45–60.

Straumann, Tobias. 2010. *Fixed Ideas of Money: Small States and Exchange Rate Regimes in Twentieth-Century Europe.* New York: Cambridge University Press.

2019. *1931: Debt, Crisis, and the Rise of Hitler.* New York: Oxford University Press.

Sumner, Scott. 2015. *The Midas Paradox: Financial Markets, Government Policy Shocks, and the Great Depression.* Oakland: Independent Institute.

Thorpe, Andrew. 1991. *The British General Election of 1931.* New York: Oxford University Press.

Toniolo, Gianni. 2005. *Central Bank Cooperation at the Bank for International Settlements, 1930-1973.* New York: Cambridge University Press.

Tooze, Adam. 2014. *The Deluge: The Great War, America and the Remaking of the Global Order, 1916-1931.* New York: Viking.

Urban, Scott and Tobias Straumann. 2012. "Still Tied by Golden Fetters: The Global Response to the US Recession of 1937-1938." *Financial History Review* 19 (1): 21–48.

US Gold Commission. 1982. *Report to the Congress of the Commission on the Role of Gold in the Domestic and International Monetary Systems.* Washington, DC: Government Printing Office.

US Treasury. 1934. *Report of the Secretary of the Treasury on the State of the Finances.* Washington, DC: Government Printing Office.

1940. *Report of the Secretary of the Treasury on the State of the Finances.* Washington, DC: Government Printing Office.

2020. "Report to Congress: Macroeconomic and Foreign Exchange Policies of Major Trading Partners of the United States." https://home.treasury.gov/system/files/136/20200113-Jan-2020-FX-Report-FINAL.pdf. Accessed May 24, 2020.

Van Zeeland, P. 1938. "The Van Zeeland Report." *World Affairs* 101 (1): 48–58.

Vanthoor, Wim. 2005. *The King's Eldest Daughter: A History of the Nederlandsche Bank 1814-1998.* Amsterdam: Boom.

Waight, Leonard. 1939. *The History and Mechanism of the Exchange Equalisation Account.* Cambridge: Cambridge University Press.

Whitaker, John K. and Maxwell W. Hudgins. 1977. "The Floating Pound Sterling of the Nineteen-Thirties: An Econometric Study." *Southern Economic Journal* 43 (4): 1478–85.

Wicker, Elmus. 1971. "Roosevelt's 1933 Monetary Experiment." *Journal of American History* 57 (4): 864–79.

Williams, John H. 1943. "Currency Stabilization: The Keynes and White Plans." *Foreign Affairs* 21 (4): 645–58.

Williamson, Philip. 1992. *National Crisis and National Government: British Politics, the Economy and Empire, 1926-32.* Cambridge: Cambridge University Press.

Index

Tobias Straumann, *Fixed Ideas of Money: Small States and Exchange Rate Regimes in Twentieth-Century Europe* (2010)

Forrest Capie, *The Bank of England: 1950s to 1979* (2010)

Aldo Musacchio, *Experiments in Financial Democracy: Corporate Governance and Financial Development in Brazil, 1882–1950* (2009)

Claudio Borio, Gianni Toniolo, and Piet Clement, Editors, *The Past and Future of Central Bank Cooperation* (2008)

Robert L. Hetzel, *The Monetary Policy of the Federal Reserve: A History* (2008)

Caroline Fohlin, *Finance Capitalism and Germany's Rise to Industrial Power* (2007)

John H. Wood, *A History of Central Banking in Great Britain and the United States* (2005)

Gianni Toniolo (with the assistance of Piet Clement), *Central Bank Cooperation at the Bank for International Settlements, 1930–1973* (2005)

Richard Burdekin and Pierre Siklos, Editors, *Deflation: Current and Historical Perspectives* (2004)

Pierre Siklos, *The Changing Face of Central Banking: Evolutionary Trends since World War II* (2002)

Michael D. Bordo and Roberto Cortés-Conde, Editors, *Transferring Wealth and Power from the Old to the New World: Monetary and Fiscal Institutions in the 17th through the 19th Centuries* (2001)

Howard Bodenhorn, *A History of Banking in Antebellum America: Financial Markets and Economic Development in an Era of Nation-Building* (2000)

Mark Harrison, Editor, *The Economics of World War II: Six Great Powers in International Comparison* (2000)

Angela Redish, *Bimetallism: An Economic and Historical Analysis* (2000)

Elmus Wicker, *Banking Panics of the Gilded Age* (2000)

Michael D. Bordo, *The Gold Standard and Related Regimes: Collected Essays* (1999)

Michele Fratianni and Franco Spinelli, *A Monetary History of Italy* (1997)

Mark Toma, *Competition and Monopoly in the Federal Reserve System, 1914–1951* (1997)

Barry Eichengreen, Editor, *Europe's Postwar Recovery* (1996)

Lawrence H. Officer, *Between the Dollar-Sterling Gold Points: Exchange Rates, Parity and Market Behavior* (1996)

Elmus Wicker, *The Banking Panics of the Great Depression* (1996)

Norio Tamaki, *Japanese Banking: A History, 1859–1959* (1995)

Barry Eichengreen, *Elusive Stability: Essays in the History of International Finance, 1919–1939* (1993)

Michael D. Bordo and Forrest Capie, Editors, *Monetary Regimes in Transition* (1993)

Larry Neal, *The Rise of Financial Capitalism: International Capital Markets in the Age of Reason* (1993)

S. N. Broadberry and N. F. R. Crafts, Editors, *Britain in the International Economy, 1870–1939* (1992)

Aurel Schubert, *The Credit-Anstalt Crisis of 1931* (1992)

Trevor J. O. Dick and John E. Floyd, *Canada and the Gold Standard: Balance of Payments Adjustment under Fixed Exchange Rates, 1871–1913* (1992)

Kenneth Mouré, *Managing the Franc Poincaré: Economic Understanding and Political Constraint in French Monetary Policy, 1928–1936* (1991)

David C. Wheelock, *The Strategy and Consistency of Federal Reserve Monetary Policy, 1924–1933* (1991)

Printed in the United States
by Baker & Taylor Publisher Services